Behind the Burqa

Our Life in Afghanistan and
How We Escaped to Freedom

by
"Sulima" and "Hala"

as told to
Batya Swift Yasgur

John Wiley & Sons, Inc.

To our homeland
To the women of Afghanistan
And to Madarjan

Published by John Wiley & Sons, Inc., Hoboken, New Jersey
Published simultaneously in Canada

For general information about our other products and services, please contact our Customer Care Department within the United States at (800) 762-2974, outside the United States at (317) 572-3993 or fax (317) 572-4002.

Wiley also publishes its books in a variety of electronic formats. Some content that appears in print may not be available in electronic books.

Library of Congress Cataloging-in-Publication Data

Yasgur, Batya Swift.
     Behind the burqa : our life in Afghanistan and how we escaped to freedom / by "Sulima" and "Hala" as told to Batya Swift Yasgur.
        p.   cm.
     ISBN 0-471-26389-3 (cloth)
  1. Afghanistan—Social life and customs—20th century. 2. Women—Afghanistan—Social conditions. 3. Taliban. I. Title.
     DS371.3 .Y37 2002
     958.104'082—dc21   2002012139

Printed in the United States of America

10 9 8 7 6 5 4 3 2 1

CONTENTS

ACKNOWLEDGMENTS

We would like to thank all our friends who have supported us through our difficult times in Afghanistan, Austria, and the United States. Although we are not using your real names in this book, you know who you are and how much you mean to us.

Warm and heartfelt thanks to Eleanor Acer and all others at the Lawyers Committee for Human Rights for your dedication and fine work on Hala's asylum case and for all the wonderful work you do on behalf of other refugees and asylum seekers. We would especially like to acknowledge volunteer lawyers "Lenore" and "Kalpana" for accepting Hala's case on a pro bono basis and for helping her obtain freedom and asylum. Your compassion, warmth, and sense of humor helped us through a period of great darkness, and your legal expertise contributed to bringing us light in the form of a successful outcome. Thanks to Chris Klatell for his legal input into this book project and his loyalty and caring.

Cheryl Skafte and Alisha Horowitz at the Lutheran Immigration and Refugee Service were especially helpful with information about how to help asylum seekers in detention. Thanks also to Esther Ebrahimian and Steve Rubin, the photographer, for their roles in the original LIRS Asylum Storybook project.

Our appreciation goes to Hana Lane, our wonderful editor at John Wiley & Sons, Inc., for believing in this project and for her commitment to bringing our story to the public.

JNTRODUCTJON

J first met "Hala" in June 2001. She was one of ten asylees (individuals who had been granted asylum) whom I interviewed for a booklet to be published by the Lutheran Immigration and Refugee Service. The project was designed to inform the public about the plight of immigrants fleeing persecution who arrive in the United States without appropriate travel documents and are incarcerated in detention centers—often for years.

Like many of the other asylees I interviewed, Hala did not want her real name used. She was afraid of reprisals against her remaining family in Afghanistan and Pakistan. Of course, I honored Hala's request, and the LIRS booklet, like the present book, does not use her real name.

Working on the LIRS project transformed me and set the experiences of my own life into new perspective. Some of my problems faded to insignificance when compared to the life-and-death struggles of the asylees. Those problems that remained significant seemed easier to confront when I called upon the inspiration I had gained from the courageous people I was meeting.

All the asylees and asylum-seekers moved me deeply, with their accounts of the brutality they sustained in their own country and then the further abuses they suffered at the hands of immigration authorities in the United States. It awakened memories of stories of my Jewish ancestors fleeing countless forms of persecution, most recently the Nazi Holocaust. Turned away by country after country, many of them were left to perish. As a Jew, I share a kinship with every persecuted human being I encounter. The haunted eyes of the people I interviewed followed me through all my daily activities— writing at the computer, carpooling, washing dishes, eating dinner with friends. But of all the brave people I met, Hala and her story were what embedded themselves most deeply into my conscious- ness. Every time I left the house, free to walk the streets unmolested, free to let my hair blow in the wind, free to talk to anyone I chose, free to educate my children openly and proudly, free to pray in any manner I chose—or not pray at all—I saw an image of Hala and thousands of Afghan women, oppressed and imprisoned in their own homes. I could not forget Hala and the hundreds of asylum seekers like her, who risked their lives to come to this land of free- dom, only to find "freedom" a cruel hoax as they moldered in detention centers, locked away once again and in many cases forgot- ten. Most Americans, I found out, did not even know that this was how our country was treating asylum-seekers.

Hala's story had to be told.

I recontacted Hala and asked her if she might be interested in hav- ing the short write-up I did for LIRS expanded into a book. She is a modest and unassuming person not interested in being in the lime- light or fame, but she appeared open to the idea. So I traveled to meet her, with the intention of reinterviewing her more extensively and writing a proposal for a book.

I had met Hala's older sister the first time I interviewed Hala, but on this second visit, I got to know Sulima much better and was cap- tivated by Sulima's own story. Over hummus, stuffed grape leaves, and yogurt sauce, she told me her life history. It became clear that Sulima's journey was as compelling and unusual as Hala's and that the memoir would be more powerful if I included both sisters' sto- ries. I wanted nothing more than to be the channel through which their remarkable courage could be told to the world.

Then came September 11. Its events catapulted Afghanistan into world attention. All eyes were suddenly focused on the wild and alien terrain of this foreign country that was harboring the most dangerous and wanted man in the world. *Taliban* and *Kabul* became household words. Magazines carried photographs of women swathed grotesquely in *burqas* and fierce, bearded, turbaned men wielding whips. Westerners gasped with horror as the full implica- tions of Taliban oppression became known.

In the wake of the tragedy that struck at the heart and nerve centers of America, immigrants became the unfortunate scapegoats of Ameri- can wrath. In the minds of the American public, Afghan asylees, many of whom had fled the same egregious system that had spawned and supported the attacks on the World Trade Center and the Pentagon, were now being lumped together with their oppressors. For all of the president's admirable efforts to distinguish between the Afghan people and the Taliban supporters of Osama bin Laden, between immigrants who abused American hospitality and those who make an ongoing contribution to American society, foreigners—especially Afghans—became the target of racial slurs, and even violent attacks. Someone spray painted the word *bitch* on Sulima's plant store. Professionals working with survivors of torture told me that many of their clients were severely retraumatized, not only by the sudden, terrifying proximity of war and violence exhibited on September 11 but also by the new wave of antiforeign sentiment.

Sadly, it was not only the general public that exhibited this disturbing and distinctly un-American behavior. Even among lawmakers, the mood and spirit toward immigrants had changed. The ripple effect of these changed attitudes rebounded to asylum law. In early September, Congress had been poised to ease some of the restrictions on asylum-seekers, thereby reducing the numbers in detention centers and paving the way for a more humane and fair system for dealing with undocumented immigrants fleeing persecution. But in the wake of September 11, immigration laws became even more stringent.

It is my hope that by meeting Sulima and Hala, readers will gain insight not only into the hideous conditions under which Afghan women have lived, but also into the deplorable wrongdoing that our immigration system perpetrates upon those who come to our shores, seeking refuge from the same forces that attacked us. It is my hope that readers will lend support to women's rights movements in Afghanistan, and will also become involved in working toward change in immigration policy in our own country. You will find at the back of this book some suggestions for how you can help.

I feel honored and privileged to know Sulima and Hala and to bring their story to you. I know that you will feel equally privileged to get to know them as well.

Batya Swift Yasgur

For the sake of privacy, all names (except for internationally known leaders) and some details have been altered.

PART ONE

SULIMA

I am talking from the dark
I am talking from the very dark night
I am talking from the very dark night
If you come to my home, O my kind friend
Bring me a light
And a grate, that I may see the lucky crowd
In the alley outside

FORUGH FARROKHZAD, 1933–1967, Iran

This poem, written by a Persian woman, could have been written for Afghan women, crying for a friend to bring them light and a grate through which to see the outside world. Her prison has been our prison and her plea is our plea. Dear friend, please bring us light and a grate.

I am in Paradise.

My toes tickled by the moist, green carpet under me, I am tumbling toward the breathtaking tapestry of reds, blues, violets, and yellows. The flower beds are rich and lush. They are perfectly sculpted, a rainbow of visual magic. I am romping through the rolling landscape to the orchards. The sun kisses my cheeks, the wind laughs in my hair, and then . . . a hush. I am under the cool shade of the orchard. Crimson pomegranates, chubby golden pears, trembling to be picked, almonds and quinces . . . the ripe fruits hang over me, a ceiling of sweet delights. Birds drape me with their twittering music. A pear falls beside me. A gift from heaven as I giggle and stretch out my arms in wonder. Blissfully, I take a bite. The juice dribbles down my chin and I am transported by the peace and beauty of it all.

I will always live here, under the orchard trees, the flowers and grass a cocoon of heaven to shield me against the thorns of Earth. I close my eyes and sleep.

I am at Babajan's farm.

These are my earliest memories. I spent much of my early childhood in eastern Afghanistan, in the gardens of Babajan, my mother's father. He was a kind man, gentle and compassionate. He wore a beige *chappan*, the traditional robe, and a *karakul*, a soft oval-shaped lambskin hat. He and Bibijan, as we called my grandmother, lived with various children, grandchildren, cousins, and miscellaneous other family members in their immense mansion. I say "mansion," but actually, it was more like a compound—a series of attached town houses with a shared mosque and several indoor and outdoor bathrooms, all surrounded by a wall. It was almost a self-contained village. In our language, this is called a *qallah*.

My grandfather was not only wealthy, but also gracious and hospitable. His home was always open to wayfarers as well as to family members. "Why spend money on the inn if you can stay here?" he used to say. Consequently, his home became a haven for travelers, even those he did not personally know. This practice continued after his death, and there were always some twenty-five to thirty people at any given time eating in the guesthouse, or *mehmankhana*.

Bibijan and Babajan had a very special relationship, I am told. My grandfather had been married before, but his first wife died young. Once he married my grandmother, he never took another wife, which was quite unusual for a man of his generation and stature. The peaceful energy of their marriage pervaded the house long after his death. Just walking onto his property, I felt tension dissipate and melt away. Their home became a haven for me and remained so until I left Afghanistan in 1979.

I was born in 1954, and although I spent a great deal of time at Babajan's house, I was actually living at the home of my paternal grandparents, Aghajan and Guljan, which was also located in eastern Afghanistan. Like Babajan, Aghajan was a very wealthy and important man. He was a landowner of some real prestige and a shrewd businessman besides. He moved to eastern Afghanistan when land was cheap, then when real estate values rose, he found himself quite wealthy. Like other Afghan men of his generation and background, he did not use his wealth to acquire a new car or a new horse. Instead, he used his money to acquire more wives and yet more land.

Aghajan's estate was also quite beautiful but looked wild and unkempt. Aghajan did not believe in spending money on landscaping. The untamed quality of the property reflected much of my grandfather's personality. Under his controlled, proper exterior, a terrible temper simmered, a wildness that we all found terrifying. When I think of his garden, with its stream, its tangled flowers, its unpruned orchards, and its farmlands, I think of something that could have been beautiful had it been nurtured, but instead it was harsh and unfriendly.

Aghajan was a difficult and complex person. He could not bear to be beholden to someone else—perhaps it made him feel powerless, and Aghajan was all about power and control. So he constantly resisted accepting invitations to other people's homes. In Afghanistan, hospitality—*mehman nawazi*—is one of the most important values. Afghans become deeply offended if an offer of hospitality is refused, and they do not take no for an answer easily. So Aghajan was often forced to dine at the homes of others. On such occasions, he sent rice, sheep, and other gifts to pay them back.

As I've grown older, I've come to believe that there was another reason for Aghajan's insistence on paying his hosts for his meal. He and Babajan were distant relatives, both wealthy and prestigious. While there was no enmity or hatred between them, there was some rivalry. Babajan was known to be a generous and giving person. I believe Aghajan wanted to make the same impression on others— but he did not have the nature for it. In fact, he was quite stingy. He begrudged spending money on anything. Certainly, wayfarers and poor people were welcome on his premises—but for a price. He built a series of houses on his property. Poor people were allowed to live in these houses for free, but only in exchange for tending the orchards and helping with security around the *qallah*.

The atmosphere in his household was tense, a simmering pot of conflict. The four wives squabbled incessantly. Of course, they could not be very loud in their arguments. Women were expected to maintain a peaceful atmosphere in the house, and to remain inconspicuous. When the men were out, the wives allowed themselves the luxury of screaming, cursing, and raging, but when the men were present, they fought with silent hisses, glares, muttered laments, and pursed lips. They argued, stopped speaking to one another for a few days, then grudgingly resumed contact, only to have the cycle repeat itself. Sometimes a particular event such as *Eid*—the festive day with its message of peace and forgiveness following the end of the Ramadan fast period—would trigger reconciliation. Otherwise, the natural passage of time usually brought some softening of feelings— until the next time anyway.

Although Aghajan respected Guljan, who was his oldest wife, very much and always spoke to her, as well as to his third wife, politely and affectionately, he spent most of his time with his fourth wife, who was the youngest. And it seems that he was intimate almost exclusively with his second wife. This was bizarre because otherwise, he never spoke to her at all. In fact, he treated his second wife with the utmost contempt by day. But he visited her residence in the *qal-lah* almost every night—and far more frequently than he visited his other wives. I found this out when I was an adult, and it bolstered my impression of my grandfather as a strange, mysterious, and difficult man.

The real friction was between my grandfather and my father. Father, whom we called Abajan, had a small business as a freelance photographer, taking family portraits. The rest of his time, he devoted to his father's crops of wheat, rice, sesame seeds, and cotton—but with no form of recompense. Aghajan believed that being allowed to live rent free on his property was enough pay. In desperation, Abajan started his own sesame seed oil company.

"You are forbidden from using my seeds for this company," Aghajan said, his voice as sharp as his farming implements. "If you really feel the need for extra money—and I cannot imagine why you would, since I am allowing you to live for free on my property and eat at my table—then you must do as I did. Purchase land of your own. It is not seemly that my son should be selling oil like some peasant."

Abajan remained silent. One did not argue with a parent. One certainly did not defy a parent. The word of a parent was considered equivalent to the word of the Qur'an. Just as you could not talk back to God, you could not talk back to an elder. But Abajan reached a decision. He would move out of his father's house and seek his fortune in the big city of Kabul. And he would make it on his own. He would not accept Aghajan's hospitality, nor would he ever accept money, should Aghajan be so disposed to offer any. Never again would he be beholden to Aghajan.

My mother, whom we call Madarjan, was only too glad to leave her in-laws' home, where she had been regarded as the lowest in the family pecking order. All the wives and other daughters-in-law took their share of food, clothing, money, and other privileges first, leaving my mother to scrounge around the leftovers. For Madarjan, this was humiliating. As the daughter of a wealthy, generous man, she was used to being treated with respect and being given plenty of material comforts. My mother is a person of quiet dignity, restraint, and patience. She did not complain, nor did she turn to her own parents for help. She bided her time, suffered silently, and felt profound gratitude when Abajan decided to move to Kabul.

I was five years old when we moved to Kabul. My older brother, AbdelKarim, was nine, my younger sister, Husna, was two, and Madarjan was pregnant. Abajan began establishing his photography career in a more organized fashion. He made connections with magazines and government ministries, and slowly his business grew. But his family grew more quickly than his business, and my parents were forced to return to Aghajan's house when Madarjan gave birth to my brother AbdelAsim. Abajan needed a short period of respite when his family would be fed at someone else's expense, and Madarjan needed help during childbirth. But Abajan resisted Grandfather's attempts to pressure him into staying. Kabul was his home now. We returned to Kabul when the baby was a few weeks old and remained there for many years afterward.

It took a long time for us to get established. My father was barely eking out a living at first and had to supplement his photographer's income by buying a minibus and leasing it to a bus company. We rented a series of progressively larger homes, as my father's income gradually inched upward. When I was seven, we moved to the large house that remained in our family until long after I left Afghanistan. Meanwhile, my mother continued to have babies. When AbdelAsim was two years old, my brother AbdelZamin was born, followed by a sister, Gula, in 1964. We did not call our brothers by their full, formal names. In Afghanistan, the father picks out a prefix or suffix for all his sons that stands for some ideal or important family value, such as courage or adherence to God's will. Father chose *Abdel*, which means "servant of God." But in day-to-day conversation, we called them by their individual names—Karim, Asim, and Zamin.

In 1970, two major events occurred in the family. After a series of miscarriages, my mother gave birth to my sister Hala; and my Uncle Murid and his wife, Aunt Nasima, were killed in a car accident. My parents adopted their little daughter, my cousin Surya, who was three years old at the time. We immediately started calling Surya "sister," and indeed, that's what she was to us. No one made any distinction in the household between the biological children and the adopted sister. It was typical of my father that he assumed responsibility for his niece and raised her as his own.

The big house we settled in had six bedrooms. I shared a room with Husna. Karim had his own room. Asim and Zamin shared a room, as did Gula and Surya. The newest baby always slept with my parents in their room. As we grew older, Husna moved in with Gula, Surya, and Hala, leaving me to my own devices. The final room was occupied by Uncle Daoud and Aunt Layla. Uncle Daoud was studying at the university in Kabul. He was one of many relatives who lived with us while they were enrolled at the university, but he stayed on even once he had graduated. Visiting cousins slept on the floor in my brothers' rooms.

Our house was always overflowing with extended family members, mostly male students attending the University of Kabul. Because they were family, they were allowed to stay in the house and eat at the table with us, even though girls were present. Unrelated guests were accommodated in a smaller house separated from the main building—the guesthouse, or *mehmankhana*. These quarters were reserved for male guests who could not sit at the same table with the girls in the family. Because my father was very hospitable, the guesthouse was usually full. Often, the guests were college friends of my various cousins, but my father extended hospitality to others as well. When one of Aghajan's neighbors was going through some type of complicated legal procedure that necessitated his remaining in Kabul for two years, he was accommodated in our *mehmankhana*.

The presence of all these guests meant endless housework for the women. We did all the laundry for all members of the household, including residents in the *mehmankhana*. At mealtime, we served the guests, then withdrew. I myself started doing housework when I was about six years old. Gone were the days of freedom and laughter in the golden orchards of Babajan's estate, or even Aghajan's farm. Now I was in charge of my younger sister and baby brother. I was taught to wash cups and spent much of my day at the sink. In Afghanistan, drinking tea is like breathing air. You do it all the time. When a guest comes, offering tea is taken for granted. You don't ask if your guest wants tea, you simply serve it from a teapot, together with a pretty tray of sugar, candy, and cookies. Needless to say, the endless procession of guests led to an endless stream of dishes, which the women were endlessly washing.

At the hub of the giant, ever-changing family wheel was my father. Unquestionably the head of the household and its center, he held court in his living room or guest room when he was not working. I served countless cups of tea to countless men who came to discuss politics, religion, and current affairs with my father. Abajan was a brilliant, thoughtful, and provocative man. And, like his father, he was a character. Fierce, stubborn, opinionated, and powerfully articulate, he captivated his guests with his political insights.

Abajan was attracted to communism when I was young. He held forth for many hours to his friends about the teachings of Marx and Lenin, about economic equality among all people, about how the rich oppress the poor. He argued and debated with his friends, and often I would hear an "Aha!" of triumph as it became clear that he had made his point and a friend had no appropriate rejoinder to offer.

Abajan's charisma and unique style permeated all aspects of the household. He was always reading and educating himself, then applying his newfound knowledge to the running of the household.

"We are going to change our practices so that we will all stay healthier," he announced after dinner one evening when I was about seven—it was shortly after we had moved to our house in Kabul. "You see, when we eat directly on the floor, we can get germs into our food."

"What are germs?" Karim asked.

Abajan flashed him a dark look, as he often did when he thought Karim was asking a stupid question—which was most of the time. "They are tiny things, so small we cannot see them without special glasses. But they are in everything, and if we eat them, they can make us sick. They come into the house from the dirt on our feet, even though we take off our shoes. It is unsanitary to simply spread a cloth on the floor when we eat. I am having a special table built so that the food can be higher than the floor."

There were so many of us that several tables were built, folded, and stowed away between meals. Abajan also forbade us from using our fingers to eat. In Afghanistan, people usually eat with their hands, scooping up the food with their fingers. No one used cutlery. It was strange learning to eat with knives, forks, and spoons.

Life became more complicated in the kitchen when Abajan became convinced that fruits were contaminated with germs and had to be washed with disinfectant. Plain water wasn't good enough. He insisted that all fruits be washed with potassium permanganate and, not trusting that the women would do a thorough enough job, he took over the fruit and vegetable washing himself. Soon he insisted on being the one to buy fruits and vegetables, to be sure that only the cleanest and highest quality produce was brought into the house. I hoped that Abajan would decide that perhaps the dishes too were not being washed properly and would take over the thankless chore of dish washing, but he seemed to confine his worries to fresh fruit.

Abajan also became obsessed with our diets. "Children need a certain minimum amount of food," he told us. "You may not leave the house unless you have eaten at least this amount." He calculated the calories each of us needed in order to stay healthy, based on our weight and age, and kept careful watch over our eating. "No, Husna, you may not go to school because you have only eaten half a loaf of *naan* and a tiny daub of jelly. If you eat the rest of the bread with some more jelly, you may go."

During the fall season, Abajan would buy apples and carrots. He personally cut, squeezed, and ground them, insisting that we drink either a glass of fresh apple juice or a glass of carrot juice before school. On winter mornings, he gave us walnuts to eat after breakfast, telling us that the extra calories would help keep us warmer and that they "contained unsaturated fat, which is a healthy kind of fat."

I remember the cholera epidemic that raged through Kabul. I returned home from school to find Abajan standing outside the bathroom, a grim expression on his face. In his hand was a chamber pot.

"As long as there is illness in the town, you will all produce your *mawade ghaita* into this pot. You will show it to me before you flush it down. I want to be sure there is no blood in it. I want to be sure it looks healthy."

We exchanged glances, squirming in discomfort. Show Abajan our stools? "Do we have to?" I ventured. Although one usually did not argue with a parent, Abajan encouraged questioning—at least when we were young.

"Health comes before modesty," Abajan said, and from then on, stool checking became the protocol whenever there was an epidemic.

So Abajan was remarkably enlightened in some ways—and remarkably benighted in others. His autocratic tendencies brooked no defiance, no flexibility, and no consideration for the emotional needs of his family. He may have been advanced in his understanding of our physical needs, but he was backward in his lack of under-standing of our psychological needs.

For one thing, he picked favorites. In fact, *I* was his favorite.

"Where's my Sula?" was his first question whenever he entered the house.

"Here I am, Abajani!" I would come running out of the kitchen, my face radiating joy at being so singled out. *Abajan* means "father dear" and its diminutive, *Abajani*, means "father dearest"—which I suppose could be considered the Afghan equivalent of "daddy."

"Ah, so here's my baby!" He would scoop me up and give me a hug. "Do you want to come with me to Uncle Gum's house?"

Of course I did. Hand in hand, we would trot off to visit Abajan's best friend. I called him "Uncle Gum" because he always gave me chewing gum when I visited. We would knock on the door, and Abajan would call, "It's Nazir Obaidi and the beautiful Sulima!"

Sometimes Abajan would take me to the market to help him choose fruits and vegetables. Sometimes I would accompany him when he took photographs, and he would allow me to hold the cam-era equipment for him, my heart swelling and bursting with pride. "That's my daughter Sulima," he would tell anyone who passed by. "Isn't she smart? When I was a young man I used to say to myself, One day I will have a beautiful, smart daughter who will help me do my work."

It was intoxicating for a little girl to be so doted on by her father. I felt honored, special—and terrified. Abajan made no attempt to hide his preference for me, and Karim hated me for that. As the older son, *he* was supposed to be the favored and anointed one. Aba-jan should have been crowing over *his* accomplishments, celebrating *his* good looks and proficiency. Instead, Abajan showed obvious delight in me, and the most transparent contempt for his son. It went beyond contempt. Abajan actually pitted us against each other, fanning the fires of my brother's jealousy.

Wednesday night was schoolwork night. Once a week, we all lined up with our schoolbooks while Abajan grilled us about what we had learned. "Have you done all your homework this week? Let me see."

We opened our assignment notebooks and work sheets while Abajan pored over them.

"Karim? Why did you leave the first two questions blank?"

Karim hung his head. "I—I didn't understand the question."

"Sulima, come here."

My heart started thudding as I stepped forward. I had offered earlier that evening to help Karim with his incomplete work, but he had slapped me. "I don't need some little girl telling me the answers. I can figure things out for myself."

"What is one hundred twenty divided by sixty?"

I glanced quickly at Karim, then at Abajan. If I answered correctly, Karim would suffer and, of course, I would suffer later. If I feigned ignorance, Abajan would be angry and I would suffer anyway. The decision, though agonizing, was usually reached quickly. "The answer is two, Abajani."

Abajan scowled at Karim, then beamed at me. "Bring the flyswatter," he ordered. When I hung back, he repeated the command. "If you do not bring it right now, I will hit you with it as well."

I brought the instrument of torture from the kitchen.

"Now you hit Karim with it. A big boy like that, my firstborn. He should know the answer. He shouldn't need his little sister to help him out."

Of course, the last thing I wanted to do was to inflict any pain. First of all, I genuinely felt sorry for Karim. Schoolwork was obviously very difficult for him, and very easy for me. That wasn't his fault. And I knew that as soon as Abajan's back was turned, Karim would get back at me. Maybe if I only tapped his pants with the swatter . . . maybe if he could barely feel it, he wouldn't notice that I had done this to him? Maybe he would be gentler with me later?

Shyly, I brushed his pants with the swatter. Sometimes Abajan would see through this token gesture of discipline. "Hit him harder!" he would command. At other times, he appeared satisfied and returned to our homework assignments.

I knew I would pay dearly later. A sudden sharp blow to my ears. A kick on my shins when no one was looking. Or I would wake up one morning to find my mattress soaked. Karim, gloating and self-righteous, would point it out to my mother and say, "Sulima wet her bed." I remember Madarjan's disapproving frown, as she asked me to change my linens. And my utter helplessness. If I told her that Karim had poured water on my bed during the night, he would have simply found more sadistic ways to punish me. One day I found my allowance money missing from the can I used to keep it in and knew that Karim had stolen it—and that *there was nothing I could do about it.*

This scenario repeated itself every Monday night, when Abajan assembled all of us for his weekly lessons in manners. Each week, he lectured us on a different aspect of etiquette. "When you are invited to someone's home, you say 'hello' and 'how are you.' You do not touch anything. You do not turn on their radio without permission. If they offer food, you do not grab and stuff your face. You take only one piece. And you never go to their rooms without permission. When the food comes in, do not stare at the food as if you were starving. Just ignore the food." The following Monday, he would quiz us about last week's lesson. Husna, Asim, and Zamin answered adequately, and Abajan nodded approvingly at them. But the real drama was reserved for Karim and me. Inevitably, Karim would stumble over the question. Inevitably, I would answer correctly. Inevitably, the flyswatter would be called into play.

Sometimes, I tried to talk to Madarjan about my anger toward Karim. She counseled patience and compassion for him. "What good does it do for you to be angry at him? He is just upset because he is embarrassed. He feels bad about himself."

"He deserves to feel embarrassed for the way he's treating me," I growled.

Madarjan folded me into her arms. "Remember, Sulima, the best revenge is to be good to your enemy. Embarrass the person with your goodness. Rise above the petty differences and look for the good in everyone."

That was Madarjan's philosophy. She always encouraged us to be conciliatory, understanding, and loving, even to those who hurt us. Over the years, I have tried to come to terms with her vision of the world and its impact on me. Was Madarjan teaching me to become a doormat? Couldn't her philosophy have been caused by a culture that I was already resenting, that forced women to be submissive and allowed men to be abusive? I have struggled to understand how to apply Madarjan's humanitarian vision to the challenges I have faced in my life. Surely there must be a way to rise above pettiness and hatred, even while fighting for what you know is right. I am still working on that.

Even when I was quite young, I found Madarjan's approach to be unsatisfying, yet I found her gentle presence to be comforting. To my frustration, Madarjan did not offer concrete answers to the questions that troubled me, especially those that concerned the obviously inequitable treatment of women. Why did women have to ask men for permission to leave the house? Because that's what's right. Why did women do all the laundry? Because that's the job of women. It has always been that way. Why do women have to listen to men? The Qur'an says so. Even though we were not very religious Muslims, invoking the Qur'an always ended a question-and-answer process. The Final Authority had been cited.

So my early childhood was a mixture of fear and pride, resentment of the subservient role of women, and grudging acceptance of that role because Madarjan, whom I loved and respected, modeled quiet acceptance of that role. And also because my daddy, my Abajani, who adored me and whom I adored in return, also accepted that this was the role of women and lived his life accordingly, as the unchallenged Male Head of the Household. Inequity was the price of love, and Abajan's love was the most important of all.

2

Then Abajan changed. Every detail of that day remains branded in the crevices of my memory as if it were yesterday. I was only ten years old, but that day marked the end of my childhood.

Of course, to be quite fair, the changes did not take place all in one day. It's not as if my father, suddenly touched by the magic wand of some dark fairy, transformed from the affectionate, doting Abajani of my early childhood into the reserved, harsh father of my teen years. The changes had been setting in gradually for many months, ever since his return from Mecca.

I barely noticed Abajan's emerging fanaticism at first and I dismissed his more intensified religious observance as a phase. I was amused and mildly irritated by his new edicts and practices. How seriously could I take them? After all, he had never been a particularly religious man. Yes, he had always prayed at the mosque and quoted the Qur'an—especially to support the unfair household policies regarding girls and women. Yes, he spoke of the prophet Mohammed with reverence, as did all Afghans in our culture. But religion had never been a major focus of his life. It was communism that he generally referred to as his guiding philosophy. And his work had always commanded center stage, with religion no more than a necessary backdrop.

The trip to Mecca had not even started out as a religious pilgrimage. It was a work assignment. A local magazine had commissioned him to take photographs of the holy sites. His departure had been business as usual. No special rituals. No fanfare. No sense of solemnity. He blew me a kiss as usual, promising to bring me a treat, as he always did when he traveled. I waved good-bye to the daddy I loved and trotted off to the kitchen to help my mother wash dishes. I did not know then that I would never see my original father again.

A different man returned—A *hadji*, someone who had undertaken the *hejira*, the pilgrimage to Mecca. This site is the holiest in the world to Muslims because it is believed that Mohammed received his prophecies there. A pilgrimage to Mecca is considered an act of religious devotion and returnees are regarded as being sanctified. Many see themselves as special members of an elite and feel a new religious fervor, the weight of an awesome responsibility to be better Muslims and turn others into better Muslims too. My father was one of those men. He returned with a newfound religious commitment and zeal. He rejected his former associations and declared his renewed commitment to Islam. "At one time in my life, I believed in communism," he later said about that time in his life. "In Mecca, I came to understand that it is *badbooy,* a stinking system. It is godless. It is wrong. So I had to choose the other way, the right way. The way of Islam."

But I did not grasp the import of his religious changes. My eyes did not notice how stern and unyielding his face had become. My ears did not catch the alien harsh tones sprinkled like acid through his usual Monday night lessons in manners. I did not detect the absence of his usual phrases of endearment like "my beautiful daughter." I did not notice that I was no longer hearing his jovial voice proclaiming, "Where's my baby, where's my Sula?" I was too busy with the many daily tasks of living to pay much heed to subtle changes in my father's demeanor.

When he asked all the women of the household to start covering their hair, I reasoned that he wasn't asking for anything outrageous or dreadful. It was just a little thing, that's all. An inconvenience. So I obediently tied a scarf around my head. Sometimes it slipped, sometimes my hair tumbled out, and I simply adjusted the scarf and went about my business. Why shouldn't Sula indulge the whims of her much-loved Abajani, especially such an inconsequential request?

Until the Day of the Change. We were getting ready for dinner. It was customary for everyone to wash their hands before sitting down to eat. Adults were generally served by children, who brought them pitchers and basins and helped them wash, then cleared away their used water.

I am leaning forward to hand Abajan the basin. My scarf has slipped off my head and onto my neck. So what? I can adjust it in a minute. I move the basin toward him, then—

Wait. What's happening? Abajan is coming toward me. Just one step, but—

—but this isn't my Abajani. This is someone else. His face—that look—I've never noticed it before. Someone has put cold pebbles where his eyes used to be. Steady, don't drop the basin. Why are my hands shaking?

He takes another step. And another. I try to back up but my feet are frozen to the floor. He grabs my scarf.

"Sulima."

Who is "Sulima"? Where is little Sula?

"Yes, Abajan?"

"Do you know what I used to say to myself when I was a young man?"

Of course I know. He's told me so many wonderful things during our little outings! He's invited me into his early dreams and I have walked hand in hand with him through their corridors. "When I was your age I used to say to myself, one day I will have a lovely daughter. Then when you were born, my wish came true." "One day I will have a little girl and when she is old enough, she and I will photograph flowers together." I hear the echoes of those dreams, but—

—but the scarf is getting tighter. Tighter. I can't breathe! He's pulling me toward him. From far away, I hear his voice. "When I was young I said, if I ever have a daughter when I marry, I will make her cover her hair. And if her scarf falls off her neck, I will tie it so hard that she will choke to death."

Suddenly, he lets go. I stumble backward. Don't spill the water, hold it steady. Listen, he is talking again. "Don't ever let me catch you with your head uncovered again."

I don't remember the rest of the meal. I'm sure Madarjan soothed me by stroking my hand later. I'm sure Husna tried to cheer me up in the kitchen as we were clearing up the dinner dishes. I'm sure Karim delighted in my humiliation and added a few jibes of his own, as he always did. But I remember nothing but my father's eyes, piercing my heart like bullets of ice.

From that day on, a reign of terror fell upon the household. Cousins and uncles who were involved in Communist activities were no longer welcome in our home. We children were no longer allowed to offer an opinion that differed from my father's. We were no longer allowed to ask questions. If we made a stupid mistake, we were berated or beaten. If my mother tried to protect us, as she always did, she was criticized. We were expected to learn our lessons well and there was no room for disagreement or human error.

I learned my lessons well, but not the lessons of obedience, modesty, and religious dedication that my father hoped to teach me. I learned vigilance. I was always on guard for the next attack, the next inquisitorial question, the unexpected surge of his fury. I learned to communicate with my sisters silently, through a flick of the eyelids, a glance, a nod. Wordless messages of warning, compassion, or camaraderie. I learned the fine arts of stealth and concealment as I buried my true feelings under the scarf of filial duty.

And I learned to hate Islam. I silently declared a personal war against the religion that had poisoned my father's soul and turned him against me. All my old unanswered questions and resentments boiled to the surface, and now I made no attempt to stop them. Never again would I ask Madarjan meekly, "Why do I have to do the laundry and Karim doesn't?" Or "Aunt Layla has sweated over the stove all day but when Uncle Daoud comes home, he's served like a king." There was no point in asking these questions because I was no longer willing to accept—or even *try* to accept—the answer that "it's because the Qur'an says so" or "It has always been this way. It is the will of God." I drew my battle lines unequivocally. If that is God's will, if that's what the Qur'an teaches, then take it away. I don't want any part of it. I hate it. I will fight all my life to remove its power and give the power back to the women it has wronged. And if that's how it's always been done, then all the more reason to change things now so that there will be equality and justice in the future.

Now that I am an adult, I believe it is wrong to hate a religion. Even though I am not a practicing Muslim and never will be, I think there are some truly ethical and spiritual teachings in the Islamic faith and that the religion is not all bad. And when you hate a religious tradition, you disrespect those sincere and good people who believe in it. So after many years of pain, I have decided that I cannot blame Islam for the cruel treatment of women. People like my father—who now, ironically, would be called a "moderate Muslim," since he allowed and even encouraged his daughters to have an education—and people like today's Taliban leaders distort what the religion actually teaches. But during those years, the grotesque unfairness preyed on me and turned me bitter and angry.

My father wasn't the only tyrannical enforcer of so-called Islamic law and custom in our house. My grandfather was just as fanatical and just as frightening. It continued to rankle with Aghajan that his son would not accept money or food from him. Stingy though he was, Aghajan believed it to be his duty to share his wealth with his son and grandchildren. Abajan's continued refusal was a direct affront to Aghajan's role as patriarch of the family, and he constantly tried to prevail upon Abajan to accept gifts. But Abajan would have none of it, and he could be as stubborn as Aghajan. "My children should not see me accept handouts," he would say, refusing Aghajan's money. "Let my children see that I am working hard to take care of my family."

"It's not a 'handout' to accept the generosity of your father," Aghajan would protest. But Abajan remained adamant. To establish his role as head of the household, at least in his own city, he invited his younger brothers to live with us while they attended university. As the oldest brother, he felt responsible for them and supported them, even though this placed an additional financial burden on him and reduced the standard of living for all of us.

A formidable figure, Aghajan made no secret of his disapproval and sense of rejection. We children always tiptoed around him when he came to visit and were enormously relieved when he left. But as religion overtook the household, Aghajan's frightening presence became increasingly associated with religious domination. He was one more man who used religion as a way to oppress women.

One afternoon, Aghajan came to visit. I was sitting on my bed, doing my homework as he clumped up the steps of the front porch toward the door of the house. As he passed by my room, which was located right next to the porch, he caught a glimpse of my hair through a small opening in the curtains of my bedroom window. I had allowed my scarf to slip onto my neck as I bent over my notebook.

Aghajan exploded. He charged into the house, headed directly to my room, and flung open my door, cursing and shaking his fists.

Madarjan came rushing in to protect me, as she always did—or at least tried to do—when my father or grandfather was berating or hitting one of us. She put up a tremulous hand and tried to stop him. "Please, she's only a child," she pleaded.

"Even a child should have a sense of modesty, and ten is scarcely a baby. She is an outrage. An abomination! Your daughter is shameless. She's nothing more than a wanton hussy! She deserves to be whipped." He stomped out of the room.

"Please remember to be more careful about your scarf from now on," Madarjan whispered. Her voice wavered, thick with tears. "I am scared of what will happen to you if you don't."

I was scared too and took her words to heart. I continued to wear my scarf dutifully and to take pains to tie it tighter.

I knew my mother loved me, loved all of us. My sisters and I used to call her our *Fereshta,* our Angel, and we gratefully drank in the milk of her soothing kindness. But her submission to the cruelty of religion-crazed men served to reinforce my hatred of Islam. The daily inequities I experienced as a girl enraged me even further. Why did I have to stay home and mind the newest baby while Karim went outside? Why was I chosen to wash the endless parade of mugs produced by the legions of tea-drinking uncles, aunts, grandparents, parents, other relatives and guests while my younger brothers Asim and Zamin played with their friends? My heart was filled with rage against the religion that spawned this wrongdoing.

That is how I became a woman's rights activist at the age of ten. Of course, I didn't call myself a "women's rights activist." I had never heard such a term in my life. Nor did I have some other phrase that I applied to myself. I didn't conceptualize what I was doing. I simply acted. It may seem as though ten is awfully young to become a fighter for freedom and equal rights. Most ten-year-olds are still innocent and carefree children; successfully completing their homework is their most challenging task. Years later, when I came to the United States, I noticed that some of my daughters' American friends were still playing with Barbie dolls, even at the age of ten. But ten-year-old girls in Afghanistan were more mature than ten-year-old girls in America. Perhaps it's because they were responsible for an increasing number of household chores as they grew up, from dishes to laundry to child care of younger siblings and cousins. By ten, they had neither the interest nor the time for "playing house" or similar childish activities. In my case especially, I was catapulted into adulthood not only by the extra work I was expected to do in the household, but also by my father's religious changes and by my position in the family. I was the oldest girl and felt that I wanted to make the world a better place for my little sisters. I had clearly absorbed my father's strong sense of responsibility as the oldest child—or in my case, the oldest sister. I swore to end injustice to women. I felt it was my duty, my job on the planet. I have not stopped feeling this way, even today.

The time was right for me to become involved with women's rights. Change was afoot in Afghanistan—change that held the potential for liberating women. Even at my young age, I sensed how important that was. And I was determined to be a part of whatever was happening.

3

It was a time of unrest. It was a time of movement. It was a time of excitement and the possibility of new and lasting changes. It was a time of opportunity for women.

I was nine years old when a new Constitution was passed, calling for a democratic process in the choosing of leaders. For the first time, Afghanistan would be governed by the people. The first parliamentary election in Afghanistan was held when I was ten. One of the main election headquarters was located just a few blocks away from our house, and on my way to school, I saw the billboards urging people to vote for the candidates. It was a revelation to me to discover that there were women running for office. I pitted the messages and slogans of the female candidates against the messages conveyed to me in my household, and the result made me almost giddy with joy. Here were women who could speak in public, even in front of men! Here were women who could take part in running a government that had classically been male. Here was a chance to see a secular government that would have the power to overthrow the narrow and cruel strictures imposed by male religious authorities.

I began to sneak out of the house to join the action at the campaign headquarters. Although I was not allowed to leave the house without permission, I ignored the rules, counting on my age to protect me from punishment. I was still young enough to be considered a child, and young girls were not subject to the same restrictions as adult women. I capitalized on this freedom and left the house regularly, each time with a different lie. "I'm going to Deena's house to do homework." "I'm going to buy some cheese at the market."

Then I would slip over to the headquarters and help out with the campaign. I gathered together with the other women, standing in a crowd, holding signs and chanting slogans for various candidates. "Long live Anahita!" we shouted in unison. If I noticed someone who was not participating in the rally, I encouraged her to join in. "Come on, repeat after me. Long live Anahita!"

Anahita won, together with several other women who were campaigning. My heart nearly burst with pride, knowing that I had played a tiny part in helping her achieve this victory. Later, Anahita became an important figure in the women's rights movement, and I had the privilege of meeting her in person.

Carried away by the momentum and inspired by the victory, I began talking to other girls in school during recess—what we in America call "consciousness raising." That's exactly what I set out to do—to make my friends aware that they were being treated badly. If they recognized and acknowledged what was happening, they would be motivated to do something about it.

"Do your parents treat you worse than your brothers? Don't you think it's unfair? Do you want to do something about it?"

Some girls made faces at me, snorted, and walked away. I quickly learned not to pursue them or ply them with additional arguments to try to win them over. Instead I concentrated on girls who seemed interested in what I had to say. Soon I was able to figure out who was likely to be receptive and who was either not interested or too frightened to listen. I talked about equality with those girls I thought would be receptive.

I also brought books to my friends whose parents did not allow them to go to school, and urged them to start reading. Even at that young age, I was aware that education was important. Without education, women could never hope to be equal to men. As I grew older, I began to help friends with their reading. Many of them had never bothered to master the basics because they had internalized the attitude of their parents that there is no reason for girls to be educated.

These early efforts were important because they launched my women's rights work by giving me the opportunity to try my tiny wings on friends and equals. I learned a lot. Whom to approach and whom to leave alone. How to present an argument. How to work secretly for a cause. But most of my friends were too frightened to take action—and anyway, beyond reading, there wasn't much action I could recommend at that point. If they rebelled at home, their parents might forbid them from going out, or might beat them. So perhaps the most important thing I learned was that I needed to expand my work.

I began speaking to the mothers, sisters, and aunts of my friends, as well as to my own aunts. "It's not fair that we have to do all the housework." "Men are permitted to go in and out whenever they wish without asking their wives for permission. But we have to ask our husbands or fathers or uncles or brothers for permission to leave the house. If they say no, we cannot go out."

Challenging adults was scary at first. In Afghanistan, there is a strong ethic called *Ehteram*, requiring children to respect their elders. I was only a teenager, and while I was expected to carry out many of the responsibilities of an adult, I still was required to defer to the adults and to accord them respect. It felt presumptuous and rude to raise these questions with women old enough to be my mother. And many of these women did not respond well. Some were openly angry about my intrusion into the delicate balance they had found in their hearts between resentment of their oppression and resignation to it. Some wistfully admired my courage but refused to take action because they were afraid of being socially ostracized or physically abused by their husbands. Still others defended the customs. "It would not be safe for women to go out at night. They could be attacked." "It would not be right for a woman to wander the streets at all hours. People might think she was a loose woman. There would be gossip and scandal." "Women must behave like ladies. They can't just go ahead and do whatever they want like men can."

One woman told me that the Qur'an specifically mandated this treatment of women and we had no right to violate the Qur'an's words. She quoted a verse to prove her point.

Men are superior to women on account of the qualities with which God hath gifted the one over the other and on account of the outlay they make from their substance for them. Virtuous women are therefore obedient, guarding the unseen as God hath guarded them. But as to those on whose part you fear desertion, admonish them and leave them alone in their sleeping-places and beat them. Then if they obey you, do not seek a way against them.

Of course, this only served to strengthen my resolve. I could scarcely believe my ears. Not only were men considered superior to women, but they were actually allowed to beat and abandon their wives! This inspired me all the more to gather together other women who found these concepts as repugnant as I did.

And I did find kindred souls. Women whose eyes showed understanding and relief when I brought these matters to their attention. No longer were they suffering alone. Another woman had given voice to their private anguish, their humiliation, the haunting questions that echoed through dark, secret places in their hearts. Yes, they said. Yes, yes. We will help.

Help would be wonderful, but what to do with their offers of help? I was only a teenager, after all. I could not single-handedly forge a group of adult women into a movement and shepherd them through the steps necessary to bring changes in the treatment of women. Fortunately, at that time the first women's rights organization in Afghanistan—the Women's Democratic Organization—was formed.

The WDO could not have gotten off the ground without help from the Communist Party. During the years of my early childhood, Russia had been increasing its involvement with internal Afghan affairs as the two countries were establishing firmer economic and military ties. And Russia's involvement initially seemed good for Afghanistan—at least in my estimation. Soviet support enabled secular leaders to institute all sorts of desirable changes. In 1959, the prime minister and senior members of his government appeared in public with their wives and daughters unveiled. Women started entering the workforce in greater numbers, and there was less stigma associated with being a working woman. The Constitutional Advisory Committee responsible for mandating the election process included two female participants. The new Constitution they created granted legal equality to women and men. And the newly elected parliament included four female MPs.

I heard about the WDO and I knew that there were women involved with the new government and women working for change, but for a long time I had no idea how to get in touch with them. Ironically, it was a man—my cousin Nabi, the son of Uncle Daoud—who showed me the way. He was involved with the People's Democratic Party of Afghanistan, a movement consisting largely of students, which advocated the type of social reform taught by communism. When I was in my second year of high school, he became aware of my passion for women's rights and he suggested I meet several other women who had formed the WDO.

"How can I meet these women?" I asked.

"I will introduce you to someone who knows them," Nabi replied.

"When?" I asked.

"In a few days."

A few days passed and nothing happened. I was on my way to the bakery with the dough. Most people did not have their own baking ovens and brought their raw, prekneaded dough to communal ovens to bake. While the bread was baking, I went to my cousin's home, which was near the bakery, to find out why he had not gotten back to me.

Nabi answered the door. "Come in. There's someone here I want you to meet. I think he can help you."

I took an instantaneous dislike to the man who was sitting inside. His name, Nabi told me, was Hafizullah Amin.

"I know that you campaigned in the election and that you had to do it without your father's knowledge. I understand these family situations very well," he said right away. "You know, my brother is opposed to my nephew Assad's involvement in communism. They have terrible fights. If you get involved your father might get angry. But it is normal for young people to do what they want. My nephew certainly does and my brother opposes him." He smiled. This was supposed to make me like him, to make me feel he understood me. But there was something creepy about him. I continued listening as he babbled on. "Of course, my brother is a wonderful man. We come from a good family. We're all intelligent people. We have strong minds. We are committed to our ideals. When we want something, nothing gets in the way. My brother is not a bad person, you understand." He continued talking about his family and his brother. I could not get a word in edgewise, and by the time he paused for air, I was thoroughly disgusted. What a pompous, arrogant man! I quickly stated my reason for visiting and excused myself, saying I had to check on the progress of the bread.

To my surprise, two women who were active in the WDO contacted me a few days later. Apparently, they had received my name from Hafizullah Amin. They invited me to attend a meeting. Soon I was an active member of the WDO. At last I belonged to a group that raised awareness and educated women. At last I belonged to a group of companions whom I could share with and learn from. At last I had a context to which I could refer receptive women whom I was recruiting to the Cause. In fact, my job was to recruit new women into the organization.

I found unexpected support even in my own family. My father's sister Mariam, who was only a year older than I was, came on board. She lived with us for a while, and together, we secretly started attending meetings of the new women's group. After a few months, Mariam returned to Aghajan's house in the East to continue the work. I missed her terribly when she left. She had been my only companion and real source of understanding and support in my household.

It was especially meaningful to find companionship and support because there was so much opposition to women's rights and the WDO among women as well as men. The organization was a renegade concept in Afghanistan, an appalling concept to the established norms of the culture. In fact, the only official entity that in any way recognized and supported it was the Communist Party. The irony of having a democratic organization supported by the Communists eluded me at the time. The Communists were well aware of the power they wielded by being the sole supporters of the organization and took full advantage of the opportunity to recruit women into the Communist Party. Initially, many were reluctant and joined the Communists only because they had no choice. If they wanted the women's movement to succeed, they had to reciprocate by participating in the Communist movement. But to others, including myself, the ideology of communism, with its emphasis on equality and liberation from oppression, was attractive. It appeared to go hand in hand with our own vision of equality and liberation. It was logical to link both movements, which seemed to be working for a set of common causes. That is how I became involved with Communism.

My life began to revolve around my new friends and my women's rights work. I attended meetings regularly, disseminated literature in school, and spoke up—often in public—for what I believed. As I became more comfortable and well read, my speeches became bolder.

"Women should enjoy the same privileges as men!" I proclaimed to a group of fellow members of the WDO, and some new recruits.

"We should be allowed to hold important positions in the government. We should be allowed to leave the house without asking our fathers or brothers for permission. We should be allowed to choose a husband, even if our family doesn't like him, and we should never be forced to marry someone we don't love. And marriage should be equal. If we are not allowed to have more than one husband, then men should not be allowed to have more than one wife."

One of the new women shyly raised her hand. "But the Qur'an allows men to have many wives. Why, even the prophet Mohammed had several wives."

My heart inflamed, I took a daring leap. "Then the Qur'an is wrong. I would burn the book that allows men to marry many women, that perpetrates such a terrible injustice upon us!" I had heard Mariam say this, and it struck me as powerful and true.

On another occasion, I confessed that I was not sure I really wanted to get married, eliciting a series of gasps from some members of the audience. "This is what I want. I want to be a doctor. And I also want to work for women's rights. But unless things change, I am planning to get married. Here's why. Because without a husband, I have no freedom. I cannot go out. I cannot attend a meeting, a party, or a movie. I cannot go to a concert or go to work. I must ask my father or older brother, both of whom would be violently opposed to what I'm doing if they found out about it. Luckily, they don't know, which is why I am able to give this speech. But if I am married to a supportive partner, he will 'let' me work. He is my ticket to freedom. So think of that, sisters." My voice was rising. "In order to be free, I need the permission of a man. Do you think this is right? Do you think this is fair?"

I was wrong about one thing. I had said my father would be violently opposed to my work *if* he found out. It turned out that my father already knew exactly what I was doing. Someone told him that his daughter was a Communist, an atheist, a rabble-rouser and troublemaker. Later I learned that one of the main tattletales was my school principal, who overheard me spreading the word during recess. And perhaps there were others too. My activities had become quite well known.

I have just slipped into the kitchen through the back door. I hear his voice.
"Sulima."

I jump. Why is he here? Not to wash fruit for tomorrow, that's done by this hour. Not to squeeze juice. Certainly not to wash dishes or stir the soup. There can be only one reason. . . .

There is a rushing in my ears, a drumming of my heart. I am a big girl now. Fifteen years old. I need his permission to leave. Or a brother's or uncle's. Has he found out that I never asked anyone?

A lunge, then a cry. "Please! My arm!"

The grip tightens. "Where have you been?"

"W-with Deena. We—we were studying."

His voice is a razor of ice. "I see. And who gave you permission to go out?"

Quick, think of someone. Uncle Daoud? No, he was out earlier. Zamin? He had class today. How about—

"As I thought. You did not receive permission to leave."

Steady, I tell my voice, steady. I must say this. "Father, women should not need men to allow them to leave the house."

Ice turns to fire in the flash of his eyes, the burning grip of his hand on my arm. "Do not ever let me hear you say such blasphemous words under my roof again. No daughter of mine is going to disrespect the teachings of our ancestors, the words of the holy Qur'an. You are forbidden from attending meetings in the company of infidels and spreading their heretical message to others. People have come to tell me that my daughter is shaming our family with these obscene involvements. You will not be able to hide from me. If I hear that you have disobeyed me, I will forbid you from leaving the house for any reason at all."

I could not sleep. I was still shaking. In the privacy of my room, I stuffed my pillow into my mouth and sobbed silently. I did not want Abajan to hear me cry.

When my eyes felt as though they had no tears left to shed, I began to contemplate my predicament. It did not take long for me to reach a conclusion. I could not stop my work now. It was unthinkable. I was fighting for justice, I was fighting for a cause that was right and true. To be deterred from the pursuit of justice by fear was cowardly. It was wrong. It made me a collaborator in injustice. Abajan would not get the better of me. I would continue my work—just with greater caution. I arranged with Deena to have meetings held at her home. It was easy for me to visit her because we were in school together.

But it was only a matter of time before Abajan caught on. And not too much time, because he was suspicious. He kept me under strict scrutiny. Obviously he also had his sources outside the family who kept him informed as to my activities. Several months later, at the beginning of my junior year of high school, he stopped me in the hallway as I was leaving for school.

"Just a minute, Sulima."

"Please, Abajan, can this wait? I'll be late for school."

His hand descended on my shoulder, his fingers digging into the flesh. "You are not going to school."

I began to protest, but his grip got harder.

"You have been disobeying me. Do not think I am not aware. I have been suspicious for a long time, but now I know for sure that you have been continuing with your heretical activities." He paused, and I did not dare ask him who had told. Besides, what did it matter at this point anyway?

"You must be restrained for your own good, and for the protection of the family. You are forbidden from leaving the house for any reason. You may continue your studies at home, at least at present. Women should receive an education, if they know how to handle it. Unfortunately, some women get puffed-up ideas when they are too educated. They start to think that they are equal to men. They must be taught a lesson." The menacing quality was back in his voice. "I will give you a chance to prove that you can be a good Muslim woman who uses her intelligence correctly and does not overstep the boundaries of her proper place. I am allowing you to continue your studies in the house because I am a generous, magnanimous person, who is broad-minded and who respects women. Do not give me reason to regret it."

He expected thanks, and hating myself for it, I complied. "Thank you, Abajan," I mumbled and fled to my room.

When the newest round of shaking had subsided, I took stock of my position. Slowly, the reality of what had just happened seeped in. It was an ordinary Thursday. A school day. My friends were sitting in the classroom, studying science and math. I was in my bedroom, with finger-shaped red marks still glaring loudly from my shoulder. I glanced at my watch. Nine-thirty. Soon it would be time for morning recess. My friends would be huddled in little groups, wondering what had happened to me. Deena would be talking to Zafar about tomorrow's meeting. Then the bell would ring and class would resume. Without me.

Would I ever be allowed to leave the house again? How could I continue my life's work under my father's roof? Would I ever be allowed to go back to school? If not, how could I get into university? How could I become a doctor?

The questions were swirling, my head was aching, the world was constricting into a ball of pain and terror. The ball was spinning faster and faster, round and round, and then it exploded in a torrent of tears that left me spent and desolate.

I was under house arrest.

I must have fallen asleep because I don't remember the rest of the day. The next thing I knew, I heard doors opening and closing. Karim, Husna, Asim, and Zamin were home from school. I heard them chatting about teachers and homework, and the pain bubbled in my throat like bile, followed by rage. Pure, white-hot, cleansing rage.

I would not let him stop me. I would not let anyone or anything stand in the way of justice, equality, and liberation. Whatever it took, I would find a way.

I lay down again, and slowly a plan started to take form in my mind. I reached for the phone and dialed Deena's number.

4

"Deena, how nice to see you. What a beautiful scarf." Madarjan opened the door to Deena, who was carrying a knapsack. "You are here to study with Sulima?"

Deena nodded and adjusted the scarf on her head as she walked through the house to my room. We had agreed that all my friends would cover their hair, so as to be less threatening to Abajan.

"I will bring you some tea and cookies!" Madarjan called after her.

We hugged and I opened my chemistry book. If anyone came in, I could hide the forbidden literature under the schoolbooks.

"Did you bring *Das Kapital*?" I asked her eagerly.

She nodded and pulled the precious volume from her book bag. "We're up to Chapter five. It's your turn now."

"Good. And you can copy Chapter three of *The Prince*." Deena quickly stowed it away.

Our small contraband library—books by Marx, Lenin, Machiavelli, and other political philosophers—was carefully passed around our circle of friends and supporters. We knew we could not talk persuasively about women's rights, politics, history, and philosophy without quoting someone greater than ourselves who could provide substantiation for our views. Since none of us could afford to buy our own books, we pooled our meager funds and shared. We did not have access to photocopy machines, so each of us undertook to hand-copy a certain number of chapters from each book. Using carbon paper, we made seven copies of each chapter, then distributed them.

Madarjan entered the room with a cup of tea and a tray of cookies. Quickly, I slid *Das Kapital* under my chemistry book. Although Madarjan knew about my work, I tried to involve her as little as possible. I hated to deceive her, but I felt I was sparing her greater pain and conflict. I did not want to compromise her by having her see what we were working on. She would feel caught between Abajan and me even more than usual. I would turn her into a collaborator against him, make her betray herself, her own principles and beliefs, and I did not want to do that.

After Madarjan had left the room and we'd finished the cookies and tea, Deena stood up to leave. "Whose turn is it to come tomorrow?"

"Zafar's," I answered. "She'll pick up the chapter from me and give it to you. But she usually doesn't have time to stay. Call me, and I'll tell you what the most important pages are. Then you can tell everyone else."

"When should I call you?"

"Tomorrow after dinner. If the phone is busy, I'll call you. Remember, when I say 'multiplication,' I'm talking about the chapter in *Das Kapital*. If I give you numbers to multiply, I'm talking about page numbers in the chapter. But if I say 'division,' it means that there's nothing relevant in the chapter. So you don't need to bother."

Math had become a wonderful and versatile pretext for long conversations with my friends with all sorts of coded messages built into the various mathematical functions. Using my math book, I was able to receive and convey details about Communist propaganda, meeting places, speech assignments, and other tasks to be done. Studiously bent over the math book on my lap, I looked like the most dedicated pupil in the world.

But Abajan had his suspicions. He walked past the phone regularly, whether I was talking from the phone in the living room or the extension in Karim's room. By this time, Karim was no longer living with us. He had moved to my grandparents' house in the East to escape my father's constant pressure. But even in Karim's room, I did not have much privacy. Abajan could be lurking anywhere. And try as I might to look innocent, I was sure that my flushed face betrayed me.

I was right.

"No more phone calls," Abajan announced one night as I lifted the receiver and prepared to dial Deena's number.

"Why not?" Already, my heart was thumping. The receiver almost slipped out of my sweaty palms.

"Because I am sure you are using the phone for blasphemous purposes."

"But, Abajan, I'm just doing math. You said I should keep up with my studies."

"You have lied before. I am certain you are lying again. I cannot prove it, but I do not need to prove it. A king need not justify his actions to his subjects. In this house, I am the king and my children must obey me. Hang up the phone."

I complied.

Without use of the telephone, I felt even more isolated. Deena, Zafar, and my other friends made it their business to loyally support me and the Cause by visiting me daily, demurely covered by the required *chador*, the head scarf used for religious reasons. Abajan continued to have his suspicions, and often I caught him eavesdropping outside my door, but we spoke in whispers and low murmurs, learning to sprinkle enough chemistry and math phrases into our dialogue that he appeared satisfied and began to leave us alone.

But Father was far from satisfied and his suspicions were by no means allayed. Instead of spying on me by day, he turned his focus to my activities at night.

All of us children had a mandatory 9:00 P.M. bedtime, even in our late teen years. Abajan wanted the house to quiet down so that he could sleep soundly because he had to get up at 5:00 A.M. to wake us all for prayer. Or at least that's what he said. In reality, he spent a great deal of time prowling the house during the night, with the express purpose of catching me in illicit activities. Although he engaged in random searches of my room during the daytime, he would suddenly come knocking on my door at night. He wanted to catch me with a smoking gun.

So when I went to bed, I always locked the door. I spread my prayer rug on the floor in front of my bed and placed a Qur'an on the rug. That way, if Abajan came in, I could always say I was praying or reading the Qur'an. Although Muslims pray five times daily, it is considered a special merit to rise during the night and read the Qur'an or pray.

Then I would remove my picture of Mecca from the wall. This was a photograph taken by Abajan during that fateful trip that had changed our lives so dramatically. Behind the picture, I had taken out one brick, leaving a nice little compartment into which I stashed my books and papers. I had tried hiding them under my mattress, but Abajan had once searched there and found my papers. The beating I received was so severe I knew I had to find a more effective hiding place. I sewed a pocket into my mattress and hid the papers inside it, but they made noise when I lay down and I knew that this would not be safe either. But I felt fairly confident that the area behind the picture was as close to a perfect hiding place as possible.

Having taken my book and copying paper from the compartment, I would replace the picture of Mecca and set to work. My parents' radio had a lighted face and I borrowed it. Each night, I turned it on and used the light to copy the books. Of course, when the radio was on, the music was audible, so I had to hide everything under a thick blanket.

One night, I heard a knocking on my door.

I had trained myself to replace the papers behind the picture noiselessly. I crept over to the wall, slid the picture aside, tucked the papers into their hiding place, then opened the door.

"What were you doing?" Abajan's voice made my belly go queasy, and I felt the familiar thumping in my chest.

"*Qur'an-e-Sharif me losto,*" I answered. "Reading the Qur'an. And praying."

His eyes scanned the room. "Why did you not answer the door right away?"

"I did not want to interrupt."

He clearly did not believe me. He felt under the mattress. Nothing. He peered under the bed. Again, nothing. He pulled aside the covers and found the radio.

"Why do you have the radio under your covers?" he thundered.

"I was listening to music."

"During prayer? Do you know how disrespectful that is to God?"

Keep calm. The calmer you are, the less he'll suspect. "I covered the radio with the blanket so it wouldn't disturb anyone in the house. I couldn't hear it when I prayed."

"So why didn't you turn it off before you started?"

Steady. Calm. Think clearly. "I forgot. I was so anxious to read the Qur'an that I didn't really think about the radio."

I forced myself to meet his eye, forced myself to look nonchalant. We held each other's gaze, Father glaring at me, my face a picture of innocence. One. Two. Three. Then he unplugged the radio and tucked it under his arm.

"I'm confiscating this permanently," he told me. "There will be no more music during the night. Nor any other improper activities." He gave me another hard stare and strode out of the room.

There was no more writing that night.

By the following night, I had a new idea. I would use a candle.

Looking back on it now, I think that Someone or Something was protecting me and all of us. I could have burned down the house. I covered my night table with a blanket. The table had four legs and an open space under it, and I crouched under the table, candle in hand, copying feverishly. I managed to copy a fair number of pages before I heard the familiar knocking on my door.

Quick. No time to think. Slide away the picture. Shove the papers behind it. Put the candle on the floor. Open the door.

Abajan was staring. "Why is your face black?"

I touched my cheek and looked at my finger. It was covered with soot. My face had turned completely black from the candle smoke.

"I used the candle to read the Qur'an," I said, pointing to my little companion of light, its flame flickering innocently in its holder, illuminating the pages so sacred to my father.

Once again, he searched the room. Floor. Mattress. Bed. Dresser. Nothing. He sighed. "I cannot very well take away the Qur'an from you. Use the candle if you have to."

A tiny victory. The triumph of my pinpoint of light over the vast darkness of my life under my father's roof. The candle became my friend, my partner, as night after night, I shared noble teachings with the great thinkers and revolutionaries of history, my mind rising and dancing like the flame itself.

Soon, my picture of Mecca began to show signs of wear. The upper right corner was torn, and you could see some papers through the hole. I searched through the folder of my father's photographs until I found a suitable replacement. Still a picture of Mecca, but taken from a different angle.

Abajan was still engaging in random searches of my room. The next time he barged in, he immediately noticed the new picture.

"What happened to the old one?" he demanded.

"It tore, so I replaced it."

As soon as I said it, I knew I had made a mistake. Why would a picture, subjected to nothing more strenuous than hanging on a wall, suddenly tear? I felt the thudding again, the sinking, sick feeling in my belly, the sweat breaking out on my forehead and palms. Why had I not said I simply wanted to see a different angle of the holy site? That I found his photographs so moving, I wanted to enjoy a different one every month? Should I correct myself now, or would that be more incriminating?

"I see." His voice oozed sarcasm, like blood slowly dripping from a knife. "The picture just happened to tear, all by itself."

He strode over to the wall and wrenched the picture free. Out fell everything. The latest book I was copying, which was *A Step Ahead and Two Steps Behind,* by Lenin. My carbon paper. My notebook. My pens. A letter I was in the process of writing to Rashid, a friend and fellow socialist.

Say something. Anything. Apologize. Beg. Call upon God's mercy. I open my mouth, but my throat is as parched as the paper of the Qur'an. I try to speak, but no sound comes out.

Hands. Hands grabbing. "No, please, no!" I am being pushed onto the bed. "Abajan, don't! Not the cable, please!"

There are sounds, raw and bleeding, sounds but no words. Clothing tearing. A rhythmic whirring sound, then the thud of contact, the shock of metal against flesh. Someone is screaming—is that my voice? Then the pain, the searing pain. Again and again and again, now something slippery is trickling, gushing down my back. Again and again, and then there is a door slamming. The taste of salt in my mouth, the tears of Madarjan mingling with my dried blood as she tenderly washes my wounds.

I was confined to my bed, immobilized, for two weeks.

5

I opened my eyes. It was midnight of the following night. Abajan was sitting on my bed. Immediately, I felt my heart constrict. Was he here to beat me again?

"Abajan?" It was barely a whisper.

"You wrote some terrible things about me in that letter."

My face flushed in the dark. I had borrowed my father's fountain pen to write to Rashid, a friend in the Communist Party. I was in the process of expressing my resentment about being confined to the house, when the fountain pen had leaked all over the page. I wrote, "now my page is as dirty as my father's soul." The letter had been in the packet of papers Abajan had confiscated the previous night.

For a moment, I felt contrition. Then righteous anger surged in me. It was *his* fault that I had written these words. *He* had driven me to this hatred by his tyranny. "I'm sorry, Abajan," I mumbled.

He was silent a long time. What was he thinking? And when would he leave? I lay awake, squirming on the inside, until he rose and slowly left the room.

He came back every night after that. He would sit down on my bed and silently observe me. It was embarrassing and awkward. And even more uncomfortable because on the third night, he started to cry. I had never seen Abajan cry before. How could I comfort him? What could I say?

"Sula, Sula, I am begging you to repent before it is too late. You never know what tomorrow may bring. Pray to God and ask Him to forgive you."

Forgive me? For what? I was inflamed again with anger and any thought I had of comforting my father immediately fled—not that I would have known how to comfort him anyway.

The scene repeated itself the next night and the next. Abajan's tears were salt to the wounds he had inflicted, and each night, I counted the minutes for him to leave the room.

"You are not staying in Kabul," Abajan announced as soon as I could walk comfortably again. "You are going to your grandfather's house in the East."

Leaving Kabul? What about my work? How could I raise the consciousness of women without the organized support system of the WDO? This was the worst possible time to leave. I had already been out of the loop for two weeks and now, what would happen?

The trip was grim. I was leaving behind my friends, my work, everything precious to me. I was still aching and traumatized by my father's assault and confused by his crying spells. As I watched the streets give way to mountains as the car slowly made its way east, I allowed myself to cry again. What was I going to do?

I was greeted by a joyous Mariam, who flung her arms around me and did not let go.

"Sulima, I'm so happy you're here!"

It turned out that Mariam had been trying to organize a women's movement in the East. "I am good at talking to people," she told me while I unpacked my things. "They listen. They're impressed. I can motivate them and they want to become involved. But once they express an interest, everything falls apart. I don't know how to organize. You're just the person to help."

I brightened up. Maybe this move was the best thing that could have happened to me. Here was completely uncharted territory for my women's work. I would be breaking new ground, really making a difference. And I would not have to be accountable to my father. "Tell me what you've done and how many women there are."

"Right now, there are only girls. Kids of our age. I don't even know where to begin to get older women involved."

"Let's start by getting the girls organized. Then we can work on the women."

The two and a half months I spent in the East were among the happiest I have ever had. Although Aghajan was as fanatical and stubborn as Abajan, he did not have Abajan's vendetta against me and had no interest in following me around to supervise my activities. He didn't even know that I might engage in any "improper activities" to supervise. Abajan had not warned him about me because he assumed that once I was out of Kabul, my women's work would stop. Aghajan was old, tired, and entirely focused on his farm and his houses. He still traveled a great deal and was gone for days on end, and even when he was around, we hardly saw him. We could lose ourselves on his huge property. So long as Mariam and I did not appear to be doing anything outrageously out of line, we were left alone. Nor did we encounter any problem with my grandmother or the other wives. They doted on me and gave Mariam and me a great deal of freedom.

It was perfect. We assembled our friends and held meetings in Aghajan's orchard. This was not unusual. In the East, there were no televisions at the time and little entertainment—especially for girls. Although there were movies, young girls did not usually go by themselves. It would have been considered inappropriate. Instead, girls congregated in the orchards and took walks. They were allowed to go unaccompanied to the homes of their friends if they confined their socialization to the friend's orchard or farm.

In my case, none of my friends' parents objected to their visiting me. My grandfather was an important man, well respected by everyone. It never occurred to these parents, who usually supervised their daughters so carefully, to be concerned about their activities at Aghajan's house. So it was not difficult to invite girls over for our meetings.

Holding meetings in the orchard was quite different from holding meetings in Deena's bedroom, or in the WDO headquarters. The sun warmed our faces and delicious aromas of flowers wafted over to us, making us almost giddy with their sweetness. One of us would take turns climbing the pear trees and shaking the lush, ripe fruit to the ground. Then we would go to the stream, wash the fruit, and have a feast. It was like food of the angels. The flavor was delicate and sweet and the texture as light and airy as cotton candy. The chunks of fruit almost melted in our mouths. We lay beside the stream, eating one fruit after another, and talking. Then we picked melons and put them into a netted basket in the stream to cool. We would come back for them in the afternoon.

Meetings in Kabul had been serious, solemn affairs. But here, our meetings were filled with laughter and fun. We played *shir jangi*, a game much like Geography, only using poems instead of place names. One person recited a poem, and the next person had to find another poem that began with the last letter in the previous poem.

How we all loved poetry! We took the words of famous love poems and applied them to our revolutionary ideas.

> When you turn your eyes to me
> The beauty is so great
> You threaten me with the knife
> With getting my head removed
> But if I were afraid of the knife
> I would not dance with you
> In the circle of lovers.

Since romantic love was forbidden, the poet risked death by decapitation for pursuing his beloved. We changed the words around to suit our needs.

> When the great thinkers
> Send their words to me
> Through their books
> Their beauty is so great
> They are so true
> They threaten me with the knife
> With getting my head removed
> But if I were afraid of the knife
> I would not go to any meeting.

Not great classical poetry to be sure, but we were teenagers. This was fun. This was entertainment. We sang to one another, told stories, and dined on pears. Then we almost waddled to the house, stuffed with the sweet delight of our feast, only to find another delicious feast awaiting us. Sliced meat from a freshly slaughtered sheep, roasted in the oven with a slice of garlic. In the same oven, fresh bread was baking. When the bread came out, it was flavored with meat and garlic. We made sandwiches and ate them, the juice dripping down our faces. Then we returned to the orchard for more.

Sometimes we rewarded ourselves for a job well done. One day we had worked so hard that we treated ourselves to a movie. We pooled our money and rented the entire women's section of the movie theater. There were enough of us that it was not considered inappropriate for us to go. We sat in the upstairs area reserved for women and young children and gripped one another's hands as the plot unfolded. I still remember the movie. It was called *Khamoshi*, a word that means "silence." The lead character is a nurse who has fallen in love with a patient. The patient is a man who has gone insane with grief because the woman he loves has rejected him. The nurse pretends to be in love with him so as to give him self-confidence. He is cured, leaves the hospital, and uses his new self-confidence to win over his original beloved. But it turns out that the nurse has fallen in love with him for real. When she is asked to adopt the same strategy with another patient, she suffers a breakdown, goes insane, and is admitted to the hospital. Needless to say, we all cried copiously at the end.

But our time together was not only fun and games. We did some serious planning and organizing. We focused primarily on the school that Mariam attended. Sometimes, I accompanied Mariam to school. During recess, I talked to the girls and invited them to meetings. If I was unable to go in person, I sent Mariam to school with articles or books to distribute.

I found a wonderfully receptive audience at that school. Many teachers were delighted to have me come and raise their students' consciousness. It turned out that they had long wanted to see changes in women's rights. At last, someone was coming in to work on these issues! It was also wonderful to be back in a school environment. Although I had never stopped studying while I was at home, I did miss the interaction of the classroom. Now I was able to accompany Mariam to school and sit in on classes with her. Although she was older than I was, we were actually in the same class because she had started school—as they did in the East—at the age of seven, while I had started at age six and had skipped a grade. So I was ahead of myself and she was behind herself and we had the pleasure of being not only relatives and dear friends but also classmates besides.

Bibijan's house was much nearer to the school than Aghajan's, so I often invited girls over. By this time Babajan had passed away. Bibijan was visiting Kabul, but my mother's sister, Aunt Sheela, was living there with sundry other family members and was more than willing to help our cause. She assumed that many mothers would not be pleased with their daughters' involvement with women's rights and appointed herself as guardian of our meetings. She made sure to greet our guests at the door. If a mother accompanied her daughter to our meeting, Aunt Sheela would invite the mother to tour the house or the orchards. "Let's leave the young people alone to talk about whatever kids talk about today, shall we?"

My approach to women's rights began—and has continued to this day—with education. I passionately believe that unless women have the same educational opportunities as men, they will never be free of male oppression. Here in eastern Afghanistan, we were not talking about "equal educational opportunities" at that time. We were talking about basic literacy. Many of the poorer families did not understand the value of women's education or were downright opposed. Even among the wealthier families, girls did not understand the value of learning and many could not read.

I spoke to girls at school about how education could give them a better life. I told them stories about places where women could read and write, could hold jobs, could be free. I urged the wealthier girls to speak to their parents about encouraging poorer families, many of whom worked on the property of the wealthier families, to send their daughters to school. If a family could not afford to do so, we raised money and also helped them out with supplies such as notebooks, pens, and books. Often, the poorer families were so honored by the rich landowner's visit that they were eager to do whatever was suggested. Knowing that the rich person's child was also attending school inspired the poorer parents to accord greater value to schooling. Sometimes a mother or aunt attended the group out of sincere interest to learn, and we were thrilled to have a few adult recruits join our ranks.

I am proud to have been associated with this first women's movement in eastern Afghanistan. The movement continued to grow and flourish long after I left. Many forces contributed to its eventual destruction. In their aggressive efforts to educate the public—women and men—the Communists did not respect the needs and sense of pacing of the northern residents. Instead of being a privilege, reading became a chore, and worse, for many women it became a symbol of foreign oppression. The hatred for Soviet involvement in Afghan internal policies led to the rise of the rebels that eventually forced the Russians to withdraw—the Mujihaddin. While they were rising to power and once they took over, even the most committed women ended up staying at home rather than going to school because it was too dangerous to go out. And the rise of the Taliban squashed women's education almost entirely. Even with the current overthrow of the Taliban regime, it will be years, if not decades, before we can regroup our losses and move ahead with women's education in the East. I just hope that it will happen during my lifetime.

In August, my happy time in the East came to an abrupt and shattering end when we received terrible news. Uncle Murid, who was Abajan's brother, and his wife, Aunt Nasima, were killed in a car accident—a hit-and-run.

Abajan appeared the next day, together with other male family members who accompanied him to the cemetery. In fact, friends and family poured in from all over the country to pay their respects and offer condolences.

It was not customary for women to go to the cemetery, so the house was full with bereft female family members who stayed behind with Guljan during the burial. Even Aghajan's other wives were gentle and tried to be supportive of her. But nothing helped. Guljan remained inconsolable. She kept repeating, "I am *boora,* I am *boora,* a woman who has lost a child." She rocked to and fro moaning, *"Khawray may pe sar shoowey.* May dirt cover me and bury me."

Madarjan did not come to the funeral. She was pregnant with Hala and in poor health. The miscarriages she had sustained during the years had weakened her, and she was not up to traveling.

After the burial, Abajan came to talk to me. He was holding a typed paper. "I want you to come home," he said.

It was customary for the funeral to take place in a big city a few days after a burial in the country, so I thought he wanted me to come to Kabul for the funeral, then return to the East afterward. "So I'll be coming back to Aghajan's after the funeral?" I asked.

He shook his head. "I want you home for good."

Did this mean he had changed his mind about my schooling? I was afraid to be too hopeful, so I waited apprehensively.

It turned out that he had an entirely different motive. "We are adopting Murid's little daughter, Surya. Your mother is due to give birth any day. She is not well now, and she is not up to caring for Surya. It will be even harder once the baby is born. Your help is needed at home."

He handed me the paper. "Sign this," he commanded.

I read the typewritten words:

I, Sulima Obaidi, hereby agree to discontinue all of my heretical activities. I will no longer be associated with the Communist Party. I will no longer attend or organize meetings, or try to influence women to abandon their proper place in God's ordered universe. I will be a dutiful Muslim woman. I will obey the Qur'an and honor the message of the Prophet. I will be a dutiful daughter, and one day, I will be a dutiful and submissive wife to my husband.

I signed, of course. I had no choice. And of course, it made no difference. I was as passionate and dedicated to my own ideology as Abajan was to his. And I would no more have been able to walk away from my work than Abajan would have been able to denounce the Qur'an.

My aunt Fauziya was standing at the door of our house, a little girl peeking shyly from behind her skirt.

Aunt Fauziya hugged me with her free arm. "Sulima, I'm so glad you're back!" She nodded toward the little girl. "Surya has been staying with me at my house since—well, you know," she whispered. "But now that you're here to help your mother, she can move in with you."

I looked at the adorable little girl, her eyes huge and brown, her hair curly and soft, and right away, she became my sister. Surya disengaged from Aunt Fauziya's skirts and came over to hug me. I swept her up and hugged her tightly.

As brutal as the death of my uncle and aunt were, Surya gave me comfort and pleasure. I was overjoyed to care for her—as were Madarjan and Husna. We were all sisters now. Hala's arrival added even more joy. She was a delicious little baby, and nothing gave me greater pleasure than to hold her dimpled, chubby little fists and revel in her toothless smile.

I was even more overjoyed to find out that Abajan planned an extended trip to the North in a few days. A magazine had commissioned him to take a series of photographs of the mountains. I would be free to continue my work!

In mid-September, Abajan called me. "Sulima, I want you to go back to school to take your final exams. That way you will be counted as having finished the eleventh grade."

Abajan was sending me back to school! It did not matter that I had missed a year of school. The crucial determinant in whether a student was promoted to the next grade was how well she did on final exams. If I did well enough on my exams, I would pass eleventh grade. And maybe Abajan would relent and let me return as a full-time student for my senior year. I studied intensely and got excellent grades on my exams.

It was winter vacation, which marks the end of the academic year. In Afghanistan, vacation takes place during the winter months—beginning with the end of December and going through the end of February. I occupied myself with my women's work but with much greater caution. My friends still came to the house to plan meetings, but they were even more careful to speak loudly about academic subjects when Father was in the house. I continued copying book chapters but found a wonderful hiding place on the roof. I knew that it would never occur to Abajan to look there. I wrapped everything in many layers of plastic and weighed it down with a huge rock. My precious books and papers were safe, even from the rain and snow of winter.

"Your conduct has improved," Abajan said to me the day before school was to reopen. "You may return to school for your senior year."

"Thank you, Abajan."

School went very differently this year. The supervisor of my school, to whom my teachers were accountable, had been impressed by my test scores, especially in light of my yearlong absence from school. I was someone she wanted to keep in the student body. She also supported women's rights. She stood up for me to the principal and begged her to allow me to do my women's work unobstructed. And several teachers came forward with offers of support. For example, the recess supervisor allowed me to remain in the schoolyard even after the bell had rung if I was addressing a group of girls about women's issues.

Senior year went smoothly—in fact, it was probably the most stress free of all school years since I started my women's work, with the exception of those two and a half glorious months I spent in the East. I don't mean to suggest that I had no stress, merely that this year had fewer conflicts than previous years. But living a double life was a source of great anguish to me. I am an honest person. I do not believe in deceit, and I have been told that sometimes I am far too outspoken about my feelings and opinions because I want people to know exactly where I stand—and where they stand. Life under Abajan's roof was an elaborate, carefully thought-out, extended deceit. I had no choice, but I also felt no peace.

And there was the constant fear of Abajan. I could not forget his savage assault on me and knew that if I misstepped, it could happen again. It was like living on the edge of a volcano.

But senior year had proved to be more successful than I had feared. I looked forward to next year, when I would be starting college—or so I thought.

6

A few weeks later, all my hopes were dashed. The government, under the rulership of King Zahir Shah, closed the University of Kabul because it was a hotbed of seething radical student groups and perceived as a threat to national stability. As I stood poised on the brink of college, the college that had accepted me was closed.

"Could I please go to community college?" I begged Abajan.

He shook his head. "There is a reason the government closed the university. College is a dangerous place for the soul. It is filled with heretical ideas and anti-Islamic infidels. You have come such a long way, Sulima. You have shed the rebellious ways of your youth. I cannot allow you to be contaminated now."

In desperation, I turned to Dr. Amir Zahir, an old friend and mentor of my father. Professor, poet, and humanitarian, Dr. Zahir was one of the few free-spirited people with whom my father retained a cordial relationship. It was more than cordiality. Abajan felt deep respect for Dr. Zahir. Maybe he could intervene on my behalf.

Dr. Zahir listened patiently as I cried out my eyes to him about my entrapment and the thwarting of my goal to become a doctor. "Please could you talk to my father? He respects you."

"I'll do what I can," Dr. Zahir promised.

Abajan was furious that I had sought help outside the family—especially from someone he respected. "How dare you wash our family's dirty linen in public! And humiliate me in front of my esteemed mentor. This only proves that you have not learned respect after all. You may not go to school."

So I was confined again and it was maddening. Without school as an excuse to leave the house, I ended up staying home most of the time. Of course, I continued my women's work from the house. In some ways it was easier because I claimed to be tutoring the younger students who came to see me. Abajan's suspicions diminished. It made sense to him that I would start tutoring high school students now that I had graduated and was home full time.

It happened in 1972.

A ringing sound. The doorbell. A neighbor is there, breathless and shaking. "Come quickly! There has been an accident. Your father—"
Run, Sulima, run!
Where is he taking me? Down the steps, down the path, down the road, to the corner—
—and there I see it. The mangled ruins of my father's car, squashed against a tree. Father is—
—there. On the sidewalk. What's that on his face? Oh God, no, it can't be. Blood. It's blood! His legs are twisted like the metal of his ruined car.
I kneel beside him. Hands shaking. Tears streaming. "Abajan!"
He reaches for my hand. "Don't cry, my baby. I know who did this and I will live. Just get me to a hospital."
His eyes hold mine, and in that moment, everything falls away. Our eyes bridge the fighting, the dogma, the conflict, the pain. It is Abajani and his little Sula again, just the two of us. And nothing else matters.

I waited in the hospital with Husna. Despite having shed my Muslim beliefs, I found myself praying. Don't let him die. Please, merciful God, don't let him die. Don't let him die.

I prayed continuously. At one point, I needed to use the bathroom and did not stop praying, even there. Then I remembered. It was considered disrespectful to invoke God's name in the bathroom. It had been so long since I had prayed, I had forgotten the rules. If something terrible happened to him, would it be my fault for praying wrong? I added another prayer, an apology for having desecrated God's Name in the bathroom, and continued my internal chant. Let him live, please let him live, please God, don't let him die.

Then I caught sight of Uncle Nayk-Mohammed, one of my father's brothers, whom we called Uncle Nayk. He was walking toward the hospital exit. I ran over to him. "How is he?"

Uncle Nayk kept walking.

I grabbed him by his jacket. "Please tell me. How is he?"

He still did not answer. I looked at his face and I knew. I started to scream.

Abajan was buried in the East the next day. Between family, friends, relatives, and friends of my grandfather, the burial was enormous. Busloads of people traveled to the cemetery from all over the country.

Since only men went to the cemetery, Madarjan, my sisters, and I all stayed behind in Kabul receiving family and friends who stopped by with condolences. There were so many people that we had to go to Uncle Nayk's house, which had a living room separated from the dining room by French doors. We opened the doors to make one enormous room, almost the size of a banquet hall. As the oldest daughter, it was my responsibility to sit with the adult women—Madarjan, Aunt Sheela, Aunt Freshta, Aunt Layla, Aunt Kamila, Aunt Fauziya, assorted other aunts and cousins, and my grandmothers—and receive guests.

Then a few days later, once the family was back from the East, we held the local funeral ceremonies. It was traditional to announce on the radio during the days following a burial where and when the ceremonies would be held—men would meet at the mosque, women at Uncle Nayk's house. This was where the *fateha*, the mourning rituals, were enacted. We sat in a row, receiving guests. In the background, the *kari* chanted verses from the Qur'an.

> Thought ye that ye should enter Paradise ere God had taken knowledge of those among you who did valiantly, and of those who steadfastly endure? Ye had desired death ere ye met it. But ye now have seen it. . . . No one can die except by God's permission, according to the Book that fixeth the term of life. He who desireth the recompense of this world, we will give him thereof. And he who desireth the recompense of the next life, we will give him thereof. And we will certainly reward the thankful.

The *kari* was usually blind. Since it was difficult for blind people to find employment, they memorized sections of the Qur'an and recited them at funerals. Each time a new group of guests arrived, the *kari* started all over again. The chanting droned on and on, while the guests filed in and out.

Madarjan, who was four months pregnant, was crying into the arms of the other women. Two aunts were comforting Husna. Aunt Fauziya had gone home to Khairkhana, taking Gula and the younger children with her. They were not told the truth about my father's death. Madarjan and the other adults told them that Abajan was very ill and had gone away for a rest cure. Surya heard the truth from a friend at school and told the others. It was almost a year later.

I was expected to be strong, reliable, and responsible. I was very mature for my age. I was the oldest daughter. People expected me to be sad, to wail and cry like the other women, then to shoulder my grief with restraint and dignity. And indeed, I obliged for the first two days. I went through motions. "Please come in." "Thank you for your concern." I told myself I would be freer now.

On the third day it hit me. My father was dead. He was never coming back. We would never be able to heal the enormous rift between us now. It was too late. I could never make a proper apology for writing those terrible words about the ink from the fountain pen. I would never again be his little Sula. The center of my life was gone.

When the realization really sank in, I completely lost control. The years of pent-up rage, grief, and longing for the restoration of a loving relationship between me and my father erupted. I screamed. I cried. I raged. I stamped and roared out my agony in dark streams of curses at God for having taken my father away from me.

My family was shocked.

"You must stop talking like this," Uncle Nayk said sternly. "Repent of your sins, especially your blasphemy against God."

"We do not understand God's ways. Our minds are too small. We must accept his will," said Aunt Freshta.

I got dozens of lectures.

"All your hysteria will not bring him back." From Aunt Layla.

"Stop questioning God," Uncle Daoud said sternly.

"God gives, then He takes, you must bless Him," said Uncle Fazel, my mother's brother.

"How could God abandon nine children by taking away their father?" I moaned.

"God has kept me alive and I will take care of you," Uncle Nayk said.

I glared at him. "You may give us money, but who will give us the love of a father?"

I remained bereft for weeks, long after the friends and relatives had departed. I did not need the mourning customs to remind me of my loss. I had no desire to wear brightly colored clothing or makeup, put henna on my hands or listen to music. Even beyond the customary forty days of abstention from music, the radio and stereo were silent in our home.

I also spent a lot of time brooding over my father's cryptic statement "I know who did this." Could his death have been anything other than an accident? Could there have been foul play? He had always been an excellent driver. Why would he have suddenly lost control of the car and driven into a tree? He was a controversial and opinionated man and had antagonized many people over the years. Maybe there was sabotage involved. But eventually I came to the conclusion that I had to let the issue go. There was no way to pursue it, and allowing it to dominate my thoughts would not bring Abajan back.

We all tried to resume our normal lives but nothing felt normal. In fact, everything was falling apart. Karim, the new male head of the household, was enrolled in college, but because classes had been canceled, he had nothing to do with his time. He started drinking and partying. Most of the parties were held at our house. Madarjan, Husna, Gula, and I were expected to feed all his friends while they drank and laughed and caroused in the living room. Without Abajan's income, our own savings dwindled. Karim refused to work, and the others were too young. Karim's parties began costing us savings we could ill afford. Soon we did not have enough to eat ourselves, much less feed his ravenous guests.

"We cannot afford to stay here," Madarjan told Karim. "Something must be done."

Karim agreed, and the family moved back to Aghajan's house in the East. We rented out our house in Kabul. I accompanied them to the East, where Madarjan gave birth to Naim. I looked forward to returning to Kabul in a few months to start university. We had arranged for me to stay with Uncle Nayk while the rest of the family remained in the East. I hoped that the university would reopen in time for me to start classes. And indeed it did. I was accepted to medical school and was overjoyed to hear that school was reopening. I couldn't wait to return to the intellectual excitement and opportunity for continuing my women's work that university offered.

I was looking forward to a new beginning

I got a new beginning, all right, but not the kind of beginning I had hoped for. It was the beginning of Karim's reign of tyranny over me.

7

I was bursting with excitement. Tomorrow I would be returning to Kabul. Classes started next week. I had just started packing when Karim came into the room. He had a gun in his hand. He placed it on the table conspicuously.

"What are you doing?" he asked.

I was putting some notebooks into a bag. "Getting ready to leave tomorrow. I start medical school next week." My tone of voice implied that it really was none of his business.

"What makes you think I'm going to let you go to medical school?"

I glanced at him sharply. "What are you talking about?"

His mouth arranged itself into a smug parody of a smile. "You're not going."

I flung my book bag onto the floor. "*What?*"

"I'm the head of the household now. If I don't want you to go to medical school, you won't go."

The brute. The bully. He deserved to be slapped. He deserved to be screamed at—but I wasn't going to try any of that. Not with a gun on the table next to us. It was not uncommon for a brother to kill a sister if he believed she was being rebellious, promiscuous, or disobedient. It was considered an honor killing—a deed he had not only the right but the duty to perform in order to remove shame from the family name. Karim hated me and I wholeheartedly believed he was capable of using his gun.

Hot rage churned and seethed in my belly. "But why?" My voice rose in anguish, then broke. "Why would you do this to me?"

The cruel amusement playing around his eyes reminded me of Abajan. "Because I can," he replied.

Medical school was his flyswatter, and I, like a trapped bee, was buzzing frantically and flapping my wings as he swung at me.

Don't cry, I ordered myself. Don't add to his pleasure by showing that he has power over your feelings as well as your future. I picked up my school bag with careful casualness. "Is that all?"

"Not really. You can study biology if you want to."

Keeping my face neutral, I nodded offhandedly. "That would be nice."

Biology wasn't medicine, but at least it was an interesting subject. A respectable discipline, with a career I could follow. Best of all, I would still be allowed to go to school. I turned to leave the room, but Karim called me back. "Oh. One other thing."

I knew there had to be a catch. "What's that?"

"You have to marry Jamal."

"That *ahmaq*! Absolutely not!"

"He's not an idiot, and if you don't marry him, then you can't go to school."

"What does one thing have to do with the other?" I hissed between clenched teeth.

"Jamal is my best friend. He has wanted you for years. He said he'll kill himself if you don't marry him."

I shut my eyes, and Jamal's face swam into view. I had never found anyone so repulsive. He was short and ugly with a whining and sniveling manner that grated on my nerves like chalk on a blackboard. He also was a pest, always following me around and begging me to marry him. I could not imagine spending as much as a day with him, let alone a lifetime.

"So let him kill himself. I don't care."

"You'll care plenty if you can't go to school."

"Why are you doing this to me?" I pleaded pointlessly.

"I want to do Jamal a good turn. He is my best friend, after all."

"You don't do him any favors by marrying him off to someone who hates him," I retorted.

"And I won't have you bringing shame on the family by marrying that no-good boyfriend of yours, Rashid."

Ah, now his real motives were showing. "Rashid is not my boyfriend!"

56

"You seem to spend a lot of time with him. If he's not your boyfriend, then it's improper for you to be spending so much time with him."

I would never have admitted this to Karim, but for a while, I *had* been attracted to Rashid. We had worked side by side for the Communist cause, and we had come to care for each other. The letter I was writing about Abajan was to Rashid. Dating was not allowed in our culture, so we confined our contact to polite philosophical letters and work-related matters. If Rashid had wanted to marry me, he would have had to formally request my hand in marriage from my brother. If my brother had opposed the match, we would have had no recourse. As things turned out, however, Rashid and I had ended up backing two different leaders in the Communist Party. Since our political work was at the center of our existence and of our relationship, we could not sustain a friendship once we had developed such different political alliances. Our would-be romance came to a sad end.

I never knew why Karim was so opposed to Rashid. Perhaps it was because of Rashid's Communist involvement. Karim still regarded himself as my father's posthumous voice. Perhaps it was an extension of his need to dominate me, another arena in which he could wield his authority. Whatever the reason, I knew he hated Rashid and never lost an opportunity to say something nasty about him.

"I don't spend time with him anymore," I said.

"Then you're unattached. That's just as bad. You'll go off to university and find yourself a boyfriend. You'll engage in improper activities. You'll bring shame to the family." Karim was shouting now. "You will not go to university unless you're engaged!"

"But school starts next week! What do you want me to do, stand on the corner in front of the university, stopping every man who passes and asking him to marry me?"

He shrugged. "That's your problem. You have one month to find someone to marry."

Suddenly it was okay for me to find my own husband. The hypocrisy stunned me. "And what if I don't?"

He shrugged again. "Then I'll make you marry Jamal. Or you'll leave school. Or both."

Madarjan was sitting in the other room, overhearing everything. I am sure Madarjan's heart ached for me. But what could she do? Karim had a gun. He also had the legal right to run the family as he wished. He was the head of the household now, and even his mother was required to be subservient to him.

No sleep that night. My predicament thrust me restlessly to and fro in bed. As I tossed and turned, I ran through the list of all the eligible men I knew. Whom could I get engaged to at such short notice? Rashid was out of the question, even if Karim had approved of him. So who else was there? It was customary to try to marry within the family. My parents, for example, had been second cousins. Several of my second and third cousins had expressed an interest in me. To date, I had not even considered them. In fact, they had been nothing more than a nuisance, as I had to go through the cumbersome task of continually turning down their unwelcome offers of marriage. Now, suddenly, the bevy of would-be suitors within the family seemed welcome. One of these men would become my savior.

I carried my torment into class with me when school began, resolutely shoving it into a compartment at the corner of my consciousness as I tried to concentrate on introductory biology. I walked from one class to the next, immersed in thought.

Several months passed. Karim, who was also in college, was staying in the college dormitory while I was living with Uncle Nayk. Every time Karim came to see me about my marriage plans, I arranged to be unavailable.

The semester was about to end. In Afghanistan, the academic year runs from March through July, then the second semester begins in September. Summer break was approaching, and I began to think that Karim would let the whole thing go. I traveled east to spend time with the family and Karim arrived a few days later. There were so many people in the house—aunts, uncles, and cousins of all sorts—that Karim and I had no time alone. Karim had also come with a whole group of friends. He spent his time drinking and partying with them. I hoped that he had forgotten his threat.

The day before I left to return to Kabul, Karim caught me alone. "Well, have you found someone?"

"I'm still working on it," I said.

The look on his face frightened me. The alcohol on his breath could have set the house on fire. He was irrational, but I knew then that he was serious and I had better find myself a husband.

A few days later when I was leaving class, I saw him. Yakub. He was also a student at the university. He had indicated to several mutual acquaintances that he was interested in me. Yakub was reasonably good-looking and seemed well spoken enough. Good. Perhaps he was the solution to my problem.

But I hardly knew him. Marriage was such a major step. How could I just jump into something so serious with someone I barely knew?

But the alternative—marrying Jamal or leaving school—seemed equally unacceptable.

I brooded on it for several weeks, and toward the end of the semester, I sent Yakub a letter indicating that I reciprocated his interest and would marry him. He wrote back accepting my acceptance. I was about to inform Karim that I had obeyed him when I received news of Aghajan's death.

The next weeks were consumed by the funeral and mourning, followed by final exams, which Karim and I had both missed during the time following Aghajan's death. It was not until next semester that I contacted Karim at his dormitory and asked to see him.

He came reluctantly. "What do you want?"

"I have some news for you."

When I told him, his face darkened. "You will not marry him."

I was stunned. "But why?"

"I don't like him!"

"But you told me to find someone to marry."

"I want you to break it off," Karim said.

"But that would be wrong. I gave him my word. I told him I would marry him. And I was just doing what you asked."

Karim was enraged. "Do whatever you have to do but don't marry this man."

In desperation, I turned to Uncle Nayk. "What should I do? Karim says he won't let me stay in university if I don't find someone to marry. I've found someone and now he won't let me marry him."

Uncle Nayk sighed. "You should know your brother by now. He just wants you to marry his friend. He never thought you would go through with finding someone else."

So it had all been a game. Karim was playing with me like a cat with a mouse. But I had not forgotten Karim's threats. I realized that he would continue to control me if I did not marry. Once I was married, I would no longer be accountable to Karim but to my husband. As I told the group of girls at the WDO meeting ever so long ago, if my husband was decent—and I had no reason to believe that

Yakub was anything but honorable and decent—I would be free to continue my studies. It made sense to remain engaged to Yakub.

I was grateful for Uncle Nayk's support and relieved with my decision—for the moment. But I still lived in trepidation the remainder of the semester. Karim was leaving me alone, but I did not trust him. Who knew what lay ahead? He had not talked to me since that conversation in which I stood firm about my engagement. But maybe he was planning some sinister form of revenge. The semester crept by, each day an agony of doubt.

I tried to ignore my concerns and focus on my studies. I loved biology and looked forward to classes. I was still doing my women's rights work, and I was increasingly involved with the WDO and the Communist Party. Yakub was polite, though distant. He came for dinner at Uncle Nayk's from time to time, but otherwise we had little to do with each other. When summer vacation came, we were still engaged. I decided to stay in Kabul, remembering last summer vacation in the East. It seemed likely that Karim would not confront me at Uncle Nayk's house. I had begun to suspect that Uncle Nayk had talked to him about my right to be engaged to Yakub and that Karim, out of respect for my uncle, would leave me alone while I was at his house.

The next semester passed uneventfully, and I was beginning to relax. I was engaged, but in Afghanistan engagements can continue for as long as two years—sometimes even longer. I had gotten Karim off my back by becoming engaged, but I did not have to deal with getting married for a long time. I looked forward to my third year of college. Madarjan and the others were returning from the East. I was overjoyed at the prospect of having Madarjan back. Next year would be the best yet.

It was about midway through my much-anticipated junior year of college that Yakub began to change. Gone was the courtly suitor. No more did I see the beaming face of a man delighted to have won the hand of his longed-for bride. Instead, I encountered a savage interested in nothing more than his own pleasure.

"Come to bed with me," he demanded one night, grabbing me by the hand.

"But we're not married yet," I protested.

"We don't need to be married. We're engaged. We're almost man and wife. We can do whatever we want to."

"I'm not ready. Not until we're married."

"Well, I'm tired of waiting. You're not living with your uncle anymore. You're living at home. But your brother is still in the dorm, and he won't know what we're doing. We can do whatever we want."

"This has nothing to do with being afraid of my brother. I just don't feel right about being with a man I'm not married to."

He gave me a strange look. "You know, there are other ways to do it."

Other ways? What was he talking about?

"No," I said firmly.

He scowled and spat a curse at me. Was this the man I was to spend the rest of my life with? What had I gotten myself into?

After several months of this pressure, Yakub disappeared. Initially, I was relieved. It would be nice to think that he had vanished, never to return. That would give me the best of both worlds—an engagement to satisfy my brother, with an absentee fiancé who would make no demands on me. But I was also uneasy. Where might he have gone? What mysterious errand had called him away? Was there something lurking under the surface that could be even more disturbing than what had already emerged about him?

When he returned, he was limping and doubled over. In short, staccato syllables he explained that he had gone to visit his family in the mountains and fallen off a horse. He needed bed rest to recuperate, that was all.

Something about his story struck me as odd, but I could not identify it. Some uneasy feeling nibbled away at me. I thought and thought about it, then decided I had to let it go. My fiancé had gone to visit his family. All right, he had not consulted or informed me in advance, but that was normal in our culture. He had fallen off a horse. I knew that the horses in the mountains were almost as wild as the tribes who owned them. Yakub could easily have been thrown by a horse.

Then I got a phone call from a dear friend named Badria. "Sulima, you must come over now. Something has happened that you should know about."

Disturbed by the urgency in her voice, I dropped everything and hurried over to her house. She opened the door and pulled me inside quickly. "Don't let anyone know you're here," she whispered.

"Why not?"

"Ssh," she hissed, taking my hand and leading me into her bedroom. "What I'm about to tell you is for your own good. But no one must know about it. No one must know that I've even talked to you. Promise me."

It was strange, but Badria was my friend. She was distraught, and this was the only way I could comfort her. "I promise."

"Swear on the Qur'an." She grabbed my hand and placed it over the book.

"I swear."

"Then here's something you should know about the man you're going to marry." She broke off then resumed in a hurried whisper. "You know how Yakub was missing for ten days?"

My voice rose involuntarily. "How did you know about that?"

"Ssh, not so loud. I'll tell you. My ten-year-old cousin, Ali, disappeared at the same time. Yakub kidnapped him and locked him up in an empty house for ten days. He did—well—you know what to him."

I was stunned. Now I understood what he had meant by "other ways to do it."

"Yakub finally let Ali go. When Ali came home, he told everything to his father, my uncle. Uncle took both of Ali's brothers and they came and beat Yakub up."

So that was how he had sustained those injuries. Some horse, I thought bitterly.

"Thank you for telling me." I grasped her hand fervently. "You are saving me from a terrible marriage to someone who could kidnap and rape—" I struggled to find words. "A child molester. And who likes boys."

"What will you tell Yakub about why you're breaking off the engagement? What will you tell your family?"

"That I found out he is a *hamjens baz,* a homosexual."

She shook her head violently. "No, you can't do that. They'll ask how you found out, and you'll have to tell them about me. You promised, remember? You swore on the holy Qur'an. If you tell, Yakub may come and destroy my family. Father is dead, and there is no man in the house to protect my mother, my sister, my little brother, and me. Whatever you do, you can't tell."

"I won't tell," I reassured her, hearing my words as if from a great distance.

She walked me to the door and hugged me. "What will you say to him? What will you say to your family?" she whispered.

"I have no idea. I'll just have to figure something out."

8

It took me a few weeks to decide what to do. My third year of university was over. It was winter vacation. Karim was living at home again. I thought and thought about my dilemma. Of course I was going to honor my word to Badria. Not because I had sworn upon the Qur'an. The Qur'an meant nothing to me at the time. My word was something else. I had given my pledge, and now my honor and self-respect were at stake. To me, these were sacred and nonnegotiable. At all costs, I would protect Badria's confidence and never divulge the real reason for my decision to end my relationship with Yakub. I would have to say something else. Something true and plausible.

I contacted Yakub and said I wanted to speak to him. He came over and we went out for a walk.

"You are very quiet," he said. "Something is on your mind?"

I struggled to find words. "I've given this much thought, and I realize that I've changed my mind. I don't want to marry you after all."

Yakub looked stunned. "Why?"

"You want me to go to bed with you. You've been bothering me with your demands. I don't like that."

"Oh, is that all?" He started to laugh.

"What's so funny?" I demanded.

"You're being silly. Like a child. I have the right to ask you for this, because we are engaged. You're already my woman."

I clenched my fists against my impulse to hit him. "You're wrong. You're not respecting my feelings. I don't want to be married to someone who doesn't respect me."

He laughed again. The sound was unnerving. "Well, I don't agree to having our engagement broken off, so we are engaged."

"No we aren't."

By this time, we had reached my home again. Without even saying good night, I ran into the house.

The next evening, I was returning home from a meeting. I drew my overcoat around me. I was musing over the discussions we had at our meeting as I turned onto my street.

"Sulima! Come quickly!"

It was our neighbor's eight-year-old son. He tugged at my sleeve.

"What do you want?"

"Hurry! My sister's in the car. She's asking for you. She needs you right now!"

I hurried after the boy. His sister was pregnant, and due any day now. She must have gone into labor and needed someone to drive her to the hospital.

As I leaned into the car, I felt someone grab my overcoat. My pocketbook fell to the floor of the car. Before I knew what had happened, I found myself lying on the floor of the back. I heard a door slam, then a screech as the car started to move, picking up speed as it went.

Dizzy and stunned, I struggled to sit up. There, in the driver's seat, was Yakub.

"Wh—where did you come from? What are you doing?"

He was chuckling madly. "I paid your neighbor's boy to get you into the car. He came up with a plan that really worked. Smart kid, he is."

"Where are you taking me?"

"You don't need to know." The car was hurtling forward, faster and faster. Yakub's face was grim and set.

"Yakub, let me out of the car!"

"Why should I? I'm your fiancé. That's like being your husband. Just as you have to listen to your husband, you have to listen to me. I can take you wherever I want.'

"You're not my fiancé anymore. I told you I was breaking off our engagement."

"You never gave me a good reason."

"You've been pressuring me to have sex. I don't like that."

He snorted. "That's no reason to dishonor your word and break an engagement."

64

By this time, we had reached a house I did not recognize. Yakub stopped the car, then opened the door to the back. He grabbed me by the hand and pulled me out. "You're coming with me."

I tried to break free, but he was stronger than I was. Dragging me along, he opened the door to the house and pushed me inside, locking the door behind us.

"Where are we?"

"This is my friend's house. He said I can use it."

I wondered if this was the same place where he had imprisoned the unfortunate Ali. Then I realized with mounting horror that he planned to do with me as he had done with Ali.

My fears were confirmed as he approached me and grabbed my blouse.

"Stop it!"

"I'm going to have my way with you, " he hissed.

He held my arms and pinned me against the wall. I felt his mouth, rough and foul, against mine. He was fumbling with my clothes. Using all my strength, I pushed him away.

"Please, please, *please* don't do this to me!" I was crying now.

"Why shouldn't I?" He lunged at me again.

"Because I realize you're right. I will marry you. I promise. Just don't do this to me. Let's wait until we're married so we can do it properly."

He backed off and eyed me with obvious suspicion. "I don't believe you."

I dropped to the floor and knelt before him, bowing down and kissing his feet. "You're right about everything. I have been wrong. You're the man, you're the king, and I am your humble servant. I will marry you and then you can do whatever you want with me."

I had clearly struck a receptive chord. He looked at me, his face softening.

"Now that's the kind of talk I like to hear."

I continued babbling about how I would honor and respect him, and fulfill his every wish and desire once we were married, if he would just let me go now. He relented and helped me to my feet, kissing me again on the mouth. "I'm grateful that you've come to your senses," he said as we walked to the car. "I'll take you home now, but on one condition. You will say nothing about this to anyone."

I nodded.

"Promise. Swear."

"I promise. I swear. I won't say a word to anyone."

It was 1:00 A.M. by the time we got home. I stumbled into the house to encounter a glowering Karim.

"Where have you been? Do you know what time it is?"

"I've been out with Yakub."

"Well, don't stay out so late again next time. It's wrong for a woman to be out late."

I closed my door and pressed my hands against my throbbing temples. My head ached where it had hit the floor of the car. I felt sore from the effort of struggling with Yakub, and was still shaking from the shock and fear. My mouth where he had kissed me tasted unpleasant. I had to get out of this engagement. But how?

Maybe Karim would support me when he realized how dangerous Yakub was. Maybe he would help me to annul the engagement when he heard about tonight's events. It was uncomfortable coming to him with my tail between my legs, since he had opposed the match to begin with, but on the other hand, he was to some extent responsible for it too. If he had not given me his ultimatum, I never would have become engaged to Yakub.

I was about to leave my room and knock on Karim's door when I remembered. I had promised Yakub that I would not say anything to anyone. But maybe I could communicate without saying the words out loud. Writing was not the same as speaking, after all. And with the male head of my household on my side, I would have the authority to end the engagement.

I poured out my heart on paper to my brother, omitting no details of Yakub's outrageous behavior. I begged Karim to have mercy on me, to realize that I was engaged to a dangerous man whom I greatly feared. Before dawn, I slipped the letter under his bedroom door. Surely once he heard about Yakub's unscrupulous conduct that violated his sister's honor, he would not force me to go through with the engagement.

The next morning, I awoke to the stern visage of my brother. "Poor Yakub. He was forced to do what he did because you told him you wouldn't marry him. He had every right to exercise his male prerogative and show you who's boss. The engagement stands."

"But I can't go through with it. I'm scared of him."

In our culture, an engagement was regarded as a commitment, almost tantamount to marriage. To break an engagement would cause a scandal.

"It is out of the question to end this engagement!" Karim roared. "You will go through with this marriage, or risk bringing shame upon the entire family. I was opposed, but you didn't listen to me and now you will sleep in the bed that you have made."

"I refuse to marry him."

"You're a fickle, unstable person who will cause the destruction of all of us with your selfish ways."

I stood my ground. "You can't make me marry someone I don't want to."

"Oh, can't I? Well, you watch. You're forbidden to leave the house until you come to your senses."

Karim could forbid all he liked, but I had no intention of listening to him. I had spent my childhood defying my father, and there was no way I was going to back down and allow my brother to place me under house arrest.

The next morning I woke up and dressed as usual. But when I tried to open my door, it appeared to be stuck. I rattled the door-knob and pushed against the door, but it would not budge. It took a few minutes before the realization hit me. Karim had locked the door from the outside.

I started banging on the door with my fists. "Hello? Hello? Can anyone hear me?"

I heard the rest of the family going about their daily business. Why weren't they coming to help me? I tried again.

"Please, let me out!"

No response.

What about Madarjan? What about Asim and Zamin? Where were Husna and the others?

I later found out that Karim had threatened them. If they came to my assistance, he would shoot them, and then he would shoot me. I often think of those moments and what it must have felt like for the family—especially Madarjan—to sit by helplessly, listening to my pounding and crying.

Finally, I heard a key turn in the lock. The door opened to reveal Karim's face, dark and sinister. "I told you I would not let you leave the house until you stop this silliness and go through with your marriage to Yakub."

He was blocking the doorway. I tried to push him aside and make a run for it, but he was stronger than I. He grabbed my arm. "You're not going anywhere. You can use the bathroom while I stand guard at the door. Then you'll go back into your room. I'll bring you some food. And that's how it will be until you come to your senses. And if it goes on too long, I will shoot you."

I cursed, I fought, I screamed, but he restrained me. I begged, I cried, but he was relentless.

I was imprisoned once again.

"All right, I'll marry him."

"That's what you told him too, just to make him leave you alone. How can I believe you?"

"I'll start getting ready for the wedding."

"I'll let you prove yourself to me. But if I see you're lying, I'll lock you up forever."

During the next few months, I started to go through the motions of preparing for a marriage. Yakub and I went furniture shopping, even though we did not yet know where we would live. We bought a sofa. A few days later, a dresser. Then some odds and ends—kitchen utensils and linens. Yakub was still surly and unpleasant, but at least he did not try to abduct me again. I must have succeeded in convincing him that I was really serious about marrying him.

I came home, ostentatiously parading my purchases before Karim. He seemed satisfied, but I was frantic. I could buy only so much time by doing premarriage shopping. I would be graduating soon. Once I was no longer in school, our families would begin setting the date for the wedding. There appeared to be no way out. Karim was adamant. Yakub was relentless. The prospect of being locked in again seemed as vile as the prospect of marrying a homosexual child molester who also happened to be my would-be rapist. And there was always the possibility that one of these men would kill me. How could I get out of this?

Maybe the court would help. I could appeal to the court to order the family to break off the engagement because of Yakub's assault on me. Theoretically, forced marriages are not allowed by Islamic law. Although society and culture have a long tradition of ignoring this law, it still stands on the books. It was my only chance.

A stone-faced clerk was behind the counter when I arrived. Haltingly, I explained my predicament. I handed them a letter expressing my request. "We'll have to see," he said curtly, disappearing into another room. I heard muffled conversation, then he emerged looking stonier than before. "I'm sorry but you'll have to come back another day. The person who takes care of this is out."

Desperate, I returned the next day, only to have the same clerk repeat the same story. The next day, the clerk informed me that the appropriate papers had been mislaid. I should come back next week. But the following week, I was told that the clerks were too busy to attend to this, maybe the week after. . . . I continued to return to court, my sense of panic and entrapment continuing to mount.

"So when are we getting married?" Yakub asked.

"Soon," I promised. "When I've finished with exams."

"I can't wait forever, you know."

"Of course. But first I must graduate, and then I still have to get my wedding trousseau. That takes time."

He muttered a curse.

A few days later, Karim decided to take the entire family to the East. I suspected that he wanted to deprive me of the support and comfort of Madarjan and my sisters and make me feel even more isolated. Later, my suspicions were confirmed by Husna, who overheard Karim talking to his friends about how lonely I would feel. This time, I moved in with my Aunt Fauziya.

After Karim's departure, Yakub began pressuring me to marry him immediately. "No more excuses," he said.

"But my family is away. I want them to be there for the wedding."

"Then we'll marry in the East. That's nearer to my family anyway."

Yakub's brother had come into town, and I suspected that the two of them planned to abduct me, only this time it would be no local house to which I would be taken. Yakub had threatened to take me to the mountains, where his family lived. They were wild people, primitive, almost savages. In their world, the law of the wilderness reigned. I could be killed. I *had* to get this engagement annulled. Immediately.

It slowly dawned on me that someone had gotten to the court ahead of me. Someone had pulled some strings, bribed the officials, or used some other kind of influence to get them to keep putting me off. But who?

It could only be Karim. After all, he was the one opposed to my decision to end the engagement. Maybe Karim had raised money to bribe someone. It would have been uncharacteristic, to be sure. Karim was never one to raise money. In fact, he spent every spare coin—and many we could not spare—on alcohol and partying. But maybe his hatred for me had overridden his spendthrift ways.

How could I get to the truth?

Then I thought of Mr. Mahmoud Reza.

Chief of security of Kabul, Mr. Reza was a highly respected, influential, and important man. He had been a close friend of Abajan's, but I always felt that he did not agree with Abajan's domestic policies. When I served him tea and cookies, I sensed a kindness in his eyes that I did not perceive in the others. His voice was gentler. I heard that some of his views were more moderate. Perhaps he could help.

Mr. Reza was as courteous as I remembered him to be. He listened to my story with obvious concern. "I'm in constant danger," I concluded. "Yakub is a wild man. I don't think I will stay alive if I become his wife. Please help me annul this engagement."

Mr. Reza looked genuinely confused. "I don't know what you're talking about. Engagement? You are married to Yakub."

"Married? We're not married. There was no ceremony, I signed no documents."

"But I saw your marriage certificate. It's in the files."

"That's impossible." My voice took on a hysterical pitch. "There must be some mistake."

"I'll show you."

He disappeared into another room. I heard the sliding sound of a file cabinet opening and closing. Then he returned with a document, which he slid across the desk. "See for yourself."

I read the words with increasing disbelief. "But this is impossible! We never married. This is a forgery."

A sad look crept across Mr. Reza's face. "If I had a gold coin for every forged marriage certificate, I would be a very wealthy man. Nothing is easier than for a family to create a false document. Usually these documents are so skillfully done—like yours, which was brought in by your uncle and your brother Karim—that it's almost impossible to tell the difference between what is real and what is false."

My uncle? The shock must have shown on my face, and I could hardly make my mouth form the words. "Which uncle?"

"Your uncle Nayk-Mohammed."

Uncle Nayk? Who had promised to take care of me after Father's death? Who had supported me in my engagement to Yakub when my brother opposed it? Impossible. There had to be some mistake.

"It can't be Uncle Nayk. Are you sure?"

"It says so in the files. It always says who brought the document in."

There was a sickening ring of truth to this. It made sense. Karim could not have accomplished this on his own. He lacked the stature and prestige. Uncle Nayk was well respected, rich, and influential. With his connections, it would not have been hard to get the court to agree to whatever he wanted.

"But surely it's against the law to forge a document. Surely there is an official seal, or something, that could show this to be false."

"No one will undertake that kind of thorough investigation. Not for something like this."

"You won't do it for me? You won't compare this document to some official document and show that it's false?" My voice wavered and cracked. I hid my face in my hands.

"I cannot help you."

We sat for a long time, silent sobs shaking my body. The iron grip of my brother extended right into the court. Was there no recourse? Was my future to be held hostage to the vengeful whim of my brother and the cruel injustice of history and culture?

When I looked up, Mr. Reza was gazing at me.

"I can only give you one piece of advice. Find another man. Go to a different court and get married. Then bring an official document. I will compare it to this certificate and it will be clear that this was forged. But unless you are married to someone else, I cannot do it for you."

"But I don't have anyone I want to marry!" I cried.

Mr. Reza rose to signal the end of our discussion. "These are my terms. Take them or leave them. But my earnest advice as your friend is to take them. And to do it soon."

9

$\mathcal{I}$ returned to Aunt Fauziya's house, shattered. Once again, I was no more than a piece of property to be handed over to some new owner. I had no more choice than the sheep at the marketplace. Worse. At the slaughterhouse.

Two policemen arrived at our door the following week. They displayed a document and demanded to see me.

"We are here to arrest Sulima Obaidi for insubordination and inappropriate conduct for a woman."

"What are you talking about?" Aunt Fauziya asked.

"We have a missing persons report here. Karim Obaidi, her older brother, called to say that she has left home and is living on her own. This is inappropriate behavior for a woman."

"That's ridiculous. She lives here with my husband, my children, and me. Karim knows exactly where she is!"

"Well, you'll all have to come with us to the police station. You can tell your story there."

Several hours later, we were back home. The police had dismissed the charges and called my brother an idiot. But that did not assuage my anger, or my fear of further action by Karim. I had not forgotten the gun on the table during that first conversation about marriage. What might he do next?

I returned in my mind to the conversation with Mr. Reza. I had to find someone else to marry. But who? Again, I ran through the list of men. Who had expressed an interest in me? Tarik was loud and foul-mouthed. Basir was repulsive. But Ibrahim—

Ibrahim had always been courteous. He had been sending me letters for several years asking me to marry him. He was handsome and well spoken. Of course, that is what I had originally said about Yakub, and I was wrong, but I knew Ibrahim slightly better. He was a distant relative. His father was the nephew of Aghajan's youngest wife. Ibrahim's letters had been filled with lavish praise for my beauty and intelligence, and promises that he would do anything in his power to make me happy. Besides, he couldn't possibly be worse than Yakub.

When Ibrahim heard through the family grapevine several weeks earlier that I was having second thoughts about marrying Yakub, he came and spoke to Madarjan. I happened to have been in the house, but I was not in the room, and I had no idea why he had come to visit. Later, I found out. Madarjan told me that he had come to ask for my hand in marriage.

"But she's already engaged," Madarjan had protested.

"Even if she was married and the mother of six children, I would kiss her feet and make her a crown upon my head."

I did not consider his offer at the time, but he did not give up. Now, I reconsidered.

I sent Ibrahim a letter telling him that I had been thinking over his proposal for a long time, even during my unfortunate engagement to Yakub. I told him that I wanted to marry him. I told him I wanted to move ahead with the wedding as soon as my exams were over and I had graduated.

Ibrahim reacted with unmitigated joy. I had been the object of his desire for eight years. He understood that we could not have a formal wedding ceremony. The engagement to Yakub and the false marriage certificate necessitated immediate and secret action. Our families would find out about our marriage only after the fact.

We were married the day after graduation. We went to a court in Khairkhana, a suburb of Kabul, where Aunt Fauziya lived. Later, we would bring the marriage document to our local court so that the engagement to Yakub would be annulled.

The flowers were blooming, birds were singing. I comforted myself with the sweetness of their song. Spring was a time of hope. Maybe this would be a new beginning for me.

Ibrahim had come with Ali and Yasir, two close friends who were to serve as the required two witnesses of our marriage. We presented ourselves to the clerk and he led us into a small room. It was sparsely furnished—just a desk and a few chairs.

The clerk opened the Qur'an and began to read.

"In the name of God, the beneficent, the merciful. O, my people. Take care in performing your duty to your Lord who created you from a single being and created its mate of the same kind and spread from these two, many men and women. And be careful of your duty to God by Whom you demand of one another your rights and to the ties of your relationship. Surely God ever watches over you. . . .

"Oh ye believers, it is unlawful for you to take women as heritage against their will, and do not straiten them in order that you may take part of what you have given them unless they are guilty of manifest indecency. Treat them kindly; then if you hate them, it may be that you dislike a thing, while God has placed abundant good in it. . . .

"And if you fear a breach between you, then appoint a judge from his people and a judge from her people. If they both desire agreement, God will effect harmony between them; surely God is Knowing, Aware."

He turned to Ibrahim. "Do you want this woman to become your wife according to the law of God and the Qur'an?"

"I do," Ibrahim said.

Then he turned to me. "Do you want this man to become your husband according to the law of God and the Qur'an?"

"I do."

He handed Ibrahim a document. "Sign this in front of these witnesses."

The document, a standard marriage contract, stated that Ibrahim was taking me as his wife and that he promised to give me 100,000 afghanis in the event of a divorce. Of course Ibrahim did not have that kind of money, but grooms traditionally pledged this sum and were never expected to make good on their promise.

After the wedding, we thanked the witnesses and stood on the court steps awkwardly.

"It's strange to go home to different places now that we're married," Ibrahim finally said. "I should be carrying you on my shoulders through the city, with people throwing roses at your sacred feet."

"We can't tell our families yet. Not until we've figured out how to break it to them."

We agreed that we should not even be seen together yet. I said good-bye to my new husband, who hailed a cab. When it pulled up, he handed me some money. "Please pay the driver with this."

All the way home, I thought of the morning's events. How strange. I was a married woman now. Someone had read some verses of the Qur'an, a man had signed a document, and now I was a wife. My husband would be my ticket out of my brother's tyranny.

As the cab pulled up in front of Aunt Fauziya's house, I felt something I had never experienced before. It started as a warmth in my cheeks, then a tingling in my belly. I thought of Ibrahim again, handsome and courtly beside me, and my heartbeat quickened. By the time I had gotten out of the cab, I knew what it was.

I had fallen in love with my husband.

I did not know what to do with these feelings. They had descended upon me so quickly—from one moment to the next. They were new and unexpected . . . and completely uncharacteristic for me. Yes, I had experienced mild attractions in the past, crushes, such as the feelings I'd had for Rashid. But I had never been swept away before. When I had read love poetry, I had always thought it silly and exaggerated. I had been a person of logic. Of academic achievement. My brain had always been in charge. Suddenly, unpredictably, my heart had taken over.

I tried to understand it. Was it because of the way he looked at me, so proudly and lovingly? No one had ever looked at me that way before. Was it because I saw him as my redeemer? Was it his loyalty? He knew that by marrying me—an engaged woman with an angry brother and uncle—he would be adding complications, even danger, to his life, but he went through with the wedding anyway.

Whatever it was, it was new. It was scary. It was wonderful. It made me want to fly and sing. I could not wait to see Ibrahim again.

When we saw each other the next day, I was shy and tongue-tied at first. I behaved so differently that Ibrahim noticed. "Is everything all right?"

What could I say? "It's just—well, it's just that I love you."

"I love you too. But you said you've loved me for a long time. What makes you act differently now?'

I could not explain, so finally I said, "It's different because we're married now."

He smiled and looked deep into my eyes. I felt my heart swelling and shuddering. I ached to be able to touch him, but unmarried men and women were not allowed to touch in public, and our marriage was still secret. So we touched with our eyes, our hearts crossing the magic bridge created by our gaze.

"I want to live together soon," he whispered. "I can't survive without you another day. My heart is pining, my body is wasting away. Please take care of the court matter. Then I'll tell my family about us and you can move in with me."

I promised to do it right away.

The next day, I contacted Yakub and asked him to meet me at the courthouse.

"Oh, are we getting married? Finally? I'll be right there."

He came escorted by his brother. They were both grinning. Two swarthy men swaggered in after them. The witnesses, I supposed. A cold sweat broke out on my neck. As we walked into the building, Yakub squeezed my arm. I shuddered.

"Yakub, I'm not marrying you," I said as we walked down the hall. "We're here because I want to officially annul our engagement."

The smile on his face faded. His brother took a step forward, his fist clenched, but Yakub signaled for him to step back. "What are you talking about?"

"I am married to Ibrahim Azimi. We got married yesterday."

Yakub's brother shouted something to the would-be witnesses, who turned and left.

By this time, we had reached the clerk's office. I had called Mr. Reza yesterday, and he had informed the clerk ahead of time that I would be coming. I stepped forward. "I am here to formalize the annulment of my engagement to Yakub," I said to the man behind the desk. I handed him my marriage license. "Please look at this. It was signed in Khairkhana yesterday. Please notice that this is an official document, issued by the court. It will override the forged document you have on file here."

I thought Yakub and his brother would kill me right then. But a look passed between them. Yakub's brother backed off and sat down. Yakub stood, glowering, until the man returned with my forged license. "Which is the real one and which is the false one?" he asked.

I pointed. "This one is the real one. It says that I am married to Ibrahim Razimi. The other one is false."

The clerk tore up the forged marriage license. "This woman now belongs to someone else," he told Yakub. Then he said to me, "Go home and be a good and obedient wife to your husband."

Yakub and his brother walked ahead of me, murmuring. When they got outside, Yakub's brother said good-bye. "You are a *fahesha*, a godless bitch and a whore." He turned to leave.

Yakub was silent until his brother was out of earshot. "I'm sorry he spoke to you that way. You have every right to your happiness, even if you have hurt me and behaved dishonorably."

Another miracle. Yakub would leave me alone! "Thank you," I said fervently.

"Let me call a taxi for you."

A taxi turned the corner and Yakub signaled to it. When it pulled up to the curb, I stepped forward. The door opened. Suddenly, a hand grabbed my shirt, then my arm. Another hand came over my mouth. Hands were pushing me from behind. I was being dragged somewhere. I kicked and struggled, but the grip was steel. Before I knew what had happened, I was inside the cab. The door slammed.

I twisted my neck around. There was Yakub's brother, in the driver's seat. When he saw me looking at him, he pushed my head down until my face was buried in the passenger seat. With both his hands holding my head, I saw my opportunity. I slipped my own hand free, grabbed at his crotch, and pulled hard.

He screamed and clutched himself while I wriggled away and ran out of the car. Yakub rushed over to see if his brother was all right. I ran as fast as I could, then found another taxi. I arrived, trembling and breathless, at Aunt Fauziya's house.

"What happened?" she asked when I burst in the door.

I was about to tell her when the door flew open. Yakub and his brother charged into the living room, waving their fists. "You're *paste-baysharaf*!" Yakub's brother yelled. "You're all a bunch of lowlifes. You bring shame to Islamic society. Your mothers are pigs. She—" he pointed to me—"is a whore. If you don't make Ibrahim divorce her so she can marry my brother, I will come in the night and kill you and your entire family!"

They stormed out of the house.

Aunt Fauziya turned to me. "What are they talking about?"

My voice was small and shaky when I told her the truth about my marriage.

"I just want you to know that we are very happy for you," Aunt Fauziya said. "If you want to marry this man, and you have married him according to the laws of God and the Qur'an, then *khash bashea.* May you be blessed."

She hugged me.

"*Ilahee ba pie ham peer shawed.* May you have a long life together," she continued.

I started to cry. "I can't stay here with you anymore," I said. "I'm putting you in danger. Yakub's brother is a crazy man. He will make good on what he said and come and kill you."

"So what are you going to do?" she asked.

"I'll call Ibrahim and move in with him now."

10

Ibrahim was waiting in the car.

"How did your family react?" I asked as soon as the key turned in the ignition.

"Some of them well, some of them poorly." Ibrahim explained that his mother and sister were happy for him. They knew how long he had pined for me and had been delighted when I had accepted his offer of marriage. But his brother Yasin and his uncle Yusuf were upset. They refused to talk to him. "It's not personal," Ibrahim explained. "It has nothing to do with whether or not they like you. They simply feel our marriage was inappropriate. You already belonged to someone else. You should have taken care of your problem before marrying me."

If Ibrahim's uncle—who, incidentally, was married to my Aunt Sheela, Madarjan's sister—and Yasin disapproved, we were in trouble. Ibrahim lived with them. He anticipated my next question.

"I have arranged for us to move in with my mother, my sister Seema, and her husband, Roshan. We can live with them while I straighten things out."

Seema greeted us with outstretched arms and congratulations. "*Khash amady.* Welcome. May you be very happy together. I am honored that my home is your first wedding home."

I followed her to our room and started to unpack, but my hands would not listen to my instructions to open dresser drawers and put clothing inside them. I sank down on the bed. My head was throbbing where Yakub's brother had grabbed it, and my eyes were burning. My shoulders ached, and my knees still felt rubbery from running. My eyes started to close. I was exhausted. In the past forty-eight hours I had married, annulled an engagement, escaped being abducted, watched my aunt be threatened with her life, and moved into a new home with a new husband. I wanted to lie down and sleep, then wake up refreshed to find Ibrahim next to me. I wanted to lose myself in his arms and not have to face anyone else.

But I heard Seema calling the family to dinner. Wearily I rose. It would have been rude, almost unthinkable, for me to remain in my room during dinner. Food is the center of the Afghan household solar system. Everything revolves around serving and eating. To refuse to come to a meal is to offend the hostess. I washed my face, straightened out my hair, and went downstairs.

I had met Ibrahim's mother before, at various family events, but had never exchanged more than a few words with her. Now she came over to me. Her mouth was smiling, but her eyes held a different expression. Something unreadable. Not sadness exactly, not hostility, but definitely not joy. Her eyes did not match her words and when she hugged me, her embrace felt weak, like water running down my sides. "*Mubarak* daughter-in-law. Congratulations. Ah, how happy his father will be when he returns and sees his youngest son a bridegroom."

Ibrahim's mother, whom we called Deljan, lived with her daughter Seema and her husband, Roshan. Ibrahim's father had been absent a long time, and the family party line was that he had traveled abroad to seek his fortune. When he was established, he would send for the rest of the family. But no one had heard from him since Ibrahim was four years old, and rumor had it that he was living in Russia with a new family.

Dinner was over. The dishes had been cleared up, the food put away, and the children tucked into bed. Ibrahim and I were about to go upstairs when I felt a hand on my arm. I turned around to see Deljan gazing intently into my eyes.

"Take care of my baby," she said.

I nodded.

She was still holding my sleeve. "He has wanted you for so many years. Now he has you. He is happy and nothing makes me happier than to see my baby smile."

How sweet. She was still calling him her baby. A little knife sliced through my heart. Abajan should be here too, to tell Ibrahim to take care of *his* baby, his little Sula.

She was still talking. "But although you're smart, you're beautiful, and you come from a good family, you already belonged to someone else. You bring scandal with you. This is not what I would have wished for my darling." She pulled my sleeve more forcefully now. Her lips were shaking. "It is up to you to make up for the trouble he's going through on your behalf. Don't ever make him regret marrying you. Serve him faithfully and uncomplainingly. Grant his every wish. Never let the smile vanish from his lips. Never let the walls of your house see his eyes crying."

I nodded fervently. What more could I want than to make Ibrahim happy?

She let go of my sleeve and gave me a little push. "Go then, and do your duty."

I carried her words upstairs with me. They reverberated uneasily through the pulsating corridors of my brain. Would I know what to do? Could I really make Ibrahim happy? What if I failed him? What if—

But here he is. Ibrahim. We are alone for the very first time. His hands are strong as they move, his hair is onyx, glistening, beckoning. The echoes of his mother's words fade, overtaken by the hoofbeats of my heart, thudding wildly like a mountain horse gone mad. I hide my face. A hand touches my chin. My face is being turned to his. Can I meet his eyes? Eyes that will soon see— They are calling, pleading, I can at least try to meet their gaze, try to look into them. I gasp at what I see, the love, the light, the tenderness. He reaches over and closes the door.

I sat at breakfast the next morning, transformed. There was the intense embarrassment of having the family know that we had spent our first night as husband and wife under their roof. I caught Deljan staring at me. What was she thinking? Would she ask Ibrahim if I had really made him happy? What was Seema thinking? She was treating me as if nothing in my life had changed and everything was normal. I knew that Seema had gone through the same experience of being brought home to her husband's house. Couples in our culture did not usually rent their own place when they were first married. They moved in with the husband's family. I thought about Aunt Fauziya, about Aunt Sheela, and about Madarjan. There were questions I could never ask them.

But I also felt as though I had been touched by God Himself. Everything was different. I reverently fingered the bread dish that Ibrahim had just put back on the table. *His* hand had just touched the dish. I straightened out the bedroom in the morning, handling each article of clothing with awe because *he* had touched it. The entire house glowed with his light. I had never imagined that I could feel this way.

Before dinner the next night, Roshan rushed into the house, white and shaking. "I stopped at a traffic light. Suddenly, someone opened the passenger door. A man sat down next to me. He said he was Yakub's brother. He grabbed my arm. He said—" Roshan stopped. Clearly, Yakub's brother had used foul language that he did not want to repeat in front of the women. "He told me that I must try to separate Ibrahim and Sulima."

"We must leave at once," Ibrahim told Roshan and Seema. "Your lives are in danger if we stay here."

"But where will you go?" his mother asked. Her glare said, Look what you have done to my son.

It was arranged that we would go to Moursal, Ibrahim's cousin, until more permanent arrangements could be made.

The light that had accompanied me since the night before faded, then darkened. I was afraid to meet Deljan's eye. I was bringing pain to these good people. I was placing the family of the man I loved in grave danger. I was already unworthy of Ibrahim and bringing him sorrow instead of joy. I wanted to cry. I wanted to kneel and beg forgiveness of each of them. I wanted to die.

"Do you regret marrying me?" I asked Ibrahim.

He took me in his arms. "God forbid. When you accepted my proposal, it was as if the heavens had rained drops of honey and the earth had started dancing."

"But—"

He put his finger on my lips. "I have prayed that you would come to me all these years. My soul sings with gratitude. We will see this through together."

We had been at Moursal's house for several days, when I received a call from my brother Zamin.

Zamin and I had always been close. He was one of the few people in the family I could talk to about how Karim was treating me, and he had always listened sympathetically. He and Karim did not get along very well. He was resentful of Karim's misappropriation of family money for his own pleasures. Lately, however, Zamin and I had drifted apart. He didn't approve of my attempts to end my engagement because he too was concerned about family honor. So although there was no enmity between us, the closeness was gone.

"Can I come and visit?"

I was immediately suspicious. Zamin had been so angry when I told him I wanted to annul the engagement. Surely he would be even angrier about my marriage. He also had an old and long-standing dislike for Ibrahim. Even when they were young, they fought at family events, and as they grew older, Zamin continued to harbor anger toward Ibrahim. So there was something strange about his request to come visit me now.

"Why do you want to come see me?"

He sounded hurt. "Do I need a reason? You're my sister. I'm your brother. You are recently married. I want to come over to wish you congratulations and good luck."

I was terribly embarrassed. How could I even think ill of my brother? We had been so close. Now that my marriage was a fait accompli, he must have reconsidered his earlier disapproval. "I will be happy to see you," I said.

I told Ibrahim that Zamin was coming to visit. "But don't be here," I warned him. "I want you to be someplace else."

"Why not?"

"He doesn't like you. It will be unpleasant."

Ibrahim shook his head. "You are my goddess and my beauty. Your wish is my command. If you feel this way, I will go. But sooner or later, your brother will have to come to terms with me as your husband."

"You're right—but let me meet him alone this time. There's plenty of time ahead for the three of us to get together. We have our whole lives."

He kissed me and left.

I served Zamin tea and cookies and we chatted about this and that for a while. Finally he stood up. "I would love a tour of the house."

I shrugged. "It's just a house."

"I would like to see where my sister is living now that she is married. I want to be sure that Ibrahim is taking good care of you."

I was touched. "Of course." We started walking as I pointed out the obvious. "This is the dining room, and here is the kitchen. This is our bedroom, and here's where Moursal and her husband sleep. Over there is the children's room."

He nodded and smiled, kissing me three times on each cheek. "I approve. *Khuda qadamesha nayk kuna.* May you be very happy in your new life."

That night, Ibrahim and I were getting ready for bed when we heard a whizzing sound. Something was flying in our direction. Then there was a thud, as whatever it was bounced against the window screen. It landed in the yard with a crash. The house shuddered and the lawn burst into flame.

"Quick! Put the fire out!" Ibrahim shouted.

Now the entire house was filled with cries. Moursal's husband rushed out with a pail of water. There was more commotion, children were crying, Moursal was screaming.

I looked at the window. The storm window was open, with only a screen in place. The screen was old and sagged, so that when the homemade bomb had hit, it had merely bounced off the netting instead of sailing through into our bedroom as intended.

Moursal and her husband had no enemies—at least none that I knew of. There was only one person who could have been responsible for this attack. Yakub's brother. But how did he know where we were? How did he know what room we were in? He had never visited Moursal before. Unless—

No, it was unthinkable.

Unless someone had given him a description of the interior layout of the house and where we were sleeping. And that could only be—

No, no, *no!* It couldn't be! Zamin could not have betrayed me. Surely the reason for his visit was brotherly affection. But—

But I knew, with sickening accuracy, that my initial uneasiness had been correct. Zamin's reason for visiting me had been deceitful. Somehow, he was in cahoots with Yakub's brother.

I later discovered the truth from Husna. She had found out from her friend Fatima, whose brother was part of Karim's circle of carousers, that Karim had arranged for Zamin to be the spy. He was to scout out the house and report its layout to everyone else. Fatima had overheard her brother and Karim chortling together. They were congratulating each other over wine and cigarettes about their plan to restore the family honor. Yakub and his brother had been there as well.

My brothers! My own brothers had done this to me.

Ibrahim was shaken. "We must do whatever it takes to restore honor to Yakub's family or they'll never leave any of us alone."

"How are we going to do that?" I inquired anxiously.

"Leave that to me."

When he returned later that evening, he looked grim but resolute. "My family will give them fifty thousand afghanis, two guns, and five sheep for having stolen you from his family. In turn, they have promised to leave us alone."

I gasped. "*Azbarai Khodo!* How did you arrange that?"

"Through a mediator."

I wanted to ask who the mediator was, but suddenly I didn't want to ask. I didn't want to know. I didn't want to hear what Ibrahim's uncle and brother, who already disapproved of our marriage, had said. I didn't want to know how Ibrahim's mother, with her outspoken fears for her son's happiness, had reacted. What I already knew was enough: I had put Ibrahim's family in a terrible position. They were being humiliated—relatives of a man who had stolen another man's woman, and now it was costing them money as well. I hid my face in my hands and started to cry.

Ibrahim gathered me into his arms. "*Azizem, Janem,* Darling, Sweetheart. Don't cry. If I had to give away all the money and sheep in the world, it would not be a drop in the ocean of my love for you."

I looked into his eyes. They overflowed with so much love, so much tenderness, that I felt utterly unworthy. I buried my face in his chest.

A few days later, Ibrahim came to me with good news. "Uncle Yusuf has thought things over. He feels he was harsh and hasty when he condemned our marriage. He wants us to move back into the house."

Wonderful. And I would be living with Aunt Sheela too! But first I had a question.

"What changed his mind?"

"We went to a mediator."

"Who?"

He put his finger on my lips. "Don't worry your pretty little head about who. A family elder. That's all you need to know."

I felt a little ping! of resentment, like the snapping of a rubber band. I was being relegated to the inferior position of Wife who did not need to know the Important Financial Matters of the Men. And it was not my husband's family or society, but my husband himself who was being condescending. I was about to press the point when I thought of Deljan's warning and my own precarious position. How lucky I was that Ibrahim had stood loyally by my side and had worked things out with his uncle. That should be enough for me.

Then I thought of something else. "What about Yasin?"

"Uncle Yusuf is talking to him. He has a lot of respect for Uncle Yusuf, and I think things will be all right."

And indeed, things between Ibrahim and myself and Uncle Yusuf really were all right. More than merely all right. Uncle Yusuf and I got along splendidly. Having Sheela in the house was a bonus. It was like reconnecting with a sister. Ibrahim's initial presentation of Uncle Yusuf's disapproval had been correct. His uncle had opposed Ibrahim's handling of the issue of Yakub's honor. Once that had been resolved, Uncle Yusuf and I developed a deep and abiding respect for each other.

Yasin was another matter. He was Ibrahim's older brother and had always been nasty to Ibrahim. Uncle Yusuf told me that throughout their lives, Yasin had always bullied Ibrahim.

"Once Ibrahim came home from school with a good mark on a test. I remember how he was smiling when he walked into the house. He couldn't wait to show it to Deljan. Well, Yasin ran over to him and grabbed it. He tore it up and sprinkled the little pieces of paper all over the house. I remember how he was laughing in a mean way. Ibrahim was crying when Deljan came into the room. When Ibrahim told on Yasin, Deljan tried to hit Yasin, but he ran away. He was still laughing. Later that night, he beat up Ibrahim so badly that Ibrahim could hardly walk the next day. At least that's what I think. Ibrahim pretended he had fallen down the stairs. But I'm sure that Yasin told him if he ever told Deljan, he would get even worse."

Yasin had always taunted Ibrahim. "You can't do anything. You're a *bachay nana*, a mommy's boy. A *zancha*. A sissy." When this happened, Ibrahim would turn to Deljan for comfort and never failed to be soothed. "You're a wonderful boy, Mommy's little darling. You don't have to prove anything to anyone. Come and let me fix you some tea and candy."

Yasin was still nasty to Ibrahim and never failed to throw a barb at his younger brother. "Look at the *tanbal*. Hanging around the house like a lazy bum, freeloading off my work and Uncle Yusuf's. You're still the *banchay nana*, aren't you?" He extended the unpleasantness to include me as well. "Well, if it isn't the loser's wife. How much are you going to cost the family now?"

Every time he said this, I felt as though someone had wrenched the scab off a deep wound. Finally I appealed to Uncle Yusuf. He apparently spoke to Yasin, because the taunting subsided. I knew that Yasin did not like me, but he confined his hostility to glares and occasional snorts or chuckles when Ibrahim or I were talking.

But his comment about Ibrahim's work troubled me deeply. "Why aren't you working, Ibrahim?"

He shrugged. "I just haven't managed to find a good job yet."

Ibrahim had not finished college, but I thought that this was because he had already been working. "Why not?" I persisted.

He took both my cheeks in his hands and drew my face to his. "I don't like it when your mouth pouts," he whispered, planting a kiss on my lips. "Things just didn't come together for me, that's all."

I wanted to find out exactly what had gone wrong, but I allowed his lips to continue exploring mine. Soon, the question had vanished.

A few days later, I went to see Mr. Reza. I realized that I had forgotten to thank him for all his help in resolving my family difficulties. He was warm and courteous and expressed fatherly interest in my life. "What does your new husband do for a living?"

I was embarrassed. "He's looking for a job," I told him. The words were no sooner out of my mouth when I realized that actually, Ibrahim had not been looking for a job. But I pushed that thought aside. Surely any adult without work was looking for a job. He simply hadn't managed to find one yet.

"Does he have a college degree?"

I shook my head.

"Let me call him. I believe I can arrange for him to work as a clerk in the court."

"That would be wonderful! Thank you so much."

The next day, Ibrahim came home filled with words of praise and gratitude for Mr. Reza. "He says he was an old friend of your father's and that he wanted to do your father a good turn. I will be working in a good, steady job. I am very grateful to him."

I was still doing my literacy work. I had worried at first that Ibrahim might be unsupportive, but he proved to be wonderful. "If that's what you want, light of my life, then that is what you shall do. If I were a king, I would give you my entire kingdom."

"Are you saying yes only because it's what I want, or because you really believe in literacy for women?"

"Of course I believe in it too. If you believe in it, then I believe in it."

That was not the answer I had hoped to hear. "I had hoped you would have the same vision that I have—not because it's my vision, but because the same values and ideals are important to you too."

He kissed me on my eyelids. "Silly Sulima," he whispered, nibbling my earlobe. I moaned with delight. "What other woman has a husband who would do anything for her?"

He was right. I was being unreasonable. Once again, I had demands that were too high. I should be singing with gratitude that I had a husband who allowed me to leave the house and do what I wanted. I thought of Madarjan, who had lived her life first under Father's dominion and now under Karim's. I had nothing to complain about.

Thinking about Madarjan was painful. Karim was still trying to get back at me for marrying Ibrahim. He had forbidden Madarjan and all the others from having any contact with me. I missed Asim, Husna, Gula, Surya, and Hala. I missed Naim, my youngest brother, and his charm and sense of humor. But it was Madarjan's gentle touch and her loving brown eyes that I missed the most. I ached for her.

Karim tried in more direct ways to break up the marriage. One night, he paid an unexpected visit to Uncle Yusuf's house. I was out visiting Aunt Fauziya. He asked to see Deljan, Uncle Yusuf, and Yasin, claiming to have some important information that affected all of them.

I found out later what happened. When they were all seated, Karim said, "You should all know the type of woman you have allowed into your family. She is a whore. She is a *fahesha*. A low-down, sniveling, lying worm. Do you know that she had a boyfriend before she even became engaged to Yakub?"

When Uncle Yusuf tried to object, Karim cut him off. "You should force Ibrahim to divorce her for the sake of your family's honor. Because, mark my words, she will not stay longer than six months. Then she will find another man and run away."

When I came home and found out what had happened, I was mortified. That my own brother should attempt to humiliate me to my in-laws! Did they believe him? Their tone of voice suggested that perhaps they did. I wanted to run away and die, I was so crushed. I just hoped that in time, I would prove myself to them and they would come to realize that Karim had been wrong about me.

A few days later, there was a strange sound at the back door. It was almost as if a mouse were trying to knock. I opened it, and there were Madarjan and Husna.

"Madarjan!" I shrieked and rushed into her arms.

"Ssh!" She pulled me into the house. Husna followed and I hugged her.

"Karim does not know that we are here. We told him we were going to buy new clothing and we asked Nabi to drive us."

"You are in Kabul then?" I asked.

"No, we're still in the East," Husna said.

"But it's a seven-hour drive!" I stopped, speechless. They had done this for me. I started to cry.

Uncle Daoud's son Nabi was now a schoolteacher in the East. He had taken the day off and made this enormous trip out of love for me and for Madarjan.

I could not stop hugging Madarjan and Husna. We were all crying.

They stayed as long as they could, then there was the sound of a horn honking outside. We clung to one another, and I watched my beloved mother and sister disappear through the back door. I cried inconsolably for two days. Even Ibrahim's tender kisses and extravagant praises could not comfort me.

11

The Marxist revolution took place in 1978. I was overjoyed. I felt it was the best thing that could have happened to Afghanistan.

I don't wish to imply that the Soviet presence was all good. Far from it. As it emerged later, there was a major price tag to be paid for the communism we were importing. This new group moved rapidly to introduce major reforms, such as a ceiling on landholdings, a limited bride price, and a minimum age for marriage. Massive literacy programs were instituted, in a campaign to bring secular education to men and women, boys and girls, of all ages. Theoretically that should have been a great and positive change. But the Communists went about things in a foolish fashion. The rural population was resentful. These resentful elements, many of whom were members of the Pashtun tribes, later joined with other tribes to overthrow the Communists and reinstitute Islamic law. One day, they would form the backbone of the Mujihaddin.

"If any woman becomes the minister of women's education, it should be Sulima," Uncle Yusuf declared. "She has been educating women since she was a child. They could not choose a more appropriate person."

I was touched by Uncle Yusuf's confidence in me, although in the end I was not appointed minister of education, or even of women's education. However, I was overjoyed when I received a call from the minister of education, offering me the position of curriculum coordinator of women's educational programs. I would be working closely with the director of women's education and literacy to help found schools, motivate women to learn how to read, and create appropriate study materials for them.

I was being paid to do the work I had always done and loved so much! I could scarcely believe my good fortune. I immediately set to work organizing and formalizing what I had been doing for years. I created a curriculum and wrote a series of reading textbooks for adult education. Older women should not be subjected to the humiliation of learning from children's primers. Imagine a grandmother who had managed a complex household being forced to study the Afghan version of Dick, Jane, and Spot!

Once the books and workbooks were photocopied, it was time to put them to use. I had developed a protocol over many years of trial and error and refinement and had taught it to others. Dressed in *hijab*—modest attire—a scarf draped over my hair, I would go to the homes of villagers. I carried a copy of the Qur'an in my hand. I was invariably invited in and offered the usual fare of tea, candies, and cookies. Then I would turn to my male host.

"Do you want your women—your wives and daughters—to be better Muslims?"

Of course that brought vigorous nods from all the men. After that, I turned my attention to the women. "And do you want to be better servants of God?"

More nods, of course.

Then I would pull out the Qur'an and begin to read.

"And we sent to you an apostle from among yourselves to rehearse our signs unto you and to purify you, and to instruct you in The Book and in the wisdom, and to teach you that which ye knew not.

"They truly who hide the Scriptures which God hath sent down, and barter them for a mean price—these shall swallow into their bellies naught but fire. God will not speak to them, or assoil them, on the day of the Resurrection: and theirs shall be a grievous torment. Those are they who have bartered guidance for error."

I pointed out that anyone who seeks to bar women from learning how to read was "hiding the Scriptures" and that the Prophet was addressing everyone—men and women—when He spoke of the importance of being instructed in the Book.

My audience usually was impressed by these and other quotations from the Qur'an. At least one man would finally say, "It is not right for me to prevent my wife from Scriptural reading." And the wife would nod and agree. By the end of the evening, I had a commitment from the family to be involved in women's education in some manner—at least to allow the females in the house to be educated. Those few women who were already literate often volunteered to teach others. When volunteers were not available, the government paid for teachers. Men volunteered to arrange for a room in a mosque, school, or home for the lessons. "It is God's will," the men would say. We supplied papers, books, pens, and other items. Soon a new school would be formed.

I kept in ongoing contact with all the schools I had participated in creating. If difficulties came up—academic or interpersonal—I helped to resolve them.

These were the happiest months of my life since the summer I had spent in the East with Mariam and her friends. I was receiving acknowledgment and a salary for work I had always done and that I loved. And I believed I was participating in creating a world that would ultimately hold equality for women and men.

Of course, my reading primers contained material from sources other than the Qur'an. I hoped that I would be opening a tiny peephole that would grow and expand their horizons and eventually open the door to a new vision of the world.

My home life was as fulfilling as my work. Ibrahim and I were passionately in love. His job was going well, and he was happy. We were like two children together. We giggled, played, and bantered. We made up silly songs. We went to movies and took long scenic walks. We loved to dance, and when we were by ourselves, the radio was rarely silent. Nights were times of mystery and wonder, laughter and light. We soared like birds over mountains and valleys of beauty beyond anything I had ever imagined.

And no matter what was bothering me, Ibrahim always managed to help me feel better. Discouraged about the progress of a school? Disagreement with my supervisor? Ibrahim was there to kiss the tears away and tell me that I was a *fereshta*, an angel, and these people did not deserve me. Did my feet ache after walking through miles of dirt roads to reach someone's house? Ibrahim would bathe, then kiss, the soles of my feet, telling me that he was anointing me with sacred water because I made the land holy.

*   *   *

My stomach felt strange and bloated. I no longer felt comfortable in my clothing. I shared my concerns with Aunt Sheela.

She hugged me. "You must be pregnant."

"Impossible."

Ibrahim and I had been so careful. We used a counting method that minimized the chances of conception. But there had been this one night. . . .

"Well, when is the last time you had your *adat mahwar*?"

"I don't know. Two months?" I rapidly calculated. "No, three. No, wait a minute. Four."

"Four months? Such a long time! You know what that means."

"But I'm irregular," I argued.

She smiled and gently patted my abdomen. "*Khuda hamehet bashed*. May God bless you and the baby."

When I told Ibrahim, he swept me into his arms. "My beautiful wife is going to give me a beautiful child." He knelt down and kissed my belly.

"But Ibrahim," I wailed, "I'm not ready for a child."

"The child is ready for you." He was still beaming.

"Ibrahim! I don't want this baby."

He stood up and frowned. "I also wasn't ready. But now I'm happy. A baby is the completion of our love. A baby brings joy. Why don't you feel that way?"

"How am I going to work with a baby?"

Ibrahim shrugged.

My voice was rising. "Nothing is going to make me give up my work." I stomped out of the room.

There was a swing in our backyard. The next day, I was sailing up and down when I felt someone's hands on the chains of the swing. It was no longer moving. I turned around and saw Aunt Sheela.

"What are you doing?" I asked her.

"You should be taking care of yourself in your condition."

"I'll be fine."

"No, really." Her voice was gentle. "You have a new life inside you." She was looking at me intently. "You wouldn't overdo things on purpose to end the pregnancy, would you?"

I was shocked. "Of course not."

"Good." She smiled. "Ibrahim was worried."

My feelings toward the pregnancy changed when I started to feel the baby moving. "Ibrahim," I whispered. "Put your hand right there."

He felt it too. "It's our child!"

I had never experienced anything like this. A living being growing inside me. A child whom *I* could raise, teach about the world, share my own views with. As suddenly as I had fallen in love with Ibrahim, I knew I was in love with this new baby.

As things turned out, the pregnancy did not disrupt my work at all. If anything, it strengthened my cause. The people I visited in remote villages were impressed to see this modest, demure Muslim woman, with her obviously bulging belly, who had trudged for several hours along winding mountain paths to talk to them about education. And I was fortunate—I experienced no morning sickness, no food cravings, no weakness. In fact, I was so strong and healthy that I did not even bother to educate myself about childbirth. It's ironic to me now, looking back, that someone so involved in women's education did not educate herself about one of the most basic aspects of being a woman.

I must have been in labor for twenty-four hours before my water broke. Aunt Sheela was with me. "Something's happening." I pointed to the gushing. "And it also hurts a lot. But then the pain gets better. Then it starts hurting again. It keeps coming and going like that."

"*Azbarai Khodo!* How long has this been going on?"

I shrugged. "Maybe since yesterday?"

"Why on earth didn't you say something sooner?

I shrugged again. "I don't believe in complaining."

She turned to Ibrahim. "We've got to get her to the hospital immediately!"

Ibrahim started to cry. "Is she going to die?"

"Not if we get there right away."

By the time we arrived, I was weak and in enormous pain. I bit my lip and gripped Aunt Sheela's hand so as not to scream. "You can squeeze harder," Aunt Sheela said. But I held back. I didn't want to hurt her.

The nurse handed me the baby, smiling. "*Mubarak.* You have a beautiful little girl. Her face is *mah peshani*—just like the moon." We named her Mohabat.

I lay back exhausted but peaceful, in a way I had never known before. In my arms, a tiny, dark-haired girl was nestled. I gently touched her cheek and her lips shaped themselves into something like a smile. I was overcome by fierce, protective love like nothing I had ever experienced. My baby. This was my baby.

And indeed she was the crowning of the marriage. We brought her home from the hospital and crowed over her. We must have changed her diaper a dozen times the first night she was home from the hospital. Exhausted as I was, it was hard to sleep that first night. Lying in bed with my husband and my baby, I felt my life was complete and perfect. What greater blessing could there be?

Mohabat was a blessing. A placid little baby, she slept through the night almost immediately. I did not have to deal with any of the colic and screaming other mothers had warned me about. At six weeks, I enrolled her in a wonderful day-care center and returned to work, my heart bursting with joy.

When Mohabat was a few months old, I came home from a trip to the North to find Ibrahim sprawled on the sofa.

"How was work?" I asked him.

"I didn't go."

"Why not?"

He shrugged. "I missed you. I was sad. I decided to take off the day."

"That's not a good reason to take off from work!"

I sat down on the couch and he got up. "Of course it is. And now you're back, so I feel happier." He started walking toward the bedroom. "Come and join me in here!" he called.

I was still angry about his taking off from work. What kind of irresponsibility was this? "Not right now."

In a flash, he was at my side. I felt myself being pulled toward the bedroom.

"Stop it! You're hurting me. You're pulling my hair!"

He let go and slumped onto the bed.

"Don't you ever do that again!" I shouted. "Whatever you want to do, stay in the bedroom and do it there. Don't ever come near me to hurt me."

He was on his knees, crying. "Can you ever forgive me? It's just that I was sad. I missed you, but you didn't seem to care how lonely I felt."

He missed me that much? Maybe I had been too hard on him.

He took me in his arms and covered my face with kisses. "You know I can't live without you," he whispered, stroking my head. Soon I was willingly following him into the bedroom.

But I had not forgotten the matter of his taking off from work. I raised it again a few days later when I came home to again find him lounging on the couch. Questioning revealed that he had not gone to work.

"You can't tell me what to do!" he shouted, jumping off the couch.

"I'm not trying to tell you what to do. I just want to talk about this."

"No, what you really want is a divorce."

A divorce? How dare he! I was so angry that I heard myself say, "That's the most sensible thing that's come out of your mouth all day."

He got up and walked to the door. "All right, then. Let's go to the court right now."

Furiously, I rose to follow him, scooping Mohabat in my arms. Was this really happening? The husband who loved me was taking me to court to divorce me? I blinked back tears. Let him not have the satisfaction of seeing me cry.

"Are you sure this is what you want?" the clerk asked, looking from him to me.

My lower lip started to shake. "I—well, not really. I don't want to divorce."

"Neither do I," Ibrahim admitted.

"Then why did you say you want a divorce?" I demanded.

"Because that's what I thought you wanted."

"Well, I went along with it because I thought that's what you wanted."

The clerk began to smile. "Go home and be happy together. Be a kind husband to your wife and be a dutiful wife to your husband."

By the time we reached home, we were both crying.

"Let's never fight again," Ibrahim said, holding me tightly. "I can't bear it. I love you so much, I would die if we were not together."

I felt the same way. I was so crazed with love and passion for him that when he was drafted into the army reserves for three months, I

99

thought I would go out of my mind. Mohabat had an inflatable toy duck that Ibrahim had blown up before he left. I would not let her play with it. That duck was filled with the hallowed breath of my precious Ibrahim. No one was going to touch it and risk letting even the tiniest quantity of air out.

Twice, I couldn't stand it anymore and went to visit him at the army base, with total disregard for any danger. "I don't care," I retorted when he challenged me. "I felt like I was going to die without you."

For the first time in my life, I was utterly content. My life felt whole and satisfying. My husband, my baby, my work—everything was going well. I woke up each morning feeling blessed.

12

My happy bubble burst when Hafizullah Amin, my old adversary, rose to power. Throughout this time, he had been ascending through the ranks of the Afghan Communist Party. He started out as State Department foreign minister, then became prime minister, then assistant to the president then, in 1979, he replaced the assassinated President Nur Muhammad. My earliest impressions of him as someone who was neither humane nor honest were confirmed with every encounter. However, we had been on particularly bad terms since my second year of college, when I had challenged him during a meeting that was held at his home. I had just returned from a trip to the North and was reporting on my attempt to introduce literacy to the women there.

"So when I told them that even the Qur'an says that both men and women must be educated, I got several women to agree to talk to their husbands and enroll their daughters in school."

"You quoted the Qur'an?" Hafizullah demanded.

"Yes."

"What kind of Communist quotes form the Qur'an? Go and read the *Communist Manifesto* to them!"

"They wouldn't understand the *Communist Manifesto*," I retorted. "I used whatever I felt would work to influence the people. If you want to lead people, you have to follow their culture. You can't impose your culture upon them. You have to meet them where they are."

He banged his fist on the table. "Who are you to tell me what to do?"

"A fellow member of the Communist Party."

He pointed his index finger at me. "You're no Communist! Your father was a Muslim and you're following in his footsteps. Just another good Muslim woman."

Voices broke out. "That's not true!"

"You know Sulima better than that!"

"She's the most dedicated of all!"

He held up his hand for silence. "You're all wrong about her." Then he turned to me. "I want you to leave my home. You are not welcome here."

A hubbub of protests broke out. I raised my voice over the noise. "You can't ask me to leave a meeting because I didn't come to your home to be your guest. I came to the meeting. And if you ask me to leave and others at the meeting don't agree, then you're disrespecting not just me, but everyone else here and everything the meeting stands for." Some applause broke out. "I demand an apology. This goes against everything you're supposed to represent."

"Apologize! Absolutely not!"

"Then I'm interrupting the meeting. Nothing will proceed until I've been apologized to. You're showing no respect for anyone here, so why hold a meeting?"

He argued, but eventually he muttered an apology.

The long-standing antipathy between us continued and flared up every time we met. But after that incident, we tried to keep out of each other's way.

When I became the women's curriculum coordinator, I was able to do my work effectively and avoid him for a long time. But in 1979, when he was appointed assistant to the president, I knew I was in trouble. I tried to tread carefully, to watch what I said about him. Gone were the days of free speech. The reforms for which we had fought so hard led to a reign almost as oppressive as the one we had overthrown. Spies were everywhere. You could not air your views openly. You did your work and swallowed your feelings and your thoughts like bitter medicine. I like to speak my mind, so this was particularly difficult for me. I had endangered my life for the system that now was shutting me up. But I knew Hafizullah was up to no good. I was sure that the old animosity would continue, and I was right. I knew that he would find some opportunity to catch me out.

Shortly after he became assistant to the president, he called me to his office.

He was seated at his desk when I came in. A smug smile curled the corners of his lips. "So we meet again."

"Yes."

He studied me for a few minutes. Inwardly, I squirmed under the unkindness of his scrutiny. "You don't like me very much, do you?"

I shook my head.

"And why not, if I may ask?"

His "who, me?" act enraged me. All my carefully constructed restraint fell away. "Because you're demeaning what this movement is and what it could be. You're betraying the ideal we have fought for, some of us have died for."

His face flushed. His own carefully constructed mask of aloof amusement and chilly sarcasm fell away. "*I* am betraying our ideals? Surely you know about my furthering of land reforms, my promotion of literacy programs—in fact, the very program that pays your salary!" He was shouting now.

"The communism I fought for was not supposed to be about land reforms or teaching women to read!" I shouted back. "Sure, these things were part of it. But it was ultimately about equality for all people. About freedom. About the right to have your own point of view and to express it in public. It wasn't about putting people into jail for no reason as you do, just because they have a different opinion, or because they are associated with someone you don't like!"

The guard heard us shouting and came charging into the room, his gun pointed at me. "Leave her alone," he told the guard. "She's crazy, but she won't hurt me."

The guard glared at me fiercely. "I'll be right outside, so don't try anything funny."

When he left the room, Hafizullah spoke. His lip curled in contempt and he spat out his words. "You don't understand anything. You are still a child. You are naive and stupid. You have stars in your eyes and cotton in your head. You know nothing about the real world."

"I reject your 'real world.' The world I fought for is not filled with corruption and injustice as yours is. The world I fought for is one of freedom and equal rights. That's not naive. That's correct."

"Correct." He chuckled—a nasty, sadistic sound. "What do you know about correctness? Your father was a religious man. He worshipped the false god of Islam. You are his daughter. You have false gods of your own and you are not to be trusted. Your foundation is false, and you have not shed your childhood."

I was about to argue, but he held up his hand to stop me. He opened the door and motioned for me to follow him. We had walked a few paces down the hall when he called the guard.

"Escort this crazy woman out. She is wasting my time." The smile on his lips was chilling. It held no warmth or affection, only sarcasm and contempt.

The guard was only too glad to oblige. I was marched through the hallways and back to the street.

A few weeks later, President Nur Muhammad Taraki was assassinated, and Hafizullah Amin became president. Within days, he replaced my supervisor. I knew I was next in line.

I remember the last visit I paid to a tiny village in the North called Istalef. It is one of the most beautiful places in the world. And the people there responded beautifully. I remember the face of one particular woman I spoke to, her eager expression when she agreed to learn how to read, and her invitation to me to come back in six months so she could show me how much she had learned. I had turned away so that she would not see my tears. Six months from now I would have surely lost my job.

It took only six weeks. My new supervisor called me and informed me that I was being replaced.

I found myself obliged to report each day to the "punishment office." This was a small room filled with many others like me who, for one reason or other, had offended the Communist regime and had been deprived of jobs. We arrived in the morning, milled about aimlessly, then went home. In return, we received a meager salary. We were not allowed to be productive in any way, nor were we allowed to leave.

Once again, I was under a new form of house arrest. My passion for teaching women was again being thwarted. My ability to work for freedom and equality was again being stifled, but by the very people I had been imprisoned by my father for helping.

After a few days of stultifying boredom, I was surprised to receive a visit from Uncle Daoud, who had lived with us when I was growing up. His face was grave.

"Uncle Daoud! What a surprise. To what do I owe the honor of this visit?"

"I've come to warn you."

"Of what?"

"People in a jeep are looking for you. I believe they're going to arrest you."

"What for?" I asked, although I knew.

"They say you're speaking against Hafizullah Amin. That's enough to get you arrested."

"But—"

"Don't argue. And don't resist them. If you cooperate, you'll probably be treated better. It's my hope that they'll release you."

I felt the familiar thudding in my chest that had so often dogged me through my childhood. My eyes were burning and I rubbed tears away.

"Don't be afraid." Uncle's voice was tender. "Trust in God to protect you."

Invoking God did nothing to comfort me, but Uncle's tenderness at least calmed me a little.

Sure enough, after he left, two men in uniform came into the room. They were pointing their guns at me. "You are to follow us to this jeep. Someone in the jeep wishes to talk to you."

"Who wants to talk to me?"

The soldier who had spoken scowled. "That's not for me to say. Just come with us."

I followed them cooperatively, keeping Uncle's words in mind. We reached the street and I saw a jeep with covered windows. I peered in, trying to discern who was inside, but it was dark.

"Get in." The soldier pushed me toward the jeep and I climbed inside.

We started moving, but because the windows had been covered, I couldn't see where we were going. I fought against mounting panic and helplessness. I'm sure that keeping the windows of these vehicles covered is not only a way to ensure the secrecy of a location in which people are interrogated, but also to make the prisoner feel even more helpless, even more lost. We don't realize how much we rely on our eyes to guide and orient us until we are in darkness.

I arrived at a building that turned out to be the headquarters of KAM, the official intelligence service. I was led into a small room. It was chilly, and I clutched my coat around myself.

A man entered the room. He was carrying a folder and a clipboard. "What have you said about our president?" he began.

"I haven't said anything about him."

He pointed to the folder. "I have a report that you spoke ill of him."

"It's not true."

"I'm told that you have organized three hundred literacy teachers. What insidious tactics did you use to control that many people?"

"I didn't use 'insidious tactics.' I used their own beliefs and values to interest them in ours. I have long been involved with the education of women. I simply called upon old friends and associates."

The chair was tiny, metal, and cold, and I shifted uncomfortably as the interrogation continued. For over an hour I was questioned, accused, berated, and questioned some more.

Finally the man stood up. "You are under arrest for defying the government. You are to remain in this office until further notice."

"What's going to happen to me?" I cried.

"That is not my decision. Someone will be back for you shortly. Just stay where you are."

He was at the door when I called after him. "Please, can I speak to Assad Amin?"

Assad was Hafizullah's nephew—a good friend of my cousin Nabi, Uncle Daoud's son, who had first introduced me to Hafizullah when I was still in high school. Over the years, Assad and I had become friendly as well. He had been in medical school at the university when I was studying biology. We had worked for the Communist cause together, and although we never became close friends, we had good feelings toward one another. During the intervening years, he had worked his way up through the ranks, starting out in the health department, continuing to Intelligence, and eventually rising to become director. I had to find him, or someone who would help me reach him.

"Assad Amin is a very busy man. You can't just walk in off the street and expect that he will see you."

"But—"

He left the room.

I waited. I had nothing to read. Nothing to do. I became aware that I was hungry. The room was bare. Nothing to look at. No way to keep warm. I looked at my watch. Only a few minutes had passed since the man left, but they had already seemed like a few hours.

The minutes continued to crawl by. Every time I heard someone's footsteps in the hall, I jumped out of my seat in a mixture of relief and fear. But no one came for me.

Where were they? And what was Ibrahim doing at home now? It was evening. I should have been home from work long ago. He must be beside himself with worry. And what about Mohabat? She would be crying for me by now.

Pictures swarmed before my eyes. Everything jumbled together, a kaleidoscope of images. My father smiling, his smile suddenly turning deadly. The inside of Yakub's car. Mohabat's sweet giggles, her dimpled smile. Hafizullah's contemptuous mouth. Madarjan's loving eyes. Ibrahim's hands. My students, eagerly sounding out the alphabet. A cascade of everything I had worked for, everything I was, everything I feared, everything I loved. I rested my head on the metal desk and slept.

When I woke up, it was daylight. My bladder was bursting, demanding attention. My stomach growled angrily. I glanced at my watch. It had been over fifteen hours since I had been left in the office. Clearly, no one was coming to get me.

What to do? Staying in the room was out of the question. I needed food. I needed the bathroom. I needed to go home. Gingerly, I tested the door. It opened. Good. No one had locked it while I was sleeping.

I found the bathroom, washed my face, then set out to locate Assad Amin. I wandered the halls until I saw an open door. Some clerk was sitting behind a desk in an office. I knocked on the door and he looked up.

"Who are you?"

"My name is Sulima. I need to speak to Assad Amin."

"You just walk in here and expect to be put in touch with the director? Assad Amin is a busy and important man. I will not disturb him."

Just what yesterday's man had said.

My voice was about to break, but I knew it was important to keep it steady. If I appeared distraught, he might guess that I had been arrested and might have me hauled off to jail. "I'm an old friend of his."

The clerk was frowning. He was suspicious. He was about to say something, when I heard a familiar voice. "Sulima! What are you doing here?"

I turned toward the door. The man standing there had been a superficial acquaintance in college, someone in one of my biology classes. "Moushref? I hardly recognized you. You've changed so much since college."

He grinned. "It's the gray hair. Getting gray early runs in my family. Also the moustache. What are you doing here?"

"I was arrested." Now I allowed myself to cry. "I want to speak to Assad. I know he'll help me. We were friends in college."

"I would help you myself if I could, but I'm only a clerk. I have no power to release you. But I'll call Assad for you. Please come into my office."

I followed him and sat down while he picked up the receiver and dialed. "Assad? Oh good, it's Moushref." I heard him tell my story rapidly. Then he hung up and smiled. "He'll be right over."

Assad was outraged when he heard what had happened to me. He arranged for my immediate release. As I was thanking him profusely, he held up his hand. "No need to thank me. Just be careful."

"But I have been careful," I protested.

"You have to be even more careful. Don't talk to anyone who opposes my uncle. Don't talk about women's rights or equality or any of those things. Just be quiet, sit in the office, go home, and take care of your baby."

I was too grateful to him to argue, and too tired even if I had wanted to. I dragged myself home.

"So you're free now," said Ibrahim the next morning.

I shook my head. "I don't think it's over yet."

"But if you're careful, as Assad said—"

"You don't understand. You don't know these people. I could be as quiet as a little mouse and they would find something wrong. This isn't about breaking the law or being subjected to a just trial. It's about power. Hafizullah Amin holds the power. He hates me. I will be arrested again. I guarantee it."

Sure enough, I was arrested and interrogated again a week later. This time I was treated better. Word had gotten around that I was a personal friend of Assad and that he had arranged for my release. I was allowed to call him, and once again, he came right to my rescue.

But the third time they arrested me, Assad was displeased. "I can't keep helping you out like this. You're already on the black list and nothing I can do will change that. If I keep helping you out, I'll be blacklisted as well."

"So what should I do?"

His answer came readily. "You must leave the country."

My knees buckled and I sank into his chair. "Leave Afghanistan? But it's my home. I love this country. My family is here—"

"That doesn't matter. If you want to stay out of jail, you must leave. Jail is a dangerous place, Sulima. Terrible things happen to women there. Some never return. I won't be able to protect you next time. You can love the country from afar, and believe me, you will love it much less if you are in jail."

"How would I get out of the country at such short notice?"

"I have a plan. You and your husband should go and apply for passports. I will arrange the rest."

"How can we leave our country?" Ibrahim and I were sitting on the sofa. I couldn't stop crying.

"We have no choice. You can't go to jail and be raped. Or killed. I couldn't stand it if you were dead."

"But maybe this will pass," I argued. "Maybe something will happen to Hafizullah and the government will come to its senses."

"We can't live with a 'maybe,' Sulima."

"But I love this country!"

He stroked my hair. "So do I. But you know we have to go."

The next day, Ibrahim told me that he had also lost his job. The courts were now under the control of the government and we suspected that Ibrahim was now on Hafizullah's black list as well.

"You're right," I said to Ibrahim later that evening. "We have to leave."

He kissed me. "Don't worry. I'll be happy wherever you are. *You* are my home country."

A week later, I picked up the passports. Then I went to Assad to thank him.

"I had to bribe several people to create these documents and to keep quiet about my part in helping you."

I swallowed. "How much money did it cost you?"

"Seventy-five thousand afghanis," he replied.

"I'll pay you back as soon as we've sold our possessions. I'll also pay the government back for the loan we took last year."

Ibrahim and I had taken a loan to move into our own apartment because Uncle Yusuf and Yasin had moved to Austria and had sold the house. Although Uncle Yusuf was not employed in any official government position—he was a dentist—he had nevertheless managed to antagonize two government officials who had come to him for dental work. They had been sitting in the waiting room when they overheard him talking on the phone to a friend about his disagreement with Communist land policy. He was threatened with arrest and decided to leave the country. Since Yasin had married an Austrian woman who had been traveling through Afghanistan but who missed her family and her homeland, it made sense for Uncle Yusuf, Yasin, and their families to migrate to Austria. Ibrahim and I were glad to have our own place, even though we had needed to borrow money in order to afford it.

"That's very honorable of you," Assad said. "You don't know how many people are taking loans, then using it to move out of the country."

"I don't believe that's right," I said. "The money belongs to the people of Afghanistan. Anyone who robs the government is robbing the people. When I leave, I will have a clean conscience knowing that I have been honest."

He smiled approvingly. "But money is not the only issue. There is one other way you can repay me."

He reached into a drawer and produced a document. "Please sign this contract. It states that you agree not to return to Afghanistan until socialism has been firmly established and you have returned to your senses." He stared hard at me. "This means that as long as there is a Communist regime—which is for eternity, we hope—you are banned from returning to the country."

I was signing away my country, my love, all my hard work for women and freedom and equal rights. I felt I was signing away my life.

But the alternative—jail, possibly execution—was worse. I would not be allowed to raise my daughter. I would not be allowed to teach or work either. At least in a Western country I could walk free. I could be a mother and a wife. I could seek employment. I could live in a world where men and women were treated equally. And I could continue working on behalf of my Afghan sisters from afar.

I signed the contract.

I left Afghanistan in 1979—ironically, just a few months before the assassination of Hafizullah Amin. We had managed to obtain tickets to Germany, where we would be allowed into the country with only a passport. No visa was required. From Germany, we would have our pick of several Western countries that would be sympathetic to someone fleeing the Communists and would be only too glad to grant us asylum—as indeed happened.

We are airborne. I peer through the blurred curtain of my tears, through the tiny window of the plane. The rugged peaks, the snowcaps, the harsh and beautiful landscape of my childhood swims into view. Farther and farther away now. Tinier and tinier. A smudge. A pinpoint. A memory.

I had taken my belongings, my husband, and my daughter. I had taken my integrity, my convictions, and my soul. . . but I left my heart behind. It was still in Kabul, calling to the tormented hearts and bowed heads of women, inviting them to be free. It was still in the university, swelling with pride as my mind mastered concepts of biology. It was still romping and cavorting through Babajan's paradise garden. It would always remain there.

It is still there, waiting for me to return.

13

We arrived in Germany exhausted and shaken. I had not stopped crying through most of the plane ride. Ibrahim had sat, silent and morose, looking out the window. Mohabat was cranky. I missed Madarjan. I missed everyone. I had not even been able to say good-bye or tell them where I was. I would have to send a letter to Aunt Mariam when we were settled. She could find her way of telling Madarjan where we were. Aunt Mariam had always been our go-between and remained in that position until Karim was firmly estab-lished in a residence of his own.

Uncle Yusuf had written to us, explaining how to travel from Ger-many to Austria by train. He and Yasin would meet us at the train station. The trip lasted one day but seemed like one year. The whole experience felt surreal. People around us were talking a strange, gut-tural language. The country was green and filled not with dark-haired, gaunt men but with blue-eyed, blond-haired men. Signs were in German and English and the absence of Pashtu and Dari writing on the walls of the airport, train, and other public places made us feel even more isolated. We could figure out from the little picture which was the ladies' room and which was the men's room, but the signs for "hot" and "cold" on the faucets were in German.

When we saw Yasin and Uncle Yusuf waiting for us on the plat-form we rushed into their arms. We stood there hugging and crying while the train whistled along its way.

"Look at her!" Uncle Yusuf pointed to Mohabat. "She's so big and so beautiful!"

"Let's go to the car," Yasin said, picking up my suitcase.

Yasin and Ibrahim walked ahead of us, with their arms around each other, murmuring.

It was wonderful to be with family again. Uncle Yusuf and Aunt Sheela were warm and welcoming, as was Helga, Yasin's wife. Now Yasin had a baby and a toddler of his own, who were adorable. Hearing Pashtu again was like hearing the music of the angels. Uncle Yusuf's children had grown up and were looking strong and healthy. It was wonderful to see everyone again.

But Yasin looked none too friendly. He glared at me several times. When I was helping myself to more rice, he made it a point to say that he was offering hospitality to Ibrahim, and I was just along for the ride. Then Uncle Yusuf shot him a warning look and he grumbled, then went silent.

"We have to go home tomorrow," Uncle Yusuf said apologetically after dinner. "I wish we could have stayed a few days to help you get settled, but Yasin will have to do that."

"Home?"

"I had no chance to write and tell you, but we are now living in France. I lived here when we first arrived. I worked odd jobs and learned to speak German. But I wanted to get back to my own field. So I wrote many letters and a clinic in France agreed to let me come work as an oral hygienist. When I have worked there for six months, they will let me do a little dentistry, and eventually, maybe I can get a job there as a dentist. I may have to take another qualifying examination—I don't know yet. We moved to Paris last week."

"And you made the entire trip here just to welcome us?"

He shrugged. "Of course."

But it was more than merely duty to family. I saw the love in Uncle Yusuf's eyes. Watching him go back the next day was another loss, and I cried. Now we were alone with Yasin and his family, and there was no one to protect us.

Those first weeks of living with Yasin were like a nightmare. Their apartment was small and cramped. Normally, this is not a problem for Afghans. We are used to large families, small living quarters, and no privacy. But Yasin's increasingly obvious hostility made it awkward. Mohabat played in blissful oblivion on his floor, but I had to tread around Yasin's barbed words. It was like walking through a minefield.

Yasin's anger was not reserved for Ibrahim and me. "You *ahmaq*!" he yelled at Helga when she spilled the tea. "She's so stupid," he said to Ibrahim as Helga rushed in with a rag to wipe up the spill.

Ibrahim was remote, as if part of him was in hibernation. He moved like a robot. His face was somber and flat. The only smiles I saw from him were reserved for some private jokes he seemed to share with his brother. I had never seen him like this.

"Ibrahim, do you want to go for a walk? Helga will watch Mohabat."

"I'm tired."

"But we haven't spent any time alone since we got here—and it's been almost a month. There are obviously some things we can't do together here, since we're sleeping in Yasin's living room, but at least we can talk."

He shrugged. "What's there to talk about?"

We had never been at a loss for words. At the very least, he always had some term of endearment, or some longer litany of my virtues. He could be so extravagant in my praises that it was embarrassing sometimes. Certainly he had never run out of things to say before.

Never mind. He was under stress. I was under stress. Living in a one-bedroom apartment with Yasin's family and missing our homeland would have been stressful, even if Ibrahim had been on wonderful terms with his brother. And now, without Uncle Yusuf to protect him, Ibrahim was entirely at the mercy of Yasin's nastiness.

A few days later, Yasin had some information for us. "I have found you a room in Guertel."

"Is that a city?" Ibrahim asked.

"No, stupid. It is a region of Vienna, about a half hour from here. The landlord is a friend from work. Some people moved out of the room a few days ago."

A place of our own! Tiny, yes. Inconveniently furnished with a night table that seemed to take up almost the entire room. But ours. All ours. We might share a bathroom and kitchen with the other tenants, but we could close the door at night and be alone.

"We need to find work," I said to Ibrahim the day after we moved.

"You look. I'll watch the baby. When we have some money to pay for baby-sitting, I'll find a job too."

Perhaps Hans, our nice landlord, knew someone who was looking for a cleaning lady. I spoke to him and he introduced me to his doctor. I started cleaning the doctor's office, and then his house. Soon the doctor gave me the name of a friend who was a history professor at the Universitat Wien—the University of Vienna.

The professor, whose silver hair surrounded his face like a halo, took a paternal interest in me and asked me about my life. I tried to tell him my story, using a combination of my newly acquired though still limited German vocabulary and sign language. *Ich habe Biologie studiert. Ich bin in Afghanistan geboren. Ich bin von den Kommunisten geflohen.* I have studied biology. I was born in Afghanistan. I fled the Communists.

"Ach du lieber! And now you scrub floors?"

I nodded.

"Would you like to work in your own discipline?"

I nodded vehemently.

"My good friend Herr Doktor Hermann Schmidt is the *Institutsdirektor* of the department of biology. I will speak to him for you."

The next week, I had a part-time job as a laboratory technician in the biology department of the university. I would still need to clean houses, but at least I could work in my own field.

I burst into the room that night in great excitement. Mohabat was sleeping on the bed. Ibrahim was staring out the window, a beer can open in front of him. He had never drunk much alcohol in Afghanistan, but when we were staying with Yasin, he developed a fondness for beer.

"I got a job! A really great job, at a lab. It's exactly what I want!"

"That's nice," he said.

Why wasn't he more excited for me? I threw my arms around him and started kissing him. "Now we can pay for day care. Then you can start working too!"

He nodded. "Very nice," he repeated.

What was going on with him? I understood that he missed his home country. So did I. I understood that he had been especially unhappy at Yasin's. But we were on our own now. We had a room with a dear little garden right outside our window. We were alive. We were not in jail. We had an adorable little girl. We loved each other. What had changed?

I waited for the magic. For the light to return to Ibrahim's eyes. For the murmurings of the night and the laughter of the daytime.

But with each day, he slipped further away from me. It was like watching his soul drowning in a giant cesspool of beer.

Perhaps he was just depressed because he was not working. I enrolled Mohabat in a wonderful day care center. "Now you can look for a job," I told Ibrahim.

"You find me one," he said.

I spoke to the doctor who had been so helpful to me.

"What is your husband's training? His profession?"

"He didn't manage to finish college," I answered. "In Afghanistan, he worked as a clerk in the court."

"Has he learned any German yet?"

I shook my head. "Not much." By now I was almost fluent, although my grammar and sentence structure remained highly unconventional and colleagues at the lab were always correcting me. But at least I could make myself understood. "He has had no time," I explained. "He has been taking care of our daughter. Now that I've arranged day care, he can start to get adjusted."

"*Ach, ja.* I will see how I can be helpful."

A few days later, he had found work for Ibrahim in the loading department of a pharmaceutical company, moving boxes of medications from the factory to the trucks. Things would get better now.

Yasin came to visit us the following Saturday, together with Helga and the children. The brutal cold of winter was behind us and we were savoring the warm April sunshine. We were sitting outdoors on the grass. Ibrahim and Yasin were sipping from bottles of beer and talking in low voices while Helga and I were playing with the children.

Suddenly Yasin's voice was loud and sharp. "We know who the real man in your family is." He took another swallow of beer and pointed to me. "She does everything. She talks German. She works in a university. She finds you a job. She is smart. You—" he pointed at Ibrahim—"you are nothing but a *zancha*. Still the *bachay nana*. Fortunately, in my household, I am the man. My wife is not smart. She is stupid. She does not go out of the house to work at fancy university. She cleans and cooks, which is all she's good for."

My hand was frozen in position, where it had been hovering over the cookie I was about to give Mohabat. My body felt as though it had turned to ice. I could not bear to look at Helga, but when I finally managed to turn my head, I saw that she was crying. Helga is one of the kindest human beings I have ever met. There is not a shred of malice in her, only goodwill toward everyone she meets. She did not deserve this treatment.

What could I do? Anything I said would make it worse. I waited. Why wasn't Ibrahim saying anything? Defending his wife? Saying something nice about his sister-in-law? Come on, Ibrahim. Please.

Nothing.

Then Mohabat started to cry and pointed to the cookie. Helga's baby needed a diaper change, and she went indoors to the bathroom.

"Why didn't you say anything to Yasin?" I demanded after they had gone home.

"It was not my place to interfere between them."

"What about defending me? He said terrible things about your own wife."

Ibrahim shrugged and opened another bottle of beer.

The next morning. I squint into the room. Darts of pain drive my eyelids shut. My head is going to explode. I fall back against the pillows. It is nine, but I cannot imagine getting up.

Wait, what about Mohabat? She'll be hungry. I must feed her.

A sound. What's that? A clatter, a giggle. A little girl eating breakfast. Ibrahim is feeding her. Good. I close my eyes again.

A sheet of light falls onto my face. Ibrahim has opened the blind. "Time to get up!"

"Hey, close that blind! I don't want to get up yet."

"It's morning. Only a tanbal lies around in bed all day."

"I'm not feeling well." I roll over, reach for the cord, and close the blind.

He yanks it open. "I don't believe you."

"Ibrahim! I've never lied to you. I have a terrible headache. Please let me go back to sleep." I close the blind.

Is this Ibrahim? My beloved Ibrahim? Are these hateful words coming out of the same mouth that had whispered all those wonderful things to me? The same mouth that had planted such sweet kisses on mine? Is this a nightmare? A hallucination?

No dream, no hallucination. I know this, because my cheek is stinging. Ibrahim has slapped me.

"Ibrahim!"

He was on his knees on the floor beside the bed. "I am so sorry. I don't know what came over me. You're my *janem*, my *fereshta*, my darling, my angel, the love of my life, the light in my sky. I would never, never hurt you. I am so, so, so sorry."

"Something is wrong, Ibrahim." I was crying. "You're not the same person you used to be."

"It's just hard being in a new country. I miss home. I miss my mother. I miss my old friends from work. I miss hearing Pashtu in the streets. I hate that we had to run away, like frightened animals in the night."

We talked for hours. By the time we had finished, my headache was gone and I was filled again with the warm glow of our union and our love. We had talked. We had worked things out. The old Ibrahim was back. Everything would be all right.

I came back from work the next week to find Ibrahim lounging on the bed, two open beer bottles on the floor beside him. His mouth was slightly agape, and he was snoring. I shook him angrily. "Why aren't you at work?"

He opened his eyes and scowled. "I didn't like the job. It's not for my honor to drag boxes around."

"But we need the money!"

"You're making a lot of money in that hoity-toity place of yours." His speech was slurred. "Do you know, I tried to call you during my lunch break? I thought maybe I could have lunch with my wife. But no, you were out of the office for lunch. Bet you had lunch with your wonderful Herr Direktor. Bet you slept with him after that."

"How could you say that?" I burst into tears. "We had a meeting of all the laboratory employees to talk about new policies for handling cell cultures. They took us all out to lunch. It was part of work."

"So you're eating in a fancy restaurant while I'm slaving to move boxes around. What kind of wife does that? I was right to quit."

I softened. He was working so hard. After a job as a clerk in a court, it must be humiliating to do menial labor. I must try harder to find him more appropriate work. I must try harder to be more understanding. I must be more patient with him and allow him to adjust. I put my arms around him and stroked his face. "Poor darling. I will help you find something more fitting for a man of your stature."

He started kissing me and crooning in my ear. It was a long time before I rose to pick up Mohabat from her day care center.

The doctor had no leads for me this time. Ibrahim still didn't speak the language well, which limited employment possibilities. But then I saw a sign hanging at the university. There was a job opening for a security guard at one of the museums near the university. It was not on the same level as being a clerk in a court, but at least it was not manual labor. Even better, Ibrahim and I could meet for lunch more easily when I was free. We could take walks in the *Burgarten*. This was the new beginning we needed. Now things would really work out.

Two weeks later, we returned from work to find Yasin waiting in our room. "You have to move from here," he said.

"Why?" Ibrahim asked.

"Because I had a fight with Hans. You can't stay here."

"What does your fight have to do with our staying here?" I demanded. "We've paid our rent. We can stay."

He shot a dark glance at me, then at Ibrahim. "Do you let your wife talk back to you like that? Explain to her what family honor means. That you dishonor me by staying in a residence owned by a man who has treated me badly. If you handle her correctly, you will make her understand."

"You shouldn't speak to my brother like that," Ibrahim said when Yasin had left.

"He shouldn't speak to us like that!" Heat was boiling in my belly like the kettle in the kitchen upstairs. "Who is he to tell us what to do? Why should we have to move just because he's had a fight?"

"He is my older brother. I owe him respect."

"He shows you no respect."

"I'm the youngest. He doesn't owe me respect." I was reminded of the old Afghan saying, It is better to be the family dog rather than be the youngest.

"Well, you can go if you like. But I've paid the rent on this place already. I'm not going."

He sneered. "Now I understand. You are sleeping with Hans. That is why you want to stay."

My breath caught. "How dare you? You ought to be ashamed of yourself, accusing me like that. You know how much I love you! I would never, never be unfaithful!"

Ibrahim's face was dark and ugly with rage. "No, you're carrying on with him. How did you seduce him? Did you come home when I was at work? Maybe that's where you go when you're not in the lab for lunch."

"And what would that make you? A *murdagau daouz*, a pimp!"

He moves toward me. One step. Two steps. I am not Sulima the grown-up, mother of Mohabat, former literacy teacher, now employee of the Universitat Wien. I am little Sula. I am holding a basin. A man with eyes of coal is coming toward me. His fist is clenched. Who is he?

He raises the fist.

"No! Ibrahim, no!"

Knuckles meet flesh. I am falling down, down, there is a thump on my head and then he is upon me. Fist against eye, fist to cheek, I hear a distant, choked sound like a rusty chain. Get off, get off! Push, push harder, but he pushes harder still. Hands pinning shoulders to the floor, something pressing harder, harder against my neck. His knee. Gasping, choking, begging, please, I can't breathe, I can't breathe.

And someplace in the background, the sound of a little girl crying.

Suddenly, I was free. Sparks were dancing like evil demons before my eyes. I tried to sit up but slumped to the floor.

"Oh my God. Oh my poor darling. What have I done to you?"

Someone was washing my face with cold water. Someone was putting ice on my eye. Someone was talking about love, about beauty, about me. Someone was crying. I opened my good eye. It was Ibrahim. "My sweetness, my love, my flower, my little lamb. What did you make me do to you?"

The cascade of words continued as he finished sponging my face. "Didn't mean to—" "Was just angry about the things you said—" "Don't know what got into me—"

I put my arms around him and clung to him. "I'm sorry I said that terrible word to you. I won't ever say something like that again."

He buried his face in my hair. "That's my girl."

We moved to another apartment the next week.

*   *   *

A kaleidoscope of fractured images. Round and round it goes.

Someone is praising me. A neighbor. "Your wife speaks such good German. You must be so proud." Later, a fist. Another black eye. Another lie to Gretchen, my friend who works with me at the lab. This time, I have bumped into the dresser corner. She looks at me, and I know she has figured out the truth. I hide my face in shame.

Two months later:

My first day of class. I have been accepted into the Ph.D. program at the university. I will be studying cell biology. They love my work in the lab and the Institutsdirektor has arranged everything. I'm soaring on wings made of ideas . . . away, away, to a realm where nothing matters but cell membranes and nuclei. I am still soaring when I reach the day care center. But I'm late because I missed the tram. Ibrahim is here, picking up Mohabat. The teacher called him, she wanted to leave. Now we are home. I am spiraling downward, my wings melting, I am on the ground. There is shouting and pounding of fists. I must abandon my studies or Ibrahim will abandon me and take Mohabat with him. It is too much for me to manage school and a baby, I tell the Institutsdirektor the next day. I'm sorry.

We had been receiving increasingly upsetting communication from family in Afghanistan. Bands of disgruntled Afghans had joined forces to form a somewhat cohesive group determined to overthrow the Communist regime. They had begun to fight even fellow Afghans who they believed to be colluding with the Communists. They had also begun to attack women and children gratuitously, raping and torturing people for no reason at all. People were trying to flee the country. Deljan, Seema, and Roshan had been successful in moving to the United States. So had Ali, Ibrahim's close childhood friend, who had served as witness to our marriage. But my own closest family had not been so fortunate. Every piece of mail seemed to bring a report of some new horror.

My hands tremble. I am holding a letter from Husna. Nabi has been killed by the Mujihaddin. Nabi, who first introduced me to Hafizullah Amin. Who had always been so good to me. Nabi, my sweet sweet Nabi.

Dead. Last month, it was my old friend Badria who died. Raped and mutilated by the Mujihaddin. Mariam wrote to tell me about it.

I am crying. Mohabat is making nice to my face. Trying to wipe away my tears. Ibrahim sneers, "Crybaby. What's all the fuss about?"

"N-Nabi. He's dead."

"Oh, him? Is that all? He's not really my cousin. Why should I care?"

The following winter, a wonderful opportunity arose. Something that seemed to offer a solution to all our problems. The entire department was invited to move to France. A university in Paris was expanding its biology division. We were a ready-made team, and they wanted us to take over their new quarters. I was the only foreigner—an asylee to boot—and arranging for me to receive an appointment at a French university involved all kinds of legal complications. But the *Instituts-direktor* was adamant. Only if Sulima comes too, he said. It took six months for the paperwork to be complete. During that time, the whole department was delayed in its move. Finally the formalities were done. An apartment was found for us in Paris. Day care for Mohabat. Education for Ibrahim. We were packed. Ready to go. I was excited. Here was a new beginning, away from the pain of Austria, away from Yasin, close to Uncle Yusuf and Aunt Sheela. A new future was awaiting us, golden and shimmering.

Then, the day before we were to leave, everything changed.

"We're not going." Ibrahim was standing in the door to our room, watching me close the suitcases.

"What are you talking about?"

"I'm going to America. Where Deljan and Seema are."

This couldn't be happening. "But everything is arranged."

"I don't like the arrangements."

"What could possibly be wrong with them?" The anguish slashed my voice like a razor.

"You've done everything. You've arranged everything. I will be living off my wife. This is unacceptable."

"You agreed to go. They have put themselves out for me, they've delayed their own plans by six months. I'm not letting them down. We're going to France."

"No, *you're* going to France. *I'm* going to America. And I'm taking Mohabat with me. I will send you divorce papers from America."

"No, wait!"

I reach for him, but he is gone. On his way to the United States. With Mohabat. Mohabat! He has taken my baby with him!

What's happening? The room, it's roaring, it's spinning, a tornado of darkness. Back home, the man can take the child. Surely the law is the same here. My baby is gone forever.

I have lost my husband. I have lost my child. There's nothing I can do about it. There's nothing, nothing, nothing left to live for.

Pills, where are those pills? Pain pills for headaches—they were right here, on the nightstand. Find them, quick. Oh no, did he take the pills too? Ah, here they are. Come, little friends, and get me out of this hell. Quick, swallow them down. A gulp of water. Lie down and wait for—

But what's that ringing sound? I must make it go away. Must have quiet. I grope. My hand closes around something hard. A phone receiver. "H-hello? Gretchen? Ibrahim, he— I won't be at work— Baby gone, and—"

Hard to talk. Words won't come out. Gretchen, I say, Gretchen, then I slide into darkness.

I woke up to find myself in a hospital, a kindly nurse leaning over me. I shut my eyes. Why did they bring me back? What was there to live for? Why were they asking me these questions? Wearily, I started to explain. My eye was black because I fell down the stairs last week. Really. The red mark on my back came from the heater in my room. Why would I be using heat in the summer? Well, the baby sometimes got cold. Did I want to call the police? Why would I want to do that?

And then I saw Ibrahim. He had been at Yasin's the whole time. "You're not in the United States!" I screamed. I threw my arms around him, my tears pouring over his shoes like blood. "You're back!"

I did not let go of his hand. "I'll do anything you want. Anything. Just don't ever go away again. Don't ever take my baby away. I will try harder to be a better wife. We will go to America if that's what you want."

I could not look the *Institutsdirektor* in the eye when I told him that I would not be joining the department in France but would be going to America instead. Why, he kept asking, why? And I couldn't tell the truth. I shrugged. "I just changed my mind." He was crushed, then angry. After all his hard work, the lengthy delay, the sacrifice of the entire department— Only Gretchen knew the truth. She understood. She was my friend. She hugged me. "Call me if you ever come back to Austria again. *Aufwiedersehen!*" My other colleagues refused to talk to me. Just yesterday we were celebrating, but today I was leaving and no one would even say good-bye.

Ibrahim stayed behind to finish packing the apartment. He would join me when I found us a place to live. He hugged me at the airport and kissed little Mohabat good-bye. "America is a land of opportunity," he said. "I can start my own business there. I can be a man again. We will be happy, like we were in the beginning."

I clung to him, crying. "I love you too. I have never felt like this about anyone or anything. I will do everything to make you happy."

14

Another long plane ride, Mohabat at my side, clutching her favorite doll. I flew across the Atlantic in a rain of tears. My destination: Pittsburgh, Pennsylvania. Where Seema, Roshan, and Deljan were living. I would stay with them until I could find a place of our own. Mohabat was cranky. "I miss my teacher. I want my friends," she cried in her funny mixture of Pashtu and German. Devastated about my shattered plans for France, exhausted and still recovering from my overdose and from the injuries of a few weeks ago, I had little patience for her.

Seema was waiting at the airport. We ran into each other's arms. "You look tired," she said finally, stepping back and eyeing me critically. "And your face is all banged up. What happened to you?"

"I fell."

She frowned then picked up my suitcase. "You look like you could use a hot bath, a hot meal, and a warm bed."

As soon as we entered the house, Deljan came to the door. She gathered Mohabat into her arms. "Look how adorable she is! My baby's little baby! Flesh of my flesh!" Mohabat began to cry and struggled to be put down.

Deljan turned a wrathful face at me. "So you've turned my granddaughter against me, just like you did to my son."

I set my suitcase down, assailed by another wave of exhaustion. Had I come to the United States for this?

"What do you mean?"

"Do you know that until he married you, he used to sleep in my bedroom, just like he did when he was a little boy? Poor baby, he got so lonely at night. I would stroke his head and say, come to Mommy. Then when he married you, he started to sleep in your bedroom. You took him away from me."

"When he comes to the United States, he can sleep in your room if that's what you want."

She shook her head, a nasty little smile playing around her mouth. "No, he'll want you. You cast some kind of spell on him, then you brought him nothing but dishonor and pain." She stomped away.

"Don't let her get to you," Seema whispered. "She's been acting very strange, ever since we left Afghanistan. She does it to me too."

"What are you doing today?" Deljan asked the next morning.

"Looking for an apartment."

"See?" She turned to Seema. "I told you she was taking Ibrahim away from us. They could live with us, but she wants to take him to her own place."

"We need some space of our own," I pleaded.

Deljan snorted. "Space. That's an American idea. In our country, we all live together."

We argued all morning. By lunchtime I was thoroughly exhausted and fed up. "I'm sorry, I don't wish to offend you. But I am going to look for an apartment. You told me to take care of Ibrahim, and I think that part of taking care of him is arranging a place where he and I can live alone."

"Then Mohabat stays with me." She stepped toward Mohabat, who hid between my legs.

"No, my daughter comes with me," I said, grasping Mohabat's hand tightly.

"Then get out!"

Had I heard right? Was Deljan kicking me out? Where would I go? I knew very little English. I certainly did not know the area. I had just arrived yesterday. I was counting on family for support and guidance in this new country. What was I going to do?

"Didn't you hear me?" she shrieked. "I said, get out right now!"

I was about halfway down the street when Seema caught up with me. She was driving a blue car. "Quick, get in!" We piled into the back. "I don't want Deljan to see that I'm helping you out."

I started to cry. "Where should I go? What should I do?"

"I have friends who own a motel. Nice people, Indians."

"I can't afford a motel."

"Leave it all to me," Seema said.

It was arranged that I would pay twenty-five dollars a night—ten dollars less than their usual rate. "But where will I get that kind of money?" I asked anxiously.

She squeezed my hand. "Don't worry. I'll take care of it."

Each day, Seema came to pick up Mohabat so that I could look for a place to live and a job. At first I was worried that Deljan would abscond with my daughter, but Seema reassured me. "I won't let Mother do anything crazy. I'll keep Mohabat with me and my own kids at all times." Evenings, she would come back with Mohabat, and a plate of food. She usually had a letter from Ibrahim with her— almost always sent overnight express. A lot of money, I knew, but on the other hand, it showed how much he loved me.

Dear Sulima,

I am heartsick and lonely here without you. When I wake up and you are not here, the sky is covered with clouds and God himself starts to cry. When I think about everything I did to you, my heart breaks. I am sorry for everything I ever did. I weep for every teardrop I brought to your beautiful eyes. Just wait until I get to America, the land of promise, and watch how happy I will make you. You are my little lamb and I will protect you and cuddle you. Stay well, my darling! I'll write more tomorrow.

Only yours,
Ibrahim

I would kiss the letters and put them into my suitcase. I had been right to leave Austria. My husband loved me. He just needed an opportunity to start life over again. I was his wife and it was my duty to support him. I just hadn't taken his needs into account. Now he would come to the States, to a nice apartment. He would open a business of his own. The magic would come back.

The first order of the day was to find a place to live. I started knocking on doors. "Do you have a room to rent?" One after another, people shook their heads when they heard I was asking not only for myself, but for two other people. But finally one woman invited me in. She was large and pale with thinning, peroxide-blonde hair. "Why, honey, I have just the room you need!" She took me down to the basement.

It was perfect. A kitchen, a bedroom, a living room and dining room, and a bathroom. All ours. A garden with gorgeous red flowers. It was dirty, but that could be remedied. I had no furniture, but having a floor under me—my own floor—and a roof over my head was worth far more than a sofa or dresser.

I swallowed. "I have to tell you something. I'm new in this country. I'm living in a motel. I don't have a job yet. I don't even have a security deposit for you."

She smiled broadly. "Never mind, honey. You just take care of yourself and that little baby girl. You'll pay me when you can."

The next day, I started cleaning with a vengeance. I bought a bottle of ammonia cleaner and a roll of paper towels and set to work. Suddenly I began feeling dizzy. What was happening? The room was spinning, the sink and wall and window where whirling around me like a top.

The landlady found me. "Are you all right? Shall I call an ambulance?" I staggered to the bathroom and vomited. "What happened?" she kept asking. Then she looked at the label on the bottle. "You got some kind of chemical poisoning, dear. Go back to your motel and rest."

Seema was willing to keep Mohabat overnight. My landlady was worried about having me walk back, so she drove me to my motel. The next day, I felt back to normal and my job search began in earnest.

I found out where the suburban areas were located, took a bus, and then walked. I went from house to house, ringing doorbells. "I am looking for work. Do you have any?"

Finally a beautiful black woman with an enormous house opened the door. "Please come in. I'll make you some tea."

Just like at home. I smiled. I did not know Americans were so hospitable.

"What can you do?" she asked me over tea and cookies.

"Anything you need," I answered, sipping the hot liquid gratefully.

"I need someone to do laundry and housecleaning. I'll pay you five dollars an hour."

Five dollars an hour? A small fortune! My cousins were all earning $3.25 an hour. "I'll take it!"

She liked me and recommended me to her friend who, in turn, recommended me to someone else. Within a few weeks, I was working every day. I earned enough money to pay my security deposit and my rent, and still had money left over for Ibrahim's arrival. Oh yes, things were working out after all.

In the evenings, Seema drove me around town and we scouted trash areas for discarded furniture. One night, we found an old table. A few days later, we found two armchairs. When we carried them down and set them up, we looked at them.

"Something isn't right," I finally said. "But I don't know what it is."

Seema stared at the chairs, then started to laugh. "They're seats from a van! They're not household furniture."

When the laughter subsided, Seema asked, "Do you want to throw them out?'

"Of course not. Now we have something comfortable to sit on."

Ibrahim arrived two weeks later. We rushed into each other's arms and did not let go. We were both crying.

"I never want to be separated again," he declared solemnly.

"Neither do I."

"And Mohabat. Look at her, she's grown so much!"

"Hello, Daddy," she said politely in English, holding out her hand.

Sitting next to him in the taxi, holding his hand—the hand that had brought me so much pleasure and so much pain—I whispered a prayer of gratitude that I had made the right decision to come to the States and reclaim our marriage. I could not be happier than when I was at his side, with my little daughter on our lap. We belonged together. We were two parts of a single soul. And from our soul had come Mohabat's.

"Let me show you the new apartment," I said.

"No, I want to see Deljan first."

I wanted to shout, no! Come home to me first! But that would have been unreasonable. It was respectful and proper for Ibrahim to want to see his mother.

Deljan embraced Ibrahim and cried over him, as he cried over her. "My baby, my beautiful, darling little boy," she kept saying. "Nothing, no one should ever come between us. No one will ever love you as I do. You are home with Mommy."

It was getting late. I had to be up early for work the next morning. I tried to discreetly signal to Ibrahim with my eyes, but he was oblivious. Finally, he yawned. "I am tired. It's been a long flight and a long day. I want to go home and get some sleep."

"You are home, darling."

"No, I want to go home to my own place, together with my wife."

When he went upstairs to say good-bye to Roshan, Deljan grabbed my arm. Her eyes were pellets of ice. "You'll never win, you know," she said. "I will give him so much love that he'll have to come to me. Mark my words, you'll see."

She was just babbling. Ibrahim was back now. He had reaffirmed his loyalty to me. He had said it tonight. No one would ever separate us again.

"The apartment is wonderful!" Ibrahim walked around. "You've done an amazing job getting it ready."

I glowed. "Thank you."

"Tomorrow, I'll start looking for a job. Everything will be different. I promise."

We tucked Mohabat into bed, then turned to each other.

The night was suffused with magic.

The next day, I let Ibrahim sleep, tiptoeing out with Mohabat. He was exhausted. He needed his rest. Tonight, I would make him a good dinner. And tomorrow he could start looking for work.

I returned home that evening to find Deljan in the kitchen. She was spooning food out of a pot and fussing over Ibrahim. "My darling was hungry. You left without giving him breakfast."

"But there's plenty of food in the refrigerator. I knew he would help himself. That's what he's always done."

"A good wife makes her husband breakfast. I knew that you wouldn't, so I came over here. I made him breakfast and lunch. Now it's time for dinner. You were gallivanting around town and you weren't home to do your duty, so it fell upon me."

"I wish you would talk to your mother," I said to Ibrahim later. We were lying in bed, my head on his chest. He was stroking my hair.

"She went through so much pain when my father left that I couldn't bear to bring her anymore."

"She's bringing us pain," I argued.

"By giving me breakfast?" He laughed. "You're being silly, aren't you? She just wants to help. She sees you work hard and she wants to take care of me."

Maybe he was right. I was overreacting. I couldn't give him the time he needed, and I should be thanking God that his mother doted on him and was willing to fill in the gaps I left. I should be grateful to her. "I'm sorry," I whispered.

"Let's not talk about this anymore." His arms circled me and he drew me to him.

I found Ibrahim a construction job through the husband of one of the women I worked for. "It's just a beginning," I said to him. "Mike says there is a lot of room for advancement and eventually you can become foreman, then manager. Eventually, you could rise to own the entire company. It's great pay, and it will get you started. Meanwhile, you can learn English."

"One thing at a time. I want to concentrate on work. Language will have to wait."

When did it start to go sour? The first day Ibrahim didn't feel like going into work? When I became pregnant again and was too sick to cook or clean? When he started drinking again? When he graduated from beer to whiskey? When he quit his job for good? When I complained about having to clean up after him and his rowdy friends, a few fellow Afghans and a few men from work, who had begun hanging out all day, drinking and eating and leaving their cigarette ashes on the floor, dishes with congealed food in the sink, and candy wrappers everywhere? Or was it when our landlady kicked us out ("you're a doll, honey, but I can't have those lowlifes hangin' around my property")? No matter. The change was gradual at first then accelerated like a mad car without brakes, careening downhill.

When I was pregnant, he started hitting me again. I don't even remember what provoked it the first time, but soon it became part of our routine. Once he choked me so badly, I thought that this time, he would finally finish off the job and kill me. Nancy, the mother of one of Mohabat's school friends, questioned me when I picked

Mohabat up from school. I sent Mohabat and Nancy's daughter Laurie ahead to the car. With great difficulty, I told her the truth.

"Why don't you call the police next time?" she asked. "They'll ask if you want to press charges. and if you do, they can put him in jail."

I shook my head. "I'm sure he won't do it again."

But it happened again when the baby, whom we named Negeen, was a few weeks old.

I am still sore from childbirth. Tired, so tired. When was the last time I had a full night's sleep? But now it is peaceful. I am holding the baby. She is nursing. She is making little contentment noises. She smells sweet. Clean. Her toes are so tiny! I nuzzle her face, warm and soft. I relax into the lovely feeling of her suckling. Ibrahim is on the sofa. His feet are on the glass coffee table. He is looking at a magazine. Starting to doze, when—

He hurls the magazine across the room. The baby startles and starts to cry. He is shouting. Waving his bottle of beer. "And don't just sit there!"

He kicks the table. Oh no, it's toppling over. It will hurt the baby! Hurry, stop it from falling, I hold my foot out and—

Something is flying at me. There is the shattering of glass. The scream of a baby in pain. The rush of blood from her dimpled little foot. I am wrapping the foot in a cloth when I see—what is it? Something dangling above my shoulder. A phone receiver.

"So what are you going to do? Call the police? Here's the phone. I've already dialed 911 for you. So you can tattle on your husband and tell them what a bad boy I've been."

But the police make people pay. Nancy said so. You had to do something about charges. Where will the money come from? Ibrahim has used our money for his parties. I hang up the phone. Must keep my voice steady. Don't frighten Mohabat anymore. "Come on, children. We're going outside."

I was sobbing on the street corner when a police car pulled up. "Is there an emergency, ma'am? Someone just called 911 from this address."

"But I hung up the phone," I said foolishly.

"We have ways of tracing a call, even when the person hangs up. We always come out to investigate. What happened to you?"

"N—nothing."

He looked as though he did not believe me. My face was streaked with tears. My baby's foot was bandaged. I was shaking, and Mohabat was clinging to me. "Well, I'll take a look around anyway, just to be sure." Ibrahim was inside.

"Police! Open the door!"

Ibrahim staggered to the door.

"What happened?"

"Everything fine."

"Then why did someone call 911?"

Ibrahim shrugged and tried to smile. I could tell how scared he was. "I call friend. I dial wrong number phone."

"Then why is this table broken? Why does this place stink like a brewery? What's all that broken glass?"

"I bump into table. Then I drop bottle."

The officer turned to me. "I don't believe his story. I think he attacked you. You can press charges against him and get the state to protect you."

There was that word *charges* again. I shook my head. The policeman asked to talk to me alone. He tried to convince me, but I refused.

"That's all right," Ibrahim said after the officer left. "You don't need to have me put in jail. I won't come near you anymore. I'm leaving you and getting a divorce."

"Don't leave!" I cried, grabbing his hand. "I still love you. We can work this out!"

He spat a curse at me and flung himself out of the room, slamming the door.

"Good, Mommy. Now he's gone. He won't hurt you anymore." Mohabat put her arms around me and hugged me.

"But I don't want him to go!" I sobbed. "I don't even know where he is."

Then I thought about it. I remembered how he had pretended to leave me when we were in Austria and had only gone to Yasin's house. Chances were that he was at Deljan's. If I wanted to, I could go right over and ask him to come back home.

But maybe it would be for the best if he left. Our marriage now was a bitter parody of our marriage in Afghanistan. The same unbridled passion, the same crazed intensity, but now it was being turned toward hatred instead of love. What was there to remain married for?

But what about love? If he could love me once, then he could love me again. Maybe the love was buried under layers of pain and home-sickness and self-hatred. Maybe I should just be more forgiving and more patient.

And it was no small matter to get divorced. I thought of a letter I recently received from Madarjan. She had written not just to me, but also to Ibrahim and the children. One of Ibrahim's and my mutual distant cousins who had briefly visited the United States had returned to Afghanistan with dismal tales of our marriage and how I, under the corrupting influence of American values, was mistreating my husband.

My dear Sulima and dear Father, and lights of my eyes, Moha-bat and Negeen,

May you be in God's keeping. Here we are all well and healthy. We wish for your health and welfare. As it had been a long time that we had not heard from you, we were very dis-tressed, especially whatever the enemies said disturbed me very much. Sometimes I wept, and sometimes I waited and resigned myself to destiny, but my heart would not submit. Every day when Mariam came to visit, I waited for a letter, but there was nothing to turn waiting into happiness. After three months of waiting the letter, which you had written with your own beau-tiful hands, arrived. I was made so happy seeing it. If the whole world were under my command, I could not be so happy. My dear Sulima, as I do not know how to write letters, I will end here. But may my heart be ransom for all your lives. Many greetings; you lighted up my eyes with your first letter. I kiss dear Mohabat and Negeen on the eyes. Finally, I entrust you all to God and say good-bye, hoping to see you soon.

Your suffering mother

I thought of Madarjan crying after hearing about our marital problems. I would have to write and say there had been a misunder-standing. And to try harder. I could not possibly hurt her more.

But Nancy and some other American friends were encouraging me to end the marriage. When they would hear that he had left me, they would sing psalms of gratitude. They would encourage me never to take him back.

I called Uncle Yusuf in France. "What should I do?"

"Go and bring him home. Tell him you love him and you will do whatever he wants."

"Sometimes I think I should get a divorce. But then I think of Madarjan and how humiliated she would be. I've already caused my family so much pain—"

"These are the right thoughts, Sulima. Divorce is not proper for a Muslim wife. Try to bring your husband back." He paused. "There are things you should know about the family. I did not know these things when my brother married Deljan." He paused again. "Deljan's father was a crazy person. A *dewana*. He did terrible things. He used to marry fourteen-year-old girls, virgins, then cut their private area after the first night so no one else would ever want them. Of course, he no longer wanted them either. So he would take another girl." He sighed. "Ibrahim's mother is the daughter of one of those girls. My brother left her, although he did not go through a formal divorce. It would have brought shame to the family. You must find a way to stay loyal and work this out."

It was exactly what I wanted to hear. I still loved Ibrahim. I did not want to get divorced. So I went to Deljan's house and begged him to return. When he left, Deljan's gaze was triumphant. "It's only a matter of time," she whispered.

This time, there was no apology. There had been no apologies since the second or third time he hit me in the United States. But I went down on my knees and apologized to him. "I'll try harder. I'll be a better wife. I promise. Here, let me make you *korma chalau* for dinner."

Later that night, we were in bed. We had made up, and Ibrahim had been affectionate—almost his old self. Mohabat was asleep in her little cot, Negeen was nestled in my arms, nursing. Ibrahim's arm was around my shoulder, gently stroking my skin.

"Could there be anything better than this? We're together again. We love each other. We have healthy, beautiful children. We are in a free country."

He withdrew his arm and looked at me bitterly. "Yes. We could have more money. Then things would be good."

The coldness in his tone chilled me. I finished nursing, put the baby into her cradle, and turned over. But it was a long time before I fell asleep.

*   *   *

"Can we try counseling?"

Ibrahim had just beaten me up again, then stormed out, swearing that he was leaving for good. For the third time in six weeks, I went to Deljan's house to tell him how much I loved him and beg him to return. We had a semireconciliation. No apology from him, no tender words of regret and love, but a gruff statement that we should try not to fight anymore.

"Can we try counseling?" I repeated.

His face reddened. His veins bulged. I thought he would hit me again.

"Counseling is for crazy people. I am not a *dewana*. I never want to hear about it again."

Ibrahim left a few months later. Negeen was a year old. I remember that he was not present for her first birthday and that I refused to make a party, even though Mohabat wanted me to. He had left to go to his mother's several more times and I continued to go to her house and beg him to return. But this time, he was not at his mother's. A call from Deljan informed me that he had gone back to Austria. Roshan had driven him to the airport.

"So now you're on your own." The smug pleasure in her voice oozed through the telephone.

Uncle Yusuf pleaded with me to call Ibrahim and ask him to come back. This time, I refused. "I don't need him for money. I don't need him for pleasure. I certainly don't need to be hit all the time. I can manage on my own. If he wants me, he'll have to come back to me."

I held out for two months.

During all this time, while my marriage was collapsing, my business had been growing and thriving. I had started with housecleaning, but I found myself taking care of my employers' houseplants. One of the women I worked for said I had a "green thumb" and asked if I wanted to trim her rosebushes and weed her flower beds.

Maybe it was the memories of Babajan's farm, but I never felt more at home or at peace than when I was working in the garden, planting flower beds and trimming bushes. Then one of the families had a party and asked me to do the flower arrangements with roses from their backyard. They told all their friends, and soon I had a small business bringing flowers to parties and arranging them, and taking care of houseplants. I was still cleaning houses and offices. Sometimes I handled as many as five jobs in a day. It was hard to do all this juggling when Ibrahim was still around. Once he left, it became even harder. I was taking care of Mohabat and Negeen single-handedly. I missed Ibrahim terribly. He stalked the corridors of midnight, sometimes tender and chivalrous, sometimes dark and brooding, sometimes with an arm outstretched, sometimes with a fist clenched. And I would cry and cry until my head throbbed and my eyes had run out of tears. I don't know how I found the strength to go from day to day.

One day there was a knock at the door. It was Deljan. Roshan was with her.

"Our car broke down nearby." Roshan's voice was apologetic. "I was hoping we could use the phone and wait here until the tow truck shows up."

Deljan scowled. "I came to spend time with Mohabat and nobody else." Then her expression changed. She crooned, "Come to Grandma!"

How dare she! But I controlled myself. *Ehteram* was a teaching so fundamental that it continued to run through my blood even when the elders did not deserve respect. I waited on Deljan hand and foot. I brought her tea and cake and a stool for her to rest her swollen legs. She had developed some type of vein problem and needed to keep her feet elevated as much as possible. I sat with her and told her stories of the cute things Mohabat had done.

When the tow truck finally showed up, Deljan turned to me. "I have been really rude to you, but you treated me like a queen. You have embarrassed me with your kindness."

I thought of Madarjan.

But the next time I saw Deljan, she was her old self again.

I received a letter two months later. When I saw Ibrahim's handwriting, my heart turned over and my hand shook as I held the envelope. "I want you here with me. A wife's place is with her husband. Come back to Austria. Listen to my orders and do as I say or I will file for divorce."

I wrote an impassioned letter in response to his, reminding him of how good things had been at the beginning of our marriage, and of everything he had done to me since. I concluded,

> All your life, when something good happened, you took the credit. And when something bad happened, you blamed me. So go ahead and get the divorce. While you're at it, go and sign the document of your *bay ghairati* because you are someone who has lost everything. Your country. Your wife. Your pride. I still love you. I want to live together in peace and happiness. But I will not beg you to come back and I will not abandon everything I have worked for so hard to build just because you tell me to.

The phone rings. I hear his voice. My letter has reached some deeply buried interior reservoir of love. He wants to come back to the United States. He wants our marriage to work out. "I love you. You are still my angel, the love of my life, the light of my days."

Everything falls away. The rage, the terror, the contempt. His voice, his precious voice, the voice that had crooned to me in the night under the jeweled Afghan sky vanquishes the demons of memory and fear. The music of his voice bridges the gap of pain and rage and my heart runs across, singing, to meet his. Yes, yes, yes, please come home. Please.

Call Uncle Yusuf, he says, tell him that you really do need me.

I'm on the phone with Uncle Yusuf in the wink of an eye. He has been telling Ibrahim that I won't take him back because I don't need him. Good, he says, you have set me straight.

I hang up. My heart is dancing, flying to Austria on wings of love above clouds of promise. This time, I will make it perfect.

I had saved enough money to put a down payment on a house. No more living in tiny apartments. Only the best for Ibrahim and me. My business was booming. Everything seemed to be going perfectly—with one glitch. I was unable to obtain a visa for Ibrahim. Since my tourist visa had expired and I had neglected to formally request asylum, Ibrahim could not obtain a visa.

I applied for asylum and started the process of trying to make arrangements for Ibrahim's return. I tried every avenue I could think of. I wrote to Amnesty International, the United Nations, my

congressmen and senators, the president himself. I even had Mohabat write a letter to President Reagan about how much she missed
her daddy—something she balked at, but I insisted. I knocked on
every door . . . no response. It would be absolutely impossible for
Ibrahim to return to the United States at this point.

"So go and join him in Austria," Uncle Yusuf advised. "If he is
willing to change then it's up to you to make it happen."

I had already moved into the house, and while the process
dragged on, I had been renting out rooms and doing home
improvements. I was so proud of myself! The house was pretty, the
children were happy, and I was so eager for Ibrahim to see everything I had done for him. For us. With a heavy heart, I put the
house on the market. I bade a sad farewell to the good people who
had employed me.

It was then, in 1989, that the Soviet Union withdrew from
Afghanistan. Suddenly the move, which had so distressed me,
became a move of hope and opportunity. It was the perfect time to
wrap up my affairs in the United States. Now I could go back home!
I wrote to Ibrahim eagerly, and he said yes, we'll go back.

Now my fingers flew through packing, selling my car, dialing the
Realtor. Austria was no more than a stopping point en route to my
home. And there, Ibrahim would be in his element again. We had
started out in Afghanistan and had a good life there. When we
returned, nothing could go wrong.

This was the first plane ride I really wanted to take. I was meeting
my beloved. And we were going home.

I was assaulted by images as soon as I got off the plane. Even the
German writing on the airport signs stabbed me with the memories
they held. Why had I come back? What was I getting into now?

But when Ibrahim greeted me at the airport, he was different. No
alcohol on his breath. No five-o'clock shadow. His smile sent my
heart spinning and his touch set me on fire. He showed me around
his apartment—which was not far from where we had lived the first
time. "See? Here's the kitchen. And look now nice the living room
is, and how it looks out onto the garden." The apartment was clean.
No beer cans or cigarette ash. Ibrahim was beaming.

That night, birds sang songs of love in a German studded with stars.

*   *   *

We did not return to Afghanistan. Our families warned us to stay away. It was too dangerous. Anarchy reigned everywhere. The Mujihaddin were tearing through the country, raping and pillaging. Relatives of ours were being killed right and left. Our family was spending much of its time running and hiding. "Anyone who can get away from here should, and anyone who is away should not even think of coming back."

So we stayed in Austria and enjoyed the best eighteen months since we had left Afghanistan. Ibrahim had learned to speak German and had found himself a job in the mailroom of a pharmaceutical company. I could not return to the biology department, but my German and typing skills were good, so I found a job as a secretary in the history department of the university. The children were content. I started volunteering for the Red Cross and raising money for Afghan refugees. I visited pharmaceutical companies and arranged for donations of antibiotics to be sent to the Red Cross in Afghanistan. I also did fund-raising for Indonesian street children.

We were a real family during that time. We even took a vacation together. We traveled through Europe, visiting Uncle Yusuf in France and touring Rome, Switzerland, and Germany. Although Yasin and Helga were still living in Austria, Yasin had backed off. Helga confided in me that it was Yasin who was initially responsible for Ibrahim's decision to reclaim the marriage. "What, are you going to let your wife stay in another country, making a lot of money, and sleeping around? Get her back here with you, where she belongs." Ibrahim had listened to his brother—and, unexpectedly, had shown himself able to stand up to Yasin afterward. He seemed truly committed to protecting his newly reclaimed marriage.

When Husna came to Holland, we helped her to get settled. I thought my heart would burst with joy to see her again! She brought me news of Madarjan, whose high blood pressure had become a more serious problem, and of everyone else.

"Asim is a doctor now. He's married and has a baby. Karim works in a factory as an engineer, Gula wants to be a veterinarian, Hala wants to be a doctor. . . ." She also told me horror stories about the brutality and lawlessness of the Mujihaddin. I worried terribly about the family and redoubled my efforts to raise money for those back at home.

In 1991, we received word that Ibrahim's visa had cleared and we could return to the United States.

Now everything was beyond perfect. Ibrahim was sober, and we were happy together. I had discovered that I could make good money in America. I looked forward to a joyous future together with Ibrahim, the past now well behind us, in the land of plenty and freedom.

15

This time, I had made arrangements with Nancy to stay at her house until I could buy a house of our own. I was not going to let Deljan get her tentacles around my husband again.

Everything seemed to be going well. I found a house right across the street from Nancy. Some of my old employers had already found other help, but most were thrilled to see me back. "My rosebushes have missed you," said one of them. Mohabat was thrilled to be back in her old school, with her old friends, and Negeen acclimated well. Best of all, I was pregnant again. I saw the new baby as tangible proof of our love and our future.

"You should start your own business." I had been hearing this for years but was not in a legal position to do so until our immigration issues had been sorted out. Now I considered it. Housecleaning was draining, thankless work. But caring for houseplants and doing flower arranging and landscaping were endlessly rewarding. I decided to open a flower store. I did not have enough money, but Gretchen—who had always said that if I needed anything I could turn to her—lent me $10,000. Nancy lent me the rest. I signed the lease and began construction on the store, which had originally been a restaurant and needed significant reconstruction to be turned into an attractive flower store. Every new accomplishment was a brick in our house of love—

—or so I thought.

But this time, the downward spiral came so fast that I was completely unprepared. Deljan had been furious that Ibrahim and I had stayed with Nancy instead of with her. She was putting daily pressure on Ibrahim to leave me. Ibrahim hated the new house. "It was bought with woman's money," he said. Every time the bank called about the mortgage, or a credit company called and asked for me, it set him off. "I'm the man of the house. They should be talking to me!"

"You don't speak English," I pointed out. "And last time, when the man called and said he wanted to talk about our mortgage, you didn't even know what a mortgage was."

He hit me for that. And for complaining that it was too much for me to clean up after all his friends, who were again leaving their debris all over the house. And for forgetting to iron his nice shirt. "You have a job and you want me to go to a job interview looking like a slob." I knew he had no job interview. When he was not carousing with his friends, he was spending his days at Deljan's, drinking and watching television with her. He hit me for taking the children out without him on Sundays, and he hit me for leaving them at home where they made noise and bothered him and his friends during their drinking parties.

This latest round devastated me more than any of the others. Things had been so good in Austria. We had been so happy together. When, how, had things gone so spectacularly wrong?

I tried to hold everything together. I was pregnant and throwing up. I had bought the store. I had to deal with the construction. With getting the children to and from school. With housecleaning, which I was still doing because the store was not yet open. With my flower business. But I was slipping. Mohabat lied to me, claiming to have some after-school project she was working on with her teacher. I went to the school to pick her up. She was not there, and her principal said she had left long ago. I was frantic and hysterical. Could she have been kidnapped? Raped? Killed? Should I call the police? It turned out that she had gone with some friends to the mall. When she returned, instead of hugging her and thanking heaven that she was all right, I spanked her and screamed at her. My God, I thought, I'm turning into Abajan. I still have not forgiven myself for that.

It was a treadmill of sorrows. And it was speeding up. Faster, faster, I was running, panting, and running some more.

The baby, whom we named Masuda, was born prematurely—only eight months. Tiny and brave, she struggled to breathe until she could draw breath on her own and I could take her home. I struggled to nurse. To change diapers. To read bedtime stories to Negeen. To help Mohabat with her homework. To get back to work. To be mother and father to this new child, whose father was barely willing to look at her. "Oh. Another girl."

Was there nothing I could do except stand by helplessly, watching the horror show unfold? It occurred to me that Saber, Ibrahim's favorite cousin, had moved to the United States and had recently come to our area. Saber always said he loved me like a sister, and I felt the same way about him. Maybe he could help. Ibrahim respected him and he cared for both of us. Perhaps he could mediate between us.

Saber had known about our marital problems—who didn't? But he felt it was not his place to interfere. Now I approached him. "Ibrahim won't go to a professional for counseling," I said. "He thinks counseling is just for mentally ill people. Would you be willing to mediate between us?"

"Of course," he answered. "I'll speak to Ibrahim tomorrow."

It was Sunday. The baby was two months old. Ibrahim was watching television on the couch. The children and I were at Nancy's for lunch. "Mohabat and Laurie, please go and bring Ibrahim a sandwich," Nancy said.

The two girls trotted across the street. When they came back, the brown paper bag was still in their hands. "He's not home," Mohabat said.

Nancy frowned. "That's impossible. We've been right here in the front room. We would have seen him leave."

"Please try again," I said.

They rang the bell and knocked, but he did not answer.

Could he have passed out? It would not be the first time I came home to find him in a stupor, surrounded by a haze of alcohol. "I'll go check," I said. I rummaged in my pocket for the key. "Oh, no! I left it across the street."

"Never mind," Nancy said, "I'll get my spare."

She returned with a worried look on her face. "It's not on the hook where it usually is."

Laurie flushed. "I'm sorry, Mom. I borrowed it last week and left it at their house." She pointed.

"Oh, Laurie!" Nancy's voice was reproachful.

"That's all right, honey." I stroked her hair. "I'll just bang on the door until he gets up and answers."

Nancy jumped up. "We'll come with you."

We rang and knocked until Ibrahim peered out of the door. His eyes were suffused with red, his hair was tousled, his face was a mass of dried liquor and stubble. "You go away. I just want her." He pulled me in after him and locked the door.

"Go to the bedroom." His speech was slurred.

"But—"

"I said, get into the bedroom *now!*"

On the bed. Quick, push him away. Too strong. Can't move. Choking, gasping for air. There is a cracking sound. A gush of red. "My nose!" The words won't come out. Palm meets cheek, with a whump and a slap. Slap! Slap! Something moves in my mouth. Hard and small. A tooth. He has knocked out my front tooth!

"Why did you bring our private business to Saber? How dare you speak ill of me to someone I care about?" Whump!

Then there is a glint of something bright. Something silvery. Long, sharp, and—

—scissors, open, oh no, no, my neck, not my neck! "Wa—" That gurgle, is that my voice? "Wat—Water."

Amazingly, he gets up to bring me water. But by time he is back, everything is dark. I have passed out.

Nancy called the police as soon as Ibrahim pulled me into the house. When they came, they saw that my face and ears and nose were bleeding and my teeth were broken and slippery with blood and saliva. "She eat raw rice, it hurt teeth," Ibrahim explained as they handcuffed him and led him away.

Deljan bailed him out of jail.

I got a restraining order against him.

Two weeks later, I was looking out of the window late at night. I was not sleeping well and I had taken to sitting by the window and crying during the night. I saw him driving to and fro in front of the house. He looked lost and lonely and sad. I called to him. And he came home to me.

A child is shouting. It is Mohabat. "Don't let him in! Don't take him back!" He tries to slap her, but I stop him. She is only a child. She has seen her mother hurt. She will feel differently when she sees how different you are. It will be different this time, I say to her. And to him—won't it?

"A mediator? You've never agreed to counseling before."

"This time it will be different." His voice was broken, he had been crying. "I'll see Ali. He's not in the family, he's just a friend. He's not some kind of doctor for crazy people. He will help us as a friend. He likes you. He also likes me. He will be fair."

A mediator. The Qur'an said that when a couple had problems, they should try mediation. Finally, Ibrahim was willing to go! More than willing. It was his suggestion this time. A little twinge of hope leaped in me like a grasshopper in summer. Every time we reconciled, we did it by ourselves. We had never tried mediation or counseling. This time would be different. We had someone to help us through.

Ali meant well. I knew how much he cared about me. I knew how much he cared about Ibrahim. He had witnessed our wedding and wanted to help save our marriage. He tried his best, but he was not a professional. He tended to lecture us, rather than engage us in an interactive process. Sometimes he would go off into some reminiscence from his own life that distracted us from whatever we were working on.

"When you're angry at Sulima, tell her in words. Say, I am angry. My father used to do that with my mother. He never hit her, he just explained what was bothering him. Then she listened to him.

"When you have accomplished something, try not to make Ibrahim feel that you were the one who did it.

"You must find a job. You can't complain that your wife earns all the money if you're sitting around drinking and refusing to work. I had an uncle who never went to work, and he was very depressed from being at home all the time.

"When Ibrahim asks you to do something, try to listen without arguing. I know that when my wife argues with me, I get angry and it's hard for me to remember to speak respectfully."

His ideas were very basic, tinged with culture and with love for us. I was weary but willing to try his suggestions. If this was the price I would pay for sparing my family the pain of my divorce, for salvaging my marriage to the man I loved, I was willing to pay it. I nodded.

I called my flower store Babajan's Paradise. I surveyed the storefront proudly. The words GRAND OPENING were written in puffs of mums over the door—red, orange, gold. The puffs of autumn color were right for November. Ibrahim and I had been back together since summertime. We were still talking to Ali. Ibrahim had managed to learn how to curb his fists, though not his tongue. He still cursed me out when he had been drinking. I was trying to be good and to avoid provoking him. I even thought of closing the flower store. Would it make him feel inferior that I owned a business, while he was still working odd jobs—when he worked at all? But we had no other steady income. I had to open this store. I had paid for construction, had taken loans. I could not back down now. And Ibrahim was trying so hard. The sessions with Ali were helping. I was sure he would be supportive.

Ten o'clock. Time to open the store. One person comes in, just to browse. Says good luck and leaves. Then someone else comes in. She wants to buy roses for a patient in the hospital. My first sale. Ah, here comes someone else.

The store is filling up. I am running from cash register to flower vases, giving prices, chatting with customers.

Then I see him. "Ibrahim!" I call. He comes in and looks around. "This is my husband," I say proudly.

There is a chorus of "oohs" and "ahs." What a wonderful wife you have. Didn't she do a great job on the store? Look at the flower arrangement she just made me, isn't it pretty?

Ibrahim's face is stone. He nods. He turns around. He walks away.

Before work the next day, I went to the bank to deposit the first day's earnings. I was bursting with pride. I handed the envelope to the teller, who gave me a receipt. I looked down, and the balance in the account was—

—$232.58. The amount I had just deposited.

There must be a mistake. A computer error. "Please check my balance," I said to the teller. "I know I had much more than this in my account."

He punched some buttons on his computer. "Twenty thousand dollars was withdrawn from the bank yesterday."

This was not the first time Ibrahim had taken money. Several times over the years he had vanished with a sum of money that I had earned. I tried to overlook it, although Nancy had always been outraged. "What, does he come back to you only when he's hungry?" Now I wished that I had listened to her. This was a huge amount of money, and it was not even mine. Half of it belonged to Gretchen and the other half to Nancy.

Ibrahim was gone when I got home.

I left the girls with Nancy and hurried to Deljan's house. I was sure he was there, and I was right.

"Ibrahim, we need to talk."

He was on the couch, a beer in his hand. "About what?"

Deljan stormed into the room. "You are here to take away my son again?"

"I need to talk to him about something."

"Why don't you go to your fancy store and talk to the men there?" He hauled himself off the couch, staggering. "All right, we'll go home."

I waited until we were in the car. "What did you do with the money?"

"It's my money just as much as yours."

"No it's not. I'm the one who took out those loans, not you."

"The bank account is in both of our names."

I was shouting now, the rage and grief of years exploding in a cascade of molten words. "That's because I don't believe in 'mine' and 'yours.' When I married you, everything was 'ours.' Every penny I saved was for us. Every penny I earned was for us and our children. You squandered the money on your own pleasures—drinking, partying—but that's not what I've slaved for."

We were home and I was still shouting. "I borrowed that money from two good friends. My name is at stake here. And my honor."

Now it was his volcano shaking, trembling, growing, rising, and exploding in a flash of burning thunder. "How dare you talk to me like that? Make me sound like a pimp? You little whore!"

He's coming after me. His strides are heavy, his shoes make a thumping noise on the floor. Quick! Get away. Run! Run!

He blocks the doorway. I slip under his arm and bolt into the kitchen. If I can get to the back door—

—but he's faster. He locks the door. Something is in his hand. Something long. It has a wooden handle, silver blade.

Move, Sulima. He is coming after you with an axe. Divert his attention. Scream. Distract him. Point at the stove. Look, quick, over there! Look! Did it work? Yes, he's looking. Now run. Fast. Faster! To Nancy's. Oh, no, he's catching up. Faster, faster, get to Nancy's, yes you're on the path, you're on the steps, you're at the door, and—

—let me in! Help!

And then I'm inside. The door is locked. The phone is in my hand. I am calling the police.

For the last time.

16

J took the children and moved into a women's shelter. They were kind and gentle with us, but their schedule was too restrictive and conflicted with my complicated work and child care arrangements. Anna, a compassionate volunteer, invited us to move in with her until the ponderous legal proceedings could be complete and Ibrahim could officially be barred from the house. We lived at her house for two months. I will never forget her kindness.

I came home once during that time, to collect some clothing and toiletries. The baby was in day care and the children were at school. The food in the refrigerator smelled vile. The dishes in the sink were covered with green scum. I leafed through the mail. A phone bill for $1,400—Ibrahim had been calling Yasin in Austria. An electricity bill for $236. Where was I going to get this kind of money?

And then I saw him. He had been in the house the whole time. He let loose a stream of the vilest curses I had ever heard. "Your mother is a *fahesha!* Your family is the scum of the earth!"

And suddenly, I knew I must speak too. "You're been attacking me all these years. You've said terrible things. You've almost killed me. I have tried to be a dutiful wife and I've never spoken back. It's time to tell you the truth. *You* are the scum of the earth. You're like the dirt on the dishes you left me in the sink. Your mother is the *fahesha!* There is no lower human being than you—if you can be called human at all."

Oh my God, what had I said? Such terrible things. And what was he going to do to me? His fist was clenched and—

—and I ran to Nancy's house.

"Nancy," I sobbed. "I just said something terrible to Ibrahim. I said—" I was so embarrassed, I whispered it in her ear.

Nancy hugged me and kissed me on each cheek. "It's about time. I can't tell you how proud I am of you."

Proud? I was an outrage. A disgrace to my family and to everything I stood for. I rushed back to Ibrahim. "I'm so sorry I said those terrible things."

"No." He held up his hand, and for a moment, there was a glint of the old tenderness in his eyes. "I deserved that. For the first time, you said the truth about me, and I deserved to hear it."

He picked up his suitcase.

"I hope you will marry someone with no sister, no brother, no family, no one else, who can be there only for you. And I wish you happiness."

When we came home from Anna's, the house was cold and dark. They had shut off our heat and electricity. We turned on the water faucet. Nothing. They had turned off the water. I picked up the phone receiver. It was dead.

It took days to straighten things out. No one—not at the electric company, not at the water company and not at the phone company—cared that it was my husband, not I, who had run up these bills. The house and everything in it were in my name. I was therefore the responsible party. I took the last of my savings to pay our utility bills and have the electricity, heat, and hot water turned back on. After much haggling, I was able to arrange an installment payment plan with the phone company, and our service was restored.

I wrote to Gretchen and told her about the money. "Forget it," she said. "Do you need more?"

"I will pay you back. I promise."

The next month Ibrahim filed for divorce on grounds of abandonment. When I was served with the papers, I wanted to die. I had let everyone down. Madarjan. My sisters. My children. I had been a terrible daughter, and a terrible wife, and now I was also a terrible mother. I was depriving my children of a father and a normal childhood. Where had I gone wrong?

I cried and brooded and paced and prayed. I took out my special box of his love letters and let their music touch my heart. "You are my goddess. I worship you." "All I want is to sacrifice myself for you." "I would die if the tiniest speck of dust brought a tear to your luminous eyes." "Your teeth are as white as pearls." He had been such a loving husband. What had I done to offend him so? And what had I done to offend God so that I could be punished so harshly?

Maybe we could try again? Ali was encouraging me to give it one more chance. So was Uncle Yusuf. I dialed Ibrahim at Deljan's house. When I heard his voice, I felt the familiar surge of joy, tenderness, passion.

"What do you want?" His speech was slurred.

"J—just to say hello. To find out how you are."

"I see. First you call the police and now you're calling to see how I'm doing? *Paste-baysharaf!*" The curse seemed to fly through the phone.

"I'm sorry. I won't call you again."

When I hung up, I was sobbing so hard I could scarcely see the receiver. But I meant what I said. I would never call him again. And I would never take him back.

Madarjan was devastated when she heard about the divorce. I am told that she took to her bed for two weeks. Once again, it had been presented to her by some of Ibrahim's cousins as my fault. Apparently Madarjan wrote to me, begging me to reconsider. Fortunately I never received her letter. I don't know if I could have remained true to my resolve if I had. I loved Madarjan too much and her pleas would have torn me apart. It was years before I had an opportunity to clarify for her the true nature of my decision.

I got a lawyer through the women's shelter. I had no money to pay her, but she said it was all right. I should pay whenever I could. I worked out an installment plan with her, and when her daughter got married, I did the flower arrangements for the bridal shower and the wedding for free.

She counseled me to fight his motion for divorce. The court agreed. For him to be granted a divorce on grounds of abandonment was patently absurd. He was ordered to pay child support. A year later, I filed for divorce on grounds of a year of separation. My request was granted.

But Ibrahim never paid so much as a dime of child support. Eventually I stopped trying. Ibrahim disappeared. I heard through the family grapevine that he had gone back to Austria and had married a German woman. I used to lie awake, tormenting myself about what they were doing together. I could not believe he could laugh with her, dance with her, and fly with her as he had with me. But with time, the preoccupation faded. It was part of the healing process I was trying to enact.

Healing. A long and painful process. We all bore the scars of those years of violence and terror—especially Mohabat. I found that I was often impatient, too strict and too overprotective. But I kept trying. I am still trying. Based on what my children say, I am succeeding.

I look at my children now. They are growing up with love and security. They will never again have to fear the eruption of a dangerous man. They will never be subservient, or watch their mother or sisters be subservient. They will grow up proud and free.

17

In 1992, a man came into my store to buy flowers for his mother's seventy-fifth birthday. He immediately impressed me as someone polite and pleasant. We chatted for a while, and I discovered that he was also interesting and thought-provoking company, and that we had many common interests. His name was Bob Beers, and he was a cell biologist. We became friends, then started dating. We were married three years later.

The marriage has been rewarding, but not without its adjustments and struggles. For both of us, this was a second marriage. We each arrived with scars and memories of our previous relationship. We are both strong personalities, and by the time we met, we each had our own well-defined personal style of living and communicating. Our culture and background were also vastly different. Bob comes from a well-established American family. His father has traced their roots right back to the *Mayflower*. He is the only child of a devoted and doting widowed mother, while I, of course, come from an enormous and highly complicated family. It took him months just to figure out who's who. "So let me get this straight. The brother-in-law of your aunt on your mother's side married your second cousin once removed on your father's side?" The complex relationships among my family members were entirely new to him. And although I had already been in the United States for a number of years, becoming part of a family as tiny and self-contained as his was new to me as well. And then there were our children. Blending our families—his two sons and my three daughters—created another set of challenges.

But there is a powerful bond between us, and we are deeply committed to each other. My daughters love him as a father, and I love his sons as if they were my own. Our children regard one another as siblings. I could not wish for a more devoted father for my girls. Bob has also been unfailingly welcoming toward all of my family members. The mutual respect and deep caring that Bob and I feel for each other have sustained us through our rough spots and given us the ability to continue working through our issues and growing together as a couple and a family. I am grateful for all that we have and share together and for the wholehearted encouragement and support he gives me in my work.

The struggle to free the women of Afghanistan remains at the center of my life. Living in the freedom and plenty of America has not distracted me from my commitment to my oppressed sisters who remain behind. Since September 11, events have taken a dramatic turn. Although ostensibly the situation for women should be improving now that the Taliban has been overthrown, it is important to realize that, in choosing the Northern Alliance as allies, the United States has put the Mujihaddin back into power. While the Mujihaddin did not institutionalize and formalize oppression of women to the extent that the Taliban did, they nevertheless were brutal to women and to men. We cannot be sanguine about improved conditions in Afghanistan as long as the Mujihaddin remain at the helm without the additional involvement of Western countries such as the United States in the rehabilitation of Afghanistan.

Rehabilitation certainly means rebuilding the country, but more importantly, it means rebuilding the people. Providing them with economic assistance is important because it gives them capital they need. Providing humanitarian aid—food and medicine—is also crucial. But these measures are not enough. There is an old saying that it is better to teach a person to fish than to give him a fish. The Afghan people must become self-sufficient and self-sustaining. Toward that end, I believe that the key to permanent change in Afghanistan—as in other poverty-ridden countries—is to provide education to both women and men.

Education opens up new worlds. It creates a sense of possibility, of options, and of power. It enables people to work in higher-paying jobs, thereby improving not only their economic conditions but also their self-respect. More importantly, it shows people that there are innumerable other ways to live and that their constricted and grotesquely limited circumstances can change. I believe that education is the antidote to religious fanaticism and to oppression of women, whether that oppression is motivated by religious or cultural factors. An educational program that honors people's sense of pacing can eventually succeed in sowing the seeds of permanent change. Those seeds may not take root and sprout in my lifetime, but once the change occurs, there will be no turning back. My great-great-granddaughters may live free and equal in my homeland and will not be hurt as I was.

Understanding the deeply ingrained cultural origins of oppression has enabled me to take a more compassionate attitude to others—even individuals who are oppressors. Although I have gone through terrible suffering, I believe that those who hurt me were products of centuries of tradition that not only condoned but actually encouraged their behavior. They were not fully responsible for their actions. Many might have made different choices if they had known that other choices were available to them. Christ's dying words, "Forgive them, for they know not what they do," express how I have tried to come to terms with what I have seen and what I have been through. While I cannot forget, my goal is to forgive. For me, this comes from an understanding of the forces that shaped those who have hurt me.

I have come to believe that every human being contains a spark of God and that no one is beyond healing and repair. No matter what a person has done—even a terrorist—that spark can be ignited with the torch of knowledge and can eventually come to light up the world.

Those who knew me when I was younger would raise their eyebrows at my mention of God. I was an avowed and vociferous atheist through much of my life. However, over the years, my views have evolved and changed. The process started in Austria when my friend Gretchen invited me to come to church with her and to read the New Testament. What I read touched me deeply. Christ did not judge Mary Magdalene, the prostitute. He treated her with compassion. He said, "Judge not, that ye not be judged." He spoke of a man's obligation to respect women. He taught meekness for all human beings, not just for women. His gentleness and compassion did not stop him from being a man of action, a social reformer who was willing to die for his ideals. Here, finally, was a religious figure I could respect.

Over the years, I have encountered many versions of Christianity both in Europe and in the United States. I have attended church services of various denominations. Some have moved me deeply, others that are excessively dogmatic or discriminatory toward women have alienated me. Bob is Christian, and for the first years of our marriage, we went to church together every Sunday. But when the deacons forced our pastor to resign because of his outspoken views on women in the ministry, I stopped going to church. So did Bob. And I do not miss it. I am not comfortable with any form of organized religion that espouses a series of dogmas, demands adherence to rituals and traditions, imposes restrictions, and foists itself upon others.

However, although I may not be a religious person, I am a spiritual person. I have moved beyond my rejection of God and reached an understanding that God is greater than the narrow pigeonholes that religion seeks to create for Him. God cannot be confined. He dwells in my heart. I communicate with Him in my own words, not someone else's words from a prayer book or hymnal. Mahatma Gandhi is quoted as saying, "God has no religion." That is how I feel.

As I have struggled to come to terms with my life and the enormous suffering I have gone through, I have felt some measure of peace in believing that God has had a greater plan and that there has been some meaning and purpose in everything I went through. Perhaps part of the purpose is to bear witness. Telling my story provides a testimony regarding conditions that go well beyond my own personal circumstances and reflect the history and culture of an entire country. If even one reader will gain insight into the dynamics of oppression and will join the fight against human rights abuses in Afghanistan and elsewhere in the world, I will have fulfilled my mission.

PART TWO

HALA

There was light. Bright, white light. A radiance so strong, so beautiful, I had never seen anything like it before. And there, within the light, I saw Him. The Prophet Mohammed. I kissed His hand. "I have a problem," I told him. He listened. His face shone with the most tender love I had ever felt. "Do you know why you have this problem?" He asked me. "It is because you do not pray." When I woke up, I did not know what problem I had told Him about. Whether I was already facing the problem, or whether it still lay ahead of me. I only knew that if I prayed, He would help me with the problem. He would be with me. Through everything I have prayed. And He has been with me. He is with me now.

18

In some ways, it feels as though Sulima and I grew up in different families. Of course, as sisters, we share the same parents and siblings. But the sixteen-year age difference could have been a difference of sixteen decades. So much had changed in the family and in the country of Afghanistan between Sulima's childhood and mine. Religion, money, culture, family members—I grew up in a very different world.

I was born in 1970 when Sulima was sixteen years old. Unlike Sulima, who was second to oldest, I was second to youngest. Husna was fourteen, Asim was eleven, Zamin was nine, Gula was seven, and Surya was three. Naim was born when I was about two and a half. By the time I was born, my family was well established in Kabul. Although money was always tight, Abajan's photography business was successful. He had become an important and controversial person.

The household was bustling and busy when I was a baby. I was cared for more by my older sisters than by my parents. Abajan was still embroiled in terrible arguments with Sulima over her involvement with women's rights. Maybe he played with me when I was a baby, but of course, I don't remember. Madarjan was caring for seven other children and the usual crowd of relatives who were constantly in and out of the house.

Abajan died when I was almost two years old. Immediately following his death, Madarjan took us to her mother's home in the East. Sulima stayed behind in Kabul to continue her college studies. We stayed in the East through the birth of my little brother Naim in 1972. A few months later, we returned to Kabul. I was just shy of four.

Abajan's death brought an easing of the strict rules that had so terrorized Sulima when she was growing up. Although Karim was now the head of the household, he just didn't feel as strongly about Islamic law as Abajan did. Rarely was Karim mean to the younger brothers and sisters. Most of his venom was directed at Sulima. He did not get along with her, so a lot of his time went into all the conflicts and struggles they were having. Their struggles had no impact on me that I can remember.

So the women of the house stopped covering their hair. We were allowed to wear pants and short sleeves, even sleeveless dresses and shirts. Prayer became optional instead of mandatory. Soon, most of the household had stopped praying entirely. The children relaxed. We could laugh without worrying that Abajan might get angry. My sisters Husna and Gula remembered what it was like when Abajan was alive. They told me many times how different things were now.

We became more modern and more technologically advanced. We bought a television. The women still did the lion's share of the housework, but I managed to spend a fair amount of my childhood watching television instead of doing dishes. I especially enjoyed a game show called *What Is the Answer?*, which was similar to *Jeopardy*. I also watched plenty of cartoons. As we grew older, the family acquired a VCR and started to rent movies.

Madarjan was also different. From what I am told, she became less involved in the day-to-day lives of the younger children, including me. Sulima tells me that if she had a problem, like a bad day at school or an argument with a friend, she came to Madarjan for help and advice. I was more likely to turn to Husna or Gula. Of course, I loved Madarjan very much. She was a loving presence through my childhood, and she still inspires me with her gentleness. But it was my sisters to whom I was closest.

It wasn't just my family that was different. I was actually born into a very different world from Sulima's. In the 1970s, when I was growing up, the Communists were in the process of rising to power. Women were treated better and had more opportunities. That's not to say that women were equal to men. There were still many cultural traditions that discriminated against women. We still had to ask our fathers or brothers for permission to leave the house, for example. But we had the same educational opportunities as men. We were allowed to go to college routinely. It wasn't something unusual we had to fight for, as Sulima did. When Husna came of age, she attended university and studied education. Gula attended veterinary school.

The changes in the educational system started well before college. Right from the beginning of elementary school, the school I attended was different from the school Sulima attended. Schools were coed until high school. Colleges had mixed classes. The Communists had created a standardized curriculum that was taught in all schools all over the country. We learned biology, Russian, math, geography, history, Islamic religion and prayer or the Qur'an. Younger children learned prayer, and in fifth grade, they started studying Qur'an instead. Even though the Communists were opposed to religious study, they had not removed Islamic subjects from the curriculum.

I loved school. I was a good student and I felt totally in my element in the classroom. I have always loved languages and I really enjoyed Russian. But biology was my favorite subject. I had a wonderful biology teacher named Nadjia-jan. (*Jan* is a suffix added to the name of a woman as a sign of respect or affection.) Nadjia-jan taught me biology in fourth, fifth, seventh, and eighth grades. She had the rare combination of being a good disciplinarian and also a loving, warm person. She had such an inviting presence that students came to talk to her about personal as well as academic problems.

One incident in particular stands out. I was in eighth grade. My classmate Neema was being treated unfairly by Fazila, the math teacher. Neema and Fazila lived in the same household because Fazila's sister and Neema's sister were married to the same man. The rivalry between the two wives had infected their sisters. Their animosity had been carried beyond the household and into the classroom. If Neema raised her hand to answer a question, Fazila deliberately called on someone else. Even if Neema got all the answers on a test correct, Fazila gave her a lower grade.

We were all troubled by this unfairness. My best friend Adela and I decided to talk to Fazila about her treatment of Neema. Several other friends agreed, and a group of us went to see Fazila. This was tricky because *Ehteram*, or respect for elders, was deeply ingrained within us. Children usually did not speak before being addressed by an elder. Certainly, we were not allowed to directly confront an elder, especially someone in authority such as a teacher. But our sense of justice won over our sense of respect, and we took the risk.

I was chosen to be spokesperson. My heart was pounding as I approached Fazila after school.

"Excuse me," I said. "Would it please be possible for us to talk to you about something important?"

She smiled pleasantly. "Of course."

"We are upset, I mean we are sad—" At first, I stumbled over the words. Then I came right out and said it. "We are troubled about how you treat Neema. You are not fair to her. You don't call on her when she raises her hand. You give her bad grades."

She bristled. "I give her the grades she deserves. How dare you challenge me!"

"But—"

"You're just defending her because you're her friends. I'm a teacher, and you don't see her as I do. You have no right to challenge my authority or my judgment. Go home and leave the teaching to me."

We were terribly disappointed by her response. Then it occurred to me that Nadjia-jan might be helpful. We spoke to her the next day. As I expected, she listened carefully. She did *not* accuse us of overstepping our bounds. She never told us what she would do, but I suspect that she did speak to Fazila. I noticed that Neema was treated more fairly after that.

Nadjia-jan was one of the most important influences of my childhood. She was also an important part of the reason I loved biology so much. My love for biology contributed to my dream of becoming a doctor. But there was more to my dream than merely my love of the subject. I was inspired by my cousin Soofiya, who was in medical school. It was her dream to be a doctor who would treat poor people for free. Sadly, her dream never came true. She went to medical school in Russia. During her vacation, she returned to Afghanistan and found out that her fiancé had been killed in the war with the Russians. It had been a love match, and Soofiya was heartbroken. Eventually, she returned to Russia. But she remained a pale shadow of her original self. A few months later, she contracted a rare lung disease and died. She was twenty-one years old.

I loved Soofiya and I was devastated when she died. I kept her vision alive. I embellished it in my mind and made it my own. I would grow up and become a doctor. I would donate my time to helping the poor. I pictured myself working in a hospital. I would minister to a stream of poor people. I would dress their wounds and cure their diseases. Then I would go home to a small cozy house with a nice husband and some pleasant children. I didn't have anyone in particular in mind to fill the role of husband. Although I had friends who were boys, I did not have a boyfriend or any crushes. My imagined husband was shadowy and faceless, but definitely courteous and loving.

Marriage was all around me. There were always aunts, uncles, or cousins getting married. I don't remember Sulima's wedding because she married in court without a ceremony or fanfare. But I do remember the wedding of my sister Husna, which took place the year after Sulima married. Sulima was not there because Karim had barred her from participating in family events.

The wedding stands out among all the other weddings in our family. It was the first I was old enough to remember. But what I remember most is that I had been very ill with typhus during the weeks prior to the wedding. I lost a lot of my hair, and they had shaved off the rest.

"I don't want to go to a wedding with a bald head!" I had wailed.

"Don't worry, Hala." Husna had stroked my smooth scalp. "We'll sew a pretty bonnet for you."

The bonnet was sewn. That was only one of many wedding preparations going on in the household. For days, the kitchen seemed to overflow with rice, lamb, and different types of vegetables and fruits. The kitchen was busy with women cooking and preparing for the wedding.

The day of the wedding dawned sunny and warm. When I entered the club that we had rented, my breath caught with the beauty of it all. I forgot the funny thing on my head and looked around in awe. Flowers were everywhere. The tables were covered with tablecloths of blue and gold. They looked gorgeous and festive. Family members of all ages and manner of relationship were pouring in. I was overwhelmed with the number of people. The bride and groom were receiving visitors. Next to them stood Madarjan, and the groom's parents. Guests lined up to hug and kiss the bride, groom, and parents. *Mubarak, mubarak!* Congratulations!

I was six years old and brimming with questions.

"Why does the bride wear green?" I asked Surya.

"Green is a lucky color. Maybe that's because green makes us think of plants growing."

"So why did she change to white after eating?"

This went beyond Surya's storehouse of knowledge. We asked Gula, but she also didn't know. One of my aunts later explained that white was a color that modern brides wore at weddings.

Everything was fascinating. All the adult women took turns giving Husna a piece of jewelry and actually putting it on her. There was some trouble getting one of the earrings into her ear. I winced as Madarjan fumbled with the little earring hole. But Husna was brave, and if it hurt, she didn't show it. Next, the bride and groom were handed a Qur'an to kiss, and the bride walked down the aisle under the Qur'an. Everyone in the room stood up as she walked in, as if she were a queen.

At the front of the room, two of my aunts held a blanket over the heads of the bride and groom. They handed a mirror to the couple. Husna and her new husband, Kabir, gazed into it together. Then they handed it back. I wanted to ask Gula what that was about, but everyone else was quiet so I didn't want to talk. Finally, Madarjan dipped Husna's hands in henna, which turned them orange. I knew that henna was considered a holy herb and a sign of good luck.

"Is that all?" I was disappointed that there were no more interesting events in store.

"Well, there's eating of course," Gula said. "And there was a ceremony before this one. Something to do with signing a document and reading from the Qur'an. But only men went to that one."

"Why does Husna look so serious?"

"The bride is supposed to look shy and modest. A wedding is a serious occasion."

Maybe it was serious, but it was also a lot of fun. After the ceremony came the food and the dancing. Afghans love to dance, and one by one, the female family members took turns entertaining the bride and groom by dancing to the music. Most of the dancers, however, were members of the groom's family. Traditionally, the bride's family does not participate in the dancing. This is a sign of sadness that the bride is moving out of the house. I loved watching their bodies twist and wriggle. Their hands were gracefully moving to the rhythm of the music. They were mesmerizing. But when I tried to dance, my bonnet fell off. Everyone saw my bald head! I ran away, crying. Gula and Aunt Fauziya brought me back and comforted me. Soon I was on the dance floor again. Even when the bonnet fell off later, I was no longer worried. The music and dancing went on until late into the night. Then Husna moved to the house of her in-laws.

As Husna and her husband drove away, Madarjan started to cry. Then Aunt Fauziya, Aunt Kamila, and Aunt Mariam started crying. Suddenly, everyone was crying.

What was wrong? Everyone had just been so happy. We had been dancing and feasting and clapping our hands. I looked around at all the wailing women. They were daubing red eyes with handkerchiefs. I started to bawl too. Now I felt that I belonged.

Of course, for weeks afterward, I daydreamed about my own wedding. But gradually, my more important fantasies revolved around being a doctor. Becoming a wife and mother was just the backdrop.

Looking back on my early childhood, I think I was very fortunate. Until the age of six, I had a pretty normal experience, as I also did from about age nine to age fourteen. I was loved and cared for by many family members. I had plenty to eat and drink. I had a comfortable home, and I found school interesting and enjoyable. I was allowed to pursue my interests such as tutoring young children, which I did even when I was myself a child. And I was always encouraged to excel in my education. Maybe this is why I enjoyed tutoring so much. I wanted others to excel in their studies as well.

Although I grew up without a father, there were many older men who cared for me and acted in a fatherly way. Certainly there was no tyrant at the head of the household. I had educational opportunities equal to those of the boys. In our coed classes, there was no distinction made between boys and girls. Even during high school, when we were taught in separate classes, I never felt I was being taught less than the boys. I took for granted that women and men could enjoy the same education. And although I was troubled by the areas in which women were obviously being treated unfairly, I was not tormented by them as Sulima was. Maybe it's because I have a different personality. Maybe it's because I never grew up in fear of my own family. In fact, my family was always a source of love and security. Maybe it's because the role of women had greatly improved in other areas such as education. Or maybe it's because during certain crucial periods of my childhood and teen years, I did not even know if I would survive due to the fighting in the country. Getting through each day alive became more important than any other issue. Whatever the reason, I simply accepted the inequities as part of life. I did not allow them to disturb my sense of pleasure in life. Life was too short. There was too much pain and violence. I tried to gobble up any crumbs of peace and pleasure I could find.

19

Unrest had been brewing for many years. The Communists had shown great insensitivity to the needs of the people. They had tried to impose all sorts of social reforms. But the Afghan people, especially in rural areas, were just not ready for those changes. The Soviet government had also engaged in a great deal of religious persecution. This caused resentment that fermented steadily. Eventually it boiled over. Members of the northern tribes had suffered the most. They were eager for revenge and a return to Islamic law. They resented the Russian occupation and the "evil" influence of modernity on Islamic values. They were filled with hatred and out for blood. They were determined to find some way of ridding themselves of this foreign intrusion into their lives. They despised the Soviet Union and anything remotely associated with its influence.

I now know that the United States was partially responsible for what happened next. America armed these rebels. The American leaders were only too glad to help anyone fighting the Soviet Union. The American leadership encouraged the rage and hatred for Russia by using Islamic doctrines and values. I have seen a video showing President Jimmy Carter's national security advisor actually telling Mujihaddin fighters to go get the Russians because they were working for God's cause and God would be on their side.

But I knew nothing of this during my early childhood, when the Mujihaddin (the word is Arabic for "enactors of the *jihad*, or Holy War") were preparing to take arms against the Russians. Even while the violence was escalating, Madarjan and the others shielded me from understanding the full impact of the horror that was overtaking our lives. But as the Mujihaddin intensified their violent attacks, I could no longer avoid hearing about the violence. It invaded our lives. It turned everything upside down.

We were living in the East when the violence started to escalate. We had returned to the East because of Karim's plan to isolate Sulima from the rest of the family. Even when Sulima left the country in 1979, we did not move back to Kabul right away. We stayed in the East as the situation deteriorated.

The violence gathered momentum and exploded long before the Mujihaddin officially rose to power. Although they started as idealists who wanted to redeem the country from evil Western influence and foreign intrusions into ancient cultural values, their attacks soon lost any semblance of idealism. They began to destroy anyone who evoked an association with the West. This included government employees. The government was, after all, collaborating with the Communists. It also included anyone with higher education, because they believed that education was a product of the corrupt West. Soon they began random attacks on anyone they did not like. Anarchy broke out, especially in outlying areas of the country, such as the North and the East. "To them, killing a human being is just like stepping on an ant," said Madarjan.

Horrible things began happening all around us.

Aunt Mariam burst into the house. "Zarmina's husband was just killed!"

"What?" Madarjan sank into a chair. "That's the third death I've heard about this week."

Zarmina had been one of Sulima's students. Under Sulima's influence, she had become increasingly involved with working for women's rights. Her husband supported her and approved. Zarmina was also employed outside the house. She worked as a teller in a bank and volunteered in one of the schools that Sulima had founded.

"They killed him because he allowed his wife to teach and to work outside the house."

The silence that followed was punctuated by the sound of sobbing. Even though I did not personally know Zarmina, seeing Madarjan, Aunt Mariam, and Gula so distraught made me cry as well.

I did not find out the rest of the story until years later. Madarjan heard it from Zarmina's mother, who was there and witnessed the massacre. After killing the husband, they came to Zarmina's house and summoned her outside. "Just let me feed my baby," she said. They nodded and waited while she nursed her child and gave her toddler his dinner. Then she went out to them. They ordered her to stand with her back to a tree and they shot her. Then they dragged out her father-in-law and brother-in-law and shot them as well.

The terror was compounded by new and terrible poverty. People who had worked for the government lost their jobs or were killed. Educated people were not allowed to practice their professions. It was dangerous for women to leave the house and still more dangerous for them to work. But most continued to do so because they had no choice. People were starving. It became more and more common to see children with huge eyes and stick-thin limbs wandering the streets listlessly and rummaging through garbage cans. Sometimes a bomb hidden in the can would explode, and the child would lose a limb or even his life.

Amid all the mayhem, some stories of great compassion and heroism reached us. One of our neighbors, Mr. Hashemi, was a wealthy man. He wanted to take a pilgrimage to Mecca, to become a *hadji*. He withdrew all his life's savings and arranged the trip—money to bribe soldiers and border guards, and of course to pay for airfare and travel expenses. On his way out of town, he passed by a man on the street with three small children clinging to his pants. "Would you like to buy my children?" the man asked.

Mr. Hashemi was appalled. "Why are you selling your children?"

"I have no job. My wife has no job. There is no more food in the house. If I sell my children, they will have enough to eat wherever they live. And I can use the money for myself and my wife to survive."

"Please." Mr. Hashemi took out his wallet. "Take this and buy food for your family. Don't ever think of selling your children again. If you have any more problems, come and see me." He wrote his address down on a card.

Mr. Hashemi gave up the idea of his pilgrimage and instead devoted his money to helping the poor—which is what Mohammed would have wanted.

The Mujihaddin started their infamous midnight raids around that time. Late at night, they would enter the house of someone they had targeted. Then they would torture and murder the men, and kidnap, rape, and torture the women and even the children. Women began to commit suicide rather than fall into the hands of the Mujihaddin. Some begged their families to kill them. "It is better to be killed by someone I love than to be raped and tortured by those savages," my cousin told her husband. He was horrified and did not comply. "I know other men are doing it, but I could not murder someone I care for," he said. The Mujihaddin broke into his house toward dawn a few days later. He was killed, and his wife and daughters were raped.

Several years ago, I watched a boxing match on television. Every time the contender who was losing tried to stagger to his feet, the other contender punched him back down again. He kept falling down and bleeding and groaning until he could no longer move. Watching them reminded me of my extended family during that time. We spent the years between 1978 and 1980 and the years after 1985 reeling from each attack. We lost the treasures of our family. Afghanistan lost some of its finest people in the flower of their youth.

My cousin Nabi was kidnapped. He had been an excellent student and was employed as a teacher. Clearly, his profession as an educator placed him on the Mujihaddin blacklist. He had been missing for close to a week when his brother Ghani set out to look for him. His brother's story stays with me to this day because of the clear involvement of a supernatural force in the finding of Nabi's body.

Ghani scoured the area, searching for his missing brother. It had been raining. The fog made it difficult to see. The muddy ground made it impossible to find tracks. Ghani passed by a deep pit that had been dug to lay the foundation of a house that was never built. "I thought I heard someone calling my name, saying, 'Look here, look over here.'" He searched the pit, hoping to find Nabi hiding in it. Instead, he found the remains of Nabi. The body was almost unrecognizable, due to the rain and the facial injuries he had sustained prior to his death. But Ghani recognized the clothing. I had not known Nabi well. Uncle Daoud and Aunt Layla were no longer living with us when I grew up. But I knew him well enough to be upset.

I'm told that in all, seventy of our relatives were killed by the Mujihaddin over the years. Some were murdered for being government employees, others for having an education, and others just randomly.

For example, one of my second cousins heard a woman screaming for help. A member of the Mujihaddin was trying to snatch her baby. He intervened in the tug-of-war and was shot to death.

We ourselves were almost killed.

Karim was warned that the Mujihaddin were out to get him. A friend had overheard two men talking in the mosque. It turned out that not only strangers but also our own relatives were involved in the plot. Some of our half-cousins who were sons and nephews of Aghajan's second and third wives had joined the Mujihaddin forces. They had long disapproved of our branch of the family because of our involvement with secular education. Even Abajan's rejection of communism had not convinced them that we were adherents to a proper Islamic set of values. Sulima's employment by the government and her outspoken support of women's rights made us sources of shame to them and symbols of everything they hated and were trying to eradicate. "You'd better pack your bags and get out of the area," his informant advised.

Karim had no intention of being chased away so easily. He and Asim approached two friends and asked for their help. Zamin was not living with us because he and Karim did not get along. He was studying chemistry and living in Kabul with Uncle Nayk.

Karim, Asim, and their friends stacked up beds to make bunkers for hideouts. They placed a gun at every window. They amassed weapons. Then they told us to hide in the *sandali*. This is a warming oven that is unique to Afghanistan. A table is placed on top of a stove filled with hot charcoal and a thick blanket is draped around the table. People sit on mattresses and warm the lower half of their bodies under the blanket. *Sandalis* are especially common in houses where there is no central heat.

We listened to Karim. Madarjan, Gula, Surya, Naim, and I crawled under the blanket and crouched inside the *sandali*. We waited.

Karim, Asim, and their friends waited.

When midnight struck, the Mujihaddin also struck. Fifty men with grenades and guns. But Karim, Asim, and their friends leaped with remarkable speed from window to window, shooting from each window and darting to the next one. This gave the impression that there were many men in the house, not just four.

The Mujihaddin had surrounded the house. One threw a bomb that exploded on the wall separating the house from the street.

Although the structure of the house was not damaged, the windows all blew out. Madarjan's cheek was cut by a piece flying glass as she peeked out of the *sandali* to see what was going on.

"Madarjan, I'm scared," Surya whispered. Her voice was shaking.

"Ssh, baby. Just say the *Chahar Qul*, and God will help you."

I began reciting the *Chahar Qul*, which means the Four Sayings. These prayers are recited during daily prayer, but people also recite them during times of danger.

> In the Name of God, the Beneficent, the Merciful
> Say, O unbelievers
> I do not serve that which you serve
> Nor do you serve Him Whom I serve
> Nor are you going to serve Him whom I serve
> You shall have your religion and I shall have my religion
> When there comes the help of God and the victory
> And you see men entering the religion of God in companies
> Then celebrate the praise of your Lord and ask His forgiveness;
> surely He is oft-returning to mercy
>
> Say, I seek refuge in the Lord of dawn
> From the evil of what He has created
> And from the evil of the utterly dark night when it comes
> And from the evil of those who blow on knots
> And from the evil of the envious when he envies
>
> Say, I seek refuge in the Lord of men
> The King of men
> The God of men
> From the evil of the whisperings of the slinking (Satan)
> From among the *jinn* (genies) and the men.

Again and again we recited it. "In the Name of God, the Beneficent, the Merciful. . . ."

Finally, Karim managed to shoot one of the Mujihaddin who had been hiding in a tree and firing at the house. The man toppled over into the stream. That splash of death echoes through my nightmares, even today.

When the Mujihaddin saw that one of their numbers had been killed, they ran away. The attack had lasted from midnight until 5 A.M. It left me shaking and terrified. Gula, Surya, and I had been gripping one another's hands so tightly that my fingers ached.

"We must leave," Madarjan whispered. "They'll be coming back for us."

She found burqas for Gula, Surya, Naim, and me. Although these coverings for women were not yet the law—that did not happen until the time of the Taliban—women had been wearing them for generations for reasons of modesty, especially in the less-developed areas of the country, such as the East. Naim began to fuss. "This is women's clothes!" But one look from Madarjan silenced him.

"No one should be able to recognize any of us," Gula explained, helping him into the offending outfit. He grumbled but consented to put it on.

The burqas were adult-size, and we looked ridiculous in them. We could hardly walk and kept tripping. But they accomplished their purpose. We were completely unrecognizable. We made our way silently to Aghajan's house.

We were just getting settled when one of our cousins burst into the house. "You have to leave here!" he gasped. "I just came from the mosque. The Mujihaddin—they expect you to run away to here. They were talking about it after prayer. They'll come here next. If they find you here, they'll burn down the house."

"So what should we do?" Madarjan cried.

"Go back to your house in Kabul," our cousin advised. "They probably won't think of looking for you there. And I hear it's much safer in the big city."

Karim found a circuitous route home because travel along main roads was already dangerous. We returned to Kabul and discovered that my cousin was right. Order still reigned. The Mujihaddin feared the Soviets and were afraid to bring their anarchy to town. I was nine years old when we moved back into our home in Kabul.

The years between nine and fourteen passed in relative tranquility. Although there were sporadic incidents of violence when the Mujihaddin raided an area of town, for the most part, things were fairly quiet. Life returned to normal. I was a child, and I had been protected from witnessing and even hearing about most of the carnage that surrounded us in the East. So once we were settled in Kabul again, I was able to make the transition to life as a normal little girl again without much difficulty. I attended classes. I had friends. I watched television. I studied. I played. I grew older and developed normal preteen and teenage interests.

But slowly the Mujihaddin began to make inroads into Kabul as well. Their presence began encroaching on our day-to-day lives. Every day, there were more incidents of violence. Shooting in the streets. Rocket attacks. Kidnappings. Crazy things started to happen. A group of schoolchildren suddenly got very ill and two died. Poison had been placed in their drinking water. The Mujihaddin were hiding bombs in toys, pens, gift boxes, and playground equipment. You could not set foot in a bus or cab without worrying that the last rider had hidden a bomb under the seat. Children were being blown up. Soon going outside became so dangerous that we stayed home as much as possible. We had to plan even the most routine errand as if it were a major transatlantic voyage.

Although anarchy reigned for everyone, those who worked for the government and their families were most at risk. We were all frightened. What would happen to Uncle Nayk? To Uncle Daoud and my cousins, who were all government employees? How about Uncle Fazel and my brothers, all of whom were highly educated men? Karim was an engineer. Zamin was a chemist. Asim was a doctor. They were all professionals. But I was most terrified for Husna, whose husband, Kabir, worked in one of the government ministries. I remembered what they had done to Nabi. Would this happen to him?

One day, Husna came to see us. "Kabir has been in hiding," she whispered. "We have counted up our money and we have enough to get across to Pakistan. From there, we will try to go to Europe. We cannot stay here."

Husna was leaving? Impossible. She was the person in the world I was closest to. She had almost raised me! It was Husna who had helped me the day I had a fight with my best friend Adela when we were in fourth grade. I can't even remember what the fight was about, but I know that Husna had never dismissed it as "silly" or "simply children squabbling." She had inherited all of Madarjan's ability to listen and soothe. But she was also able to contribute some practical suggestions that helped me reconcile with Adela. Another time, I had a high fever. Madarjan brought me herbs and cool water.

As always her touch made me feel better. But it was Husna who had sat up with me during the night, telling me stories to distract me and lull me to sleep.

"When will you leave?" Madarjan asked.

"Tomorrow. There is no time to spare."

Tomorrow! My precious Husna, who was almost like another mother to me, would be gone tomorrow. I loved Madarjan, I loved Gula and Surya. I had wonderful, loyal friends—especially Adela, who had been my best friend from elementary school right through to the present. I was very close with many of my sisters-in-law, aunts, and cousins—especially Aunt Fauziya's two daughters. But no one had ever taken care of me as Husna did. No one had ever nurtured me so tenderly. No one had ever listened to me so carefully. No one had ever given me such loving and helpful advice.

I was inconsolable when she left. We all were. Madarjan cried for weeks afterward. So did I. We received a letter that she had arrived safely in Pakistan. A few months later, another letter arrived from Holland where she and the rest of her family had been given asylum. Sulima was helping her to get settled.

There had been heavy fighting for almost a week. We had remained close to home, so we could not get to the market. We were low on supplies. "No more *naan*," Madarjan announced at breakfast. "We're out of apples," she said at dinner the next night. When we heard that there was a lull in the fighting, Gula and I decided to replenish our dwindling supplies.

"*Ahtiat kuned!* Be careful!" Madarjan called after us.

We took the bus to the market, bought our groceries, and boarded the bus as usual to return home.

"Stop!"

It was a Russian soldier. He was holding up his hand. The driver opened the door. "What's the problem?"

"This road is blocked. There has been fighting. You must go in that direction." He pointed.

"But that's not the way to—"

"Take the passengers to Khairkhana. The roads going in that direction are clear."

Khairkhana! Although it was a suburb of Kabul, it was quite far from home. How would we ever get back?

The bus was crowded and slow. It was filled with frightened women and crying children. Most were in the same predicament as we were. As the bus groaned and labored on, we decided to go to Aunt Fauziya's house. We were very close to Aunt Fauziya, who was actually not our aunt but our mother's aunt. But she had grown up with Madarjan as a sister and we called her Aunt. Aunt Fauziya lived with Nadia and Nazifa, her daughters. Her husband had taken the remaining children to the East, where he owned some land. Nadia and Nazifa stayed behind because they were going to university in the city. They were close in age to Gula and me, and we were almost best friends.

Aunt Fauziya welcomed us with classic Afghan hospitality. Afghans take in family members and even strangers in distress. We have very different concepts of privacy and very different needs from Americans. We tend to live in large, extended family units at all times, but especially during times of crisis such as war. So we did not worry about imposing. Nor did we feel that Aunt Fauziya resented our sudden arrival. We knew that Sulima had lived with her while she was in college and that she had always been welcoming to all of us.

She hugged and kissed us three times on each cheek. "Come in, come in! Thank God you are safe."

"Thank you, Aunt Fauziya."

Nadia came in from the kitchen. "You must be terribly hungry. Let me get you something to eat."

I shook my head. "We must call home first, and let Madarjan and the others know we are all right."

We rushed to the phone and dialed home, but the line was dead.

"I can't get through," I wailed. "What should I do?"

"Let's call Asim at work," Gula suggested. Asim was a doctor. Surely the hospitals had functioning phones.

My fingers were shaking so badly I could scarcely dial. I fumbled with the numbers and waited.

Nothing.

"How about Karim? Maybe they haven't cut off phone service where he works." Karim was an engineer for a company that manufactured airline parts. Their factory was located in a completely different part of town.

This time it was Gula who tried to call. I watched her face tensely. She did not need to tell me what happened.

Nothing.

We tried everyone we knew in Kabul. Uncles, aunts, neighbors, and friends. All the lines had been disconnected.

I turned to Aunt Fauziya.

"We have to leave right away. Everyone will be frantic with worry about us."

Aunt Fauziya caught my arm as I was headed for the door. "You cannot leave today. It's far too dangerous to travel."

"But—"

"You must stay here at least until the fighting has calmed down a bit. We will listen to the radio. When they say it is safe, you can leave."

We stayed for two days but it felt like two years. Often, I thought the clock must have stopped. Every few minutes, we tried the phone again. We tried to keep busy, helping with housework and playing cards with Nadia and Nazifa, but the minutes crawled by like slugs.

On the third day, the radio reported that the fighting had subsided somewhat. We insisted on leaving. Aunt Fauziya, Nadia, and Nazifa hugged us again and again.

"*Ahtiat kuned!* Be careful!" she called after us.

My heart was pounding as we walked through the streets. There had been much less fighting in this neighborhood, and it almost felt normal. I allowed myself to pretend that there was no war at all. That we were just coming back from a little trip to visit our dear aunt in the suburbs. Coming home from a nice vacation. We waited for three hours until another overcrowded bus appeared, and it took two more hours to reach our neighborhood. Usually it was a fifty-minute ride.

Madarjan threw her arms around us, crying, "*Khudaya shuker!* You're alive! Thank God, you're alive!"

Surya, Asim, and Naim came rushing to the door, hugging us and crying.

Surya's eyes were red and swollen. "We looked everywhere for you! We tried to call everyone we knew, but most of the phones weren't working. Those people we could reach hadn't heard from you."

Asim's face was grave. "We have been to every hospital. I have personally inspected every dead body. I thank God you were not among them, but—"

Surya finished his sentence. "But we thought something much worse than death had happened to you."

We made our adjustments. We stayed home more and more, but schools were still open. My friends and I did our best to attend classes as often as possible. We still went to movies and strolled in parks as often as we could. Madarjan walked the tightrope between keeping us safe and close to home and encouraging us to lead normal lives. So days could go by when we did not leave the house, followed by weeks of school as usual. The more normal we could be, the more we could continue to believe that this was just some temporary insanity that would soon pass. Every day that we sat in class and did math or biology as usual was a statement of hope for the future.

20

The Russians pulled out of Afghanistan in 1989, but Kabul was one of the last cities to be officially taken over by the Mujihaddin. By this time, I was already in medical school. We had tuned in to radio and television reports for years, and by 1992, we were almost addicted to the news. Looking back, I think we were in a state of denial. Kabul had been such an important center of advancement and relative freedom that at first we refused to believe that it could ever fall into the hands of this bunch of savages.

We were wrong.

One day, Asim came to visit us after work. "They're here."

We did not have to ask who "they" were.

"How do you know?" Madarjan asked.

"On my way home from work, I saw strange men in town. They had beards and turbans. I'm sure they were Mujihaddin."

Most men in Kabul had become so modernized that they had stopped wearing traditional Afghan clothing, *perahan* and *tunban*, and instead were wearing Western clothes, such as suits or jeans. Most men were clean-shaven and did not cover their heads.

I felt my throat tighten. I glanced at Madarjan. She looked as peaceful as ever. If she was afraid, she did not show it. Gula, Surya, Naim, and I exchanged glances. No one spoke. Then, after a few minutes, we turned on the radio.

We heard the familiar voice of the BBC announcer. The Mujihaddin were close, terribly close, to Kabul. They were in Paghman. It was a matter of days, possibly hours, before they would take over our city.

As I watched the door open and close, I felt a chill overtake me. We had been fooling ourselves. The wild, lawless reign of the Mujihaddin was here to stay. Nothing would be the same again.

It was that night when I saw the Prophet Mohammed. He came to me in a dream, surrounded by white light. I told him I had a problem. I don't think I specified the problem, but He seemed to know what it was. He told me to pray.

When I woke up, my face and pillow were wet with tears. I had been blessed by a visit from the Prophet Himself. He knew my pain, He knew the difficulties I was facing and those that lay ahead. He understood. He had given me a path to follow. The path of prayer.

I spread my prayer rug on the floor and knelt.

In the name of God, the Beneficent, the Merciful
All praise is due to God, the Lord of the worlds
The Beneficent, the Merciful
Master of the Day of Judgement
Thee do we serve and Thee do we beseech for help
Keep us on the right path
The path of those upon whom Thou hast bestowed favors. Not the path of those upon whom Thy wrath is brought down, nor of those who go astray.

Say; He, God, is One
God is He on Whom all depend
He begets not, nor is He begotten
And none is like Him.

When I stood up, everything felt changed. I was the same, but I was different. The world was the same, but I wasn't the same person facing that world.

I had not been particularly religious before the dream. I had regarded religion with respect, but I never felt it had much to offer me. I was a child of television and movies, science and math. I had friends, and we giggled, went to parties, and had fun. After my dream, I became more serious. I undertook a voluntary fast to cleanse my soul. I started to pray five times a day, as is traditional.

My family thought this was strange at first. "Why have you changed?" Surya asked.

Madarjan just looked at me with love, but also curiosity, in her deep brown eyes.

I told them about the dream.

Madarjan's face was solemn. She touched me gently, almost reverentially, with her hand. "You are blessed to have had such a vision. But do not talk of it again. It is said that if Mohammed comes to you at night and you talk about it, He will not come back."

I never had another vision of the Prophet. But this dream sustained me through all the difficulties I faced in the weeks and years ahead.

After my dream, the family changed as well. Madarjan and Surya started to pray again. We started to study the Qur'an together. The religious faith that had been forced upon the family when Sulima was young, and that had been such a source of pain and anger, was now a source of comfort and hope.

Turning to religion provided some inner peace but did very little to lessen my fear of the Mujihaddin. The fact that I was now a practicing Muslim did not give me anything in common with the Mujihaddin just because they were also Muslims. Their version of religion and mine were completely different. Theirs was about fear and coercion. About punishment and hatred. They pretended that their cruelty was being practiced in the name of Islam—and maybe some of them really believed it—but I do not believe that Islam is about bloodshed and vengeance, nor about how large a hair covering a woman should wear, or whether her arms do or don't show. To me, religion is about one thing—the person's relationship with God. I don't believe one person has a right to tell another person what to believe, how to pray, or what to wear. I don't believe that women should be treated badly, denied an education, or forced to stay at home all the time. So I'm grateful for my dream because it gave me a different understanding of Islam. I think that if it weren't for the dream, I would have come to hate my religion because of what the Mujihaddin and later the Taliban turned it into. Because of the dream, I realized that Islam could be a force of peace and love, rather than war and hatred.

Despite the dream, I was still afraid. I was frightened that my own freedom would be limited. Would I be forced to drop out of school? What about my brothers and sisters, all of whom were professionals or students? What would happen to us?

I did not know. But during those difficult days, I prayed and fasted and hoped . . . and hoped.

The Mujihaddin stormed our city and took it over two days later. I had decided to stay home from school that day. So did Surya. In fact, most offices and schools were closed. My brother Karim attempted to go to work, but he came home a few minutes later. I knew from the stricken expression on his face that it had happened.

"The *Watan* Party has fallen. The Mujihaddin have taken over Kabul."

I rushed to the television. The announcer was telling us that the Mujihaddin were in power. And the next night, the news was reported by a female announcer. She was wearing a scarf on her head.

The Mujihaddin were still on a rampage. Employees of the former government were being killed in huge numbers. I didn't leave the house during those first few days. Madarjan, Gula, Surya, Asim, Karim and his family (by this time, Karim was married and had two children), and Naim and I stayed home. We were glued to the television and the radio. We heard but tried to ignore the shooting outside, the exploding of bombs, the cries of the wounded and the wailing of those who had lost a loved one. And we wondered, Were our own loved ones safe? Surya and I tried halfheartedly to study but it was impossible to concentrate. I must have read the same two pages in my biochemistry book a hundred times. I prayed. I cleaned the floor. I tried to keep busy. I tried not to cry.

But I awoke each day—when I slept at all—to new tales of horror. My uncle Fazel, who had been a government employee, was blinded. He was working on his car when one of the Mujihaddin put a gun to his temple. Bizarrely, miraculously, the bullet went right through his skull and came out the other side. He survived the shooting but lost his vision. Now he sits home all day, staring vacantly at the wall. Sometimes he listens to music. His wife takes care of him. He is a shell of the person he used to be. Although he is only in his late fifties, he looks as though he is in his late seventies. Maybe it would have been better if he had died.

Then Aunt Mariam's husband was killed.

The funeral stands out in my mind because it was very much like other funerals I had gone to over the years—but also very different.

As in all funerals, the burial was held on the first day after his death and the funeral on the second. Only men attended the burial, and there were two separate funeral ceremonies—one for men and one for women. The funeral was linked to others before it by the chain of familiar tradition and ritual.

But it was different because, in a sense, it was everyone's funeral. When someone dies during ordinary times, everyone is sad for the dead person, and also for the family. But when someone dies during war, people are sad not only for the deceased and the family but also for themselves. This could be their husband, father, son, or brother. This could be them. They could be next.

Many of them were next.

The Mujihaddin continued to run through the city like wild people. Using the excuse of restoring Islamic law to Afghanistan, they allowed themselves to murder, torture, rape, and steal. Of course, all of these are against Islamic law. There were random shootings all the time.

We continued to try to go about our business. We put on the newly required clothes demanded of women—clothes that conformed to the Islamic laws of modesty. Then we ventured out of our house to go to work, to university, or to the market. But we never knew if school would be open when we arrived. Many days, I reached the university only to find the doors locked and the place dark and empty. Even on days when classes were being held, I often was afraid to leave the house. You risked your life every time you left home because of the fighting in the streets. A friend of Husna's, a doctor, was caught in crossfire. Her name happened to be Gula. She had been a regular visitor to our home, and we were all very fond of her. When she died, we felt as if our own Gula or Surya had died. For years, her mother continued to cry every time she saw someone in our family. She hugged and cried over our Gula the most because of the shared name.

Women were especially at risk because the Mujihaddin grabbed and assaulted them like some kind of primitive cavemen. You could not go out often during the day because of the fighting. But you could not go out at night either. Before dawn and after dusk, the Mujihaddin roamed. They were on the lookout for unattached women whom they could fondle—at best—or, worse, kidnap, rape, and kill. Nor were you safe on the bus. Public transportation had been severely cut and was almost nonexistent. We had to walk through dangerous areas just to get to the bus.

After a while, it seemed safer to avoid dodging bullets and Mujihaddin and to just stay home. I was leaving the house less and less. Sometimes, I slipped over to my friend Adela's, but for the most part, I stayed home.

I hated being confined. I liked to go outdoors, smell the fresh air, and watch the birds. I loved movies. I especially loved my studies. As often as possible, I tried to go to school. Sometimes class was in session, but more often, the school was closed. But the memory of the pale, frightened faces of my family as they greeted Gula and me on our return the day we came home from Aunt Fauziya's house stopped me many times when I could have risked it. I did not ever want to worry them like that again.

We learned to adjust to spending most of our time in the house. And as the fighting intensified, we began spending more and more time in the basement. That way, if a rocket hit the house, we would be safe. We brought our small, portable stove downstairs, and we moved our pots, pans, and dishes down there as well. Often neighboring families who had no basement came to us for shelter.

Our family became our world. Being in such close quarters so much of the time, we were especially careful to be sensitive to one another's feelings. Remarks that would ordinarily trigger a sharp response were usually ignored.

The only person who found it impossible to ignore irritants was Karim's wife, Samira. None of us had liked her from the beginning, and the feeling was mutual. She and Karim had been working together and had fallen in love. Love matches were unconventional, but that wasn't the reason we didn't like her. She was an angry, bitter woman, always complaining about something.

"You gave me the smallest piece of bread."

"Why did you tell Omid"—her son—"that he's not allowed to play with the pencils, are they so precious? You begrudge my family everything."

We tried to humor her and to overlook as much as we could. At the best of times, this was difficult, but now it seemed almost impossible. Yet it was essential for our survival. We knew that if we fell into discord among us, we could be destroyed. We had to create a tiny haven of love and support amid the jungle of explosions, gunshots, screams, and chaos outside. So we ignored Samira's nasty remarks. And we tried to remain cheerful.

We turned on our favorite music and danced. Music had always been part of my soul, but now it became even more important. Like nothing else, it had the power to transport me to another realm, where harmony and beauty ruled and there was no suffering or pain. I enjoyed the music of Afghan exile Zahir Howida, but Ahmed Zahir was my favorite singer. He was remarkably versatile and creative, blending together Eastern and Western musical styles and instruments. Sadly, he was killed by the Communists. And when the Mujihaddin came to power, they bombed his grave. The Taliban would repeat the Mujihaddin's attack on the grave and utterly destroy it, together with the graves of several other popular singers. Ahmed Zahir remains one of the most popular performers among Afghans, even today.

During the evenings, we sat around making jokes or playing cards. We tried to keep up our university studies as best we could. I held my medical books like a talisman. Since I enjoyed teaching, I also tutored Karim's children and sometimes our neighbors' children as well. Soon we had little classes in the house.

I read a great deal of poetry—the rawness and power of the imagery spoke to me. I especially loved the poems of Forugh Farrokhzad, Nadir Nadirpoor, Bidel, and Raziq Fani. The poem "Hope or Dream" by Nadir Nadirpoor was one of my favorites.

Desiring this hidden hope
Keeps me alive
Hope or dream . . . what is it?

I have many nights
Taken to morning with this hope
And many days
When I go toward night with this dream
Maybe one of these warm days
A rock will fall from the sun

And that rock, like a burning island
Reaches our hill-like world
We become a pile of ash
Ash, which hides the power of revenge
We are dead, blood-soaked corpses
We are the children who have aged too soon
We are the old and rotten shadows of the night
We are the false mornings, false dawns
Raw in fire and horror
We are the victims of events unseen
Many nights, this hope takes me to morning
Many days, this dream takes me to night

Perhaps one of these cold days
The river will overflow its banks
And we will drown under its wild waves
From our hearts we scream
The songs of our death
Then from the fear of oblivion we struggle
To break the chains of our imprisonment
From our feet

I also wrote a good deal of poetry during that time. On paper, I could allow myself to express what was too dangerous to utter aloud.

"Imprisoned"

I am imprisoned
Imprisoned in the suffocating cage of life
Sentenced to cruelty and slavery
Nothing according to my choice
Day awaiting night
Unable to speak of my aching heart
Not a word on my lips, nor a scream
Unable to even envy another's freedom
How long shall I be inferior?
Oh death, my only savior
Liberate me from this cage
I have no more desire to live

We read to one another. We studied the Qur'an. We prayed. We hugged. We cried, then we laughed. Too much crying was dangerous. Letting a few tears leak through was like allowing a hole in a dike. We could have been utterly swept away by despair. It was dangerous to hope that all this would end soon—but it was equally dangerous to lose hope.

So we survived day to day—Karim and his wife, Samira, and their children, Asim, Naim, Gula, Surya, Madarjan, and myself. Karim moved out after a few months. He rented a house in the East. By now, fighting in the East had died down—for the most part—and it was far more dangerous to remain in the cities. Once the Mujihaddin had established themselves, they felt less need to engage in brutality, and the worst of the danger was over. So the East seemed a little safer, and Karim was ready to be on his own. It was a risky journey for him to travel with his possessions, his wife, and his children, but Samira felt miserable living with us, and she was making his life miserable. Asim also moved out to Makroraion, a suburb of Kabul, and then Zamin left Uncle Nayk's house and moved in with Asim.

In their place, Uncle Daoud moved in, together with Aunt Layla and their two youngest children, aged nine and three. The Mujihaddin had burned down their house, and they needed a place to stay. I loved playing with the children—especially little Rayta, who was three years old and adorable.

Things became even more crowded when our neighbors, the Rahimis, moved in after their house was blown up by a rocket. They brought their four children, so our classes grew and became livelier. Despite the crowding, we never felt overwhelmed or resentful of the extra people.

"We must thank God that we have a home," Madarjan always said. "If He has given us a home, it is so that we can share it with those less fortunate."

We had a home, thank God. Home would keep us safe.

But home stopped being safe.

It was February. Rayta's third birthday. Ordinarily, we would have given her presents and had a little party with cake to honor her birthday. Her eyes would have danced over delighted dimples. But not today. Today we were fleeing home—at least temporarily. We were going to Aunt Fauziya's house in Khairkhana.

It was brutally cold. You could not open your window without having your fingernails turn blue. The trees looked like crazed Afghan dancers, swaying and dipping in the wind. All night long, we had lain awake to the whistling of the wind and the crashing of explosions and guns. We had been warned the night before that there would be unusually heavy fighting in our area of Kabul. Two of the seven different factions of Mujihaddin that had taken over the city were embroiled in a bitter battle. Although they had all united to fight the Russians, once the Red Army had been defeated they started to fight one another. Each of the tribal factions wanted complete control of the city, and the radio predicted the worst fighting ever in our neighborhood. People were urged to leave the center of town and go to the suburbs.

We rose before dawn. We packed toothbrushes and a few other essentials in a bag, and set off by foot. No one spoke as our procession made its way through the city, using back roads to avoid being seen. Our breath formed puff clouds in front of our faces. The wind was whipping at our backs. We took turns carrying Rayta when she could no longer walk. Her little face was drawn and terrified.

One mile. A mile and a half. Two miles. Madarjan's breathing was labored. "Will she be all right?" I whispered to Naim. "Her blood pressure—"

"She took her pills before leaving," he whispered back.

"But the walk is so long. And the doctor said her high blood pressure could get worse."

He shrugged. What could anyone do?

Three miles, then four. We continued trudging, Madarjan's pace getting slower and slower. "Are you okay?" I asked her.

She nodded, but I could tell that she wasn't. I wished we could carry her, as we carried little Rayta.

Five miles, six . . . we continued walking until, after eleven miles, Surya pointed and shouted. "A taxi!"

Over the protests of the cabdriver, six of us piled in. Madarjan went first, of course, and the children. The rest of us continued walking until we found another cab. We drove in wordless relief the remaining four miles to Aunt Fauziya's house. When we arrived, we found out that Aunt Fauziya had traveled east to join her husband, and only Nadia and Nazifa were home, with one of their brothers.

It had been a wise move. It was definitely quieter here than it had been in central Kabul, where we lived. We organized ourselves into Aunt Fauziya's house and resumed our activities as best we could—music, dancing, telling jokes, housecleaning, playing with the children, and praying. I especially enjoyed tutoring the children. It contributed to my sense of continuity and hope. One day, this insanity would pass and these children would return to school. I felt gratified thinking that I was helping them to keep knowledge alive that they would need when that wonderful day would come. In my bag of essentials, I had packed a textbook on biochemistry. I tried to force myself to continue studying it. I don't remember a word now, but I know that going through the motions of being a medical student was important to me. It kept my hope alive that one day things would return to normal and I could return to school.

Two weeks later, we heard that the fighting had calmed down enough for us to return home. Fortunately, we were able to find a taxi and did not have to travel eleven miles on foot.

We came home to a city hushed by the aftermath of fighting. There were a few bombed-out buildings and other signs of damage. The streets were noticeably empty. People were venturing out for only the most urgent business.

We were home again.

Life fell into its normal pattern—normal, that is, for such an abnormal time. A few months later, in early spring, the situation again heated up, and we were forced to flee again. This time, conditions were more tolerable. The weather was warmer and it was easier to find a taxi. Once again, we were gone for about two weeks, then we returned home.

It was late spring now. Because it was still dangerous to go out, we continued to spend most of our time indoors. This was maddening. Spring is a beautiful season in Afghanistan. Our garden was lavishly sprinkled with a delicious feast for the eyes and the nose. The apple and cherry trees were blooming. We had several trees we called "crazy willow," that looked green and inviting. Our sunflowers stood in rows like yellow soldiers of hope. All I wanted was to take my schoolbooks or poetry notebook and drink in the beauty, instead of being stuck in the basement.

I was just beginning to test the limits of going out. I was going to classes as often as possible. I was venturing into the garden to watch the sun rise. I was visiting Adela more frequently.

But then my world blew apart even more.

Surya and I were in the living room, studying. Madarjan and Gula were in the kitchen. I don't remember where everyone else was. Suddenly there was a thundering sound and the whole house shook. I heard glass shattering and heavy objects falling. We rushed into the kitchen and saw that Madarjan and Gula were all right, but Madarjan was ashen and trembling. Gula pointed to the window. A rocket had blown the roof off the bathroom of our house. Our house was shaped like a *U*. The kitchen and bathroom were at opposite ends, separated by a courtyard. All the damage was done to the bathroom—which, fortunately, no one was using at the time. The wall and glass had fallen into the courtyard. The rest of the house was intact.

Once again, we made the pilgrimage to my aunt's house. This time, we did not take only a few overnight items. We packed everything.

But I refused to believe that we would never come back. This was my home. Although we had moved around during my childhood, our home in Kabul had always been a point of stability. Even to this day, my dreams all take place in that house. I stood looking at it, trying to photograph it with my eyes. The cherry and apple trees that had shared their sweet fragrance and fruit with me. The crazy willow that had been my friend through my growing-up years. I had daydreamed under that tree. I had written poetry, whispered the Important Secrets of my little girl's heart to Husna, and exchanged giggles and gossip with Adela and Neema. We could not be moving for good. We *had* to come back.

Impulsively, I ran back into the house. I found a little saucer, filled it with salt, and put it into my bedroom, where my bed used to stand. "I will be back," I promised the house. "And then I will use this salt to cook my first meal."

The week after we moved, our house in Kabul was destroyed by a rocket.

We continued living at Aunt Fauziya's. Her children decided to join the rest of the family in the East, and we essentially took over their house. Gradually, the danger began to subside—well, not entirely. There were still incidents and flare-ups of violence. But it was as if the Mujihaddin had proved their point. The worst of the fighting died down. People began to return to their pre-Mujihaddin activities. Classes reopened, and Gula, Surya, Naim and I returned to the university. Asim and Zamin returned to work. I managed to see Adela and Neema from time to time, if our paths crossed in college. Adela was also in medical school, but we were in different classes. Neema was in dental school. Surya was studying to be a dentist.

One day I came from class to see Madarjan leaning over Gula. She was daubing Gula's shoulder and neck with a gauze pad. Gula's face was pale. Her eyes were bloodshot. I looked at her upper arm, shoulder, and neck and nearly fainted. She had a bandage wrapped around the entire area, but it was soaked with blood.

I was alarmed. "What happened?"

Gula was about to say something, but Madarjan spoke instead. "Gula had an accident at the laboratory. Some acid splashed up and burned her. We must fix the bandage as best we can and get her to a hospital."

I shuddered. We used the same chemicals in our laboratories at medical school that Gula used in veterinary school.

I looked at Gula's face. The drawn, terrified expression disturbed me. She must be in terrible pain. I helped Madarjan, Surya, and Naim bring her to the hospital.

A few months later, Gula told us she had decided to join Husna in Holland. Although I was not as close with Gula as I had been with Husna, I was terribly upset to see her go. It was one more loss, one more anchor, taken away. "Why?" I kept asking her. "Why now?"

"Because I can't forget how dangerous it was when the Mujihaddin took over," she replied. "And because I miss Husna."

Her answers were not convincing. I sensed that perhaps she was trying to hide something. But she clearly did not want to talk about it, so I let it go. And cried to see her leave. I shed all the tears I had held back during all those years. I cried for my happy childhood and my sense of safety, both brought to a cruel end by the Mujihaddin. I cried for my uncle's eyes. I cried because it was okay to cry when your sister left and too dangerous to allow yourself to cry for all the rest.

Only years later did I find out her real reason for leaving. Her veil had slipped down, revealing her neck and upper shoulder. A

Mujihaddin fighter had thrown acid at her. Madarjan had asked her not to tell us. She did not want to frighten us further. We had been through enough. Our survival lay in continuing to leave home, continuing to pursue our studies, and trying to live as normally as possible.

This was exactly what we were doing. Asim married and moved to the East. We danced and made merry at his wedding. But even though we were trying to act normal, we were constantly on guard. After living through the devastation of the Mujihaddin's takeover, we could not relax and pretend that everything was fine. But at least, we thought, we knew what we were dealing with. Yes, the Mujihaddin were savage and corrupt. They could do anything at any time. But their attacks had dwindled to occasional, random acts of brutality. We could navigate our way around them, as one might try to pick one's way through a minefield. The worst, we thought, was over.

We were wrong.

21

The Taliban were actually second-generation Mujihaddin. Many had originally been part of the Mujihaddin forces. They were disturbed by the corruption and the un-Islamic behavior of their fellow soldiers and leaders. Several of my father's half-cousins and second cousins were among those. Others were passionate Afghan refugees, studying at *madressas* in Pakistan. Most were orphans, who were clothed, fed, and brainwashed at these religious schools. From earliest childhood, they were brought up to be fighters for God. The concept of the jihad, which had been exploited by the Americans in their strategy to turn angry Islamic Afghans into anti-Soviet troops, had taken root. Now it was being transmitted to the next generation of kids. These boys were brought up to do one thing: to fight for Islam and kill anyone they believed might stand in the way.

I'm not a political expert. I don't know what turned Taliban leaders and their army of followers into people who hated women enough to institute the cruelest, most oppressive system against women ever to exist. Some people think it may be because most of them were orphans who were brought up without the love of a woman. They were nurtured instead on the hatred taught by their version of Islam. It's ironic that the Taliban originally banded together as a group after some Mujihaddin had kidnapped and raped a young girl. They believed that the Mujihaddin were degrading Islam and decided to avenge the honor of the violated girl and the honor of their violated religion. But once they acquired power, they became the greatest violators of women ever to live.

It started in 1994 when the Taliban took over Kandahar. We crowded around the radio. Could this be true? They were closing down all girls' schools and many boys' schools too. They were insisting that all men wear beards, or risk being beaten. That women would be forced to wear not only Islamic *hijab*—long skirt down to the floor, with pants underneath—but also a burqa—a thick headpiece covering the entire head and shoulders, with only a tiny rectangle of mesh through which to see.

No, no, it was impossible. Surely they were simply using Islamic ideas to win over the people. Even their name—*Taliban*, which is Arabic for "Islamic student"—connoted a kind of humility. These people did not want to call themselves leaders or teachers, but students. Perhaps they wanted to show how devoted they were to Islam so as to gain support, and to show how different they were from the Mujihaddin. And in fact, their plan worked. At least in some cities, they were greeted with joy and gratitude as redeemers. At least at first, they were seen as devout, deeply committed Muslims who were going to restore law and order.

Madarjan was hopeful. "They can't be worse than the Mujihaddin. At least they are protecting women by keeping them in the house. At least they are bringing order back."

But I never believed that life under the Taliban could be an improvement. As I listened to the radio, icy fingers of foreboding gripped my neck. Not only would there be a new wave of fighting, but the new rulers would make our lives under the Mujihaddin seem like paradise by comparison.

I was wrong about the fighting. The day that Kabul fell to the Taliban was relatively quiet. They had already bought most of the Mujihaddin battle strongholds, and so they were able to move right in with little resistance.

But I was right about what lay ahead.

The new laws were announced over the radio during the coming days.

"Women are to wear *hijab* and burqa, by order of the Ministry for the Protection of Virtue and the Prevention of Vice."

"For their safety, women are not to leave the house unaccompanied by a close male relative."

"Men are to wear beards as long as the length of their fists."

"Adultery, prostitution, homosexuality, or lewd behavior is to be punished by death."

"Thieves will have their hands removed."

And that was only the beginning.

Fighting erupted shortly after the takeover. Mujihaddin were defending their last strongholds. Telephone and electric wires were damaged, and all service was cut off. When service was restored, we were in for another shock. When we turned on the television, we saw nothing but a gray, snowy screen. The newest announcement over the radio informed us that television was an evil product of Western influence and there would be no more television. Wealthier people who owned VCRs could perhaps make up for the loss of television by watching their movies. But a further announcement forbade all forms of entertainment—movies, pigeon flying (a favorite pastime in Afghanistan), kite flying, music, and dancing. The only legal program on the radio was the religious station that broadcast announcements of the Taliban, and teachings from the Qur'an. We were still able to tune in to Radio Pakistan and All-India Radio, and we huddled around to listen to the music. But the music held little pleasure for us. We were frightened that at any moment, some member of the newly established Religious Police could be randomly spot-checking to see who was complying with the new rules. If we were caught, we could be beaten or jailed—or maybe worse.

Those first days passed like a nightmare. It is like looking back on an illness when you have a high fever and terrible pain, and you only remember pieces of what happened, and not in the right order. Each new announcement sent me reeling further into a kind of darkness I had never known. Was this really happening? Could people like this really exist? Could my life be so changed, and in such a short time? And if they could do this right at the beginning of their regime, what might they do next?

So here I was, confined again. But this time, it was worse than it had been under the Mujihaddin. The Mujihaddin had never ordered women to remain in the house. We chose to stay close to home because it was dangerous to go out. But we could choose to go out and find less dangerous routes—as indeed I did, when I went to the university. Now there were Religious Police everywhere, just waiting to catch a woman in violation of the law.

Madarjan remained serene. "This is better than the Mujihaddin. The laws are strict and harsh, but at least we know what to expect. They're not just randomly breaking into houses and killing people. They are not raping women. If we keep all the rules, then we will be safe."

I would have preferred to take my chances. I was young. I wanted to go outdoors, even if there was a risk. The very fact that there were no rules during the time of the Mujihaddin meant that we could play Russian roulette with dodging bullets. And as the Mujihaddin began to feel more secure, some of the worst atrocities had stopped. I had become hopeful for a better future. Confinement instituted by law was, to me, much worse.

We returned to the activities that had sustained us during our earlier confinement. This time it was much harder. I did not have the heart even to go through the motions of studying. I was restless and bored. We played cards. We must have cleaned the kitchen dozens of times. We studied the Qur'an. We prayed. We listened to Radio Pakistan and All-India Radio. Monstrous questions about the future faced us. Was this forever?

Each day brought new restrictions. Women were now restricted from wearing makeup even under their burqas. They were forbidden from wearing white socks, high-heeled shoes, and later, from wearing any shoes that make noise, and from wearing nail polish. If your window faced the street, you had to paint it black, then cover it with a thick curtain so that male passers-by could not catch a glimpse of the women inside the house. A woman was required to sit in the backseat of the car unless the driver was a close male relative, such as a father, brother, or son. Prayer became mandatory. Places of business had to be closed at times of prayer.

The first time I wore the burqa, I thought I would die. We were going to my Aunt Mariam's house. It was the *sale wafaat*, the anniversary of her husband's death. She lived in a different part of town. We took a taxi. As I looked out the window, I saw other cloaked women hurrying through the streets several paces behind their male escorts. As for me, the sense of entrapment and the heat seemed unbearable. My head felt squashed and tight and a headache was snaking its way around my skull. It was like being under a shroud. Sounds were muffled. I could barely see and after a few minutes, it became hard to breathe. I discovered that if I clutched the burqa close to my face, the covering around the head tightened. The mesh then stood right against my eyes and nose, and I could see and breathe more easily.

Before leaving the house, I looked in the mirror and could not recognize the swathed thing that I saw. I could not see my own eyes beneath the mesh. I could not see my face. I was indistinguishable from any other woman on the street. A nonperson. A moving, covered object.

We began hearing terrible stories. A friend's cousin was beaten, then lost his license for owning a store because he had forgotten to close his store during *waqte namaz,* prayer time. Another man was shot for failing to appear in the mosque for prayer three days in a row. A neighbor's eight-year-old niece had her fingers cut off because she was wearing nail polish. Each new horror story seemed to drive another nail into the coffin of our hope.

Medical care for women became almost nonexistent. Women were forbidden from working in any capacity, even as doctors and nurses. Since about half the Afghan doctors were female, this reduced available medical care for everyone. Male doctors were forbidden from examining female patients, but women were forbidden from leaving the house to go to female doctors. The result was that women began dying of preventable and curable illnesses. We were terrified of becoming sick.

Some female doctors continued to see patients from their home. Generally, they tried to confine their practice to female patients, who arrived escorted by a close male relative. However, several female doctors broke the law and treated men, and some male doctors broke the law and treated women. If they were caught by the Taliban, they were tortured or killed on the spot.

A couple of hospitals with wards to treat women remained open, but most female doctors had difficulty reaching the hospital, and the male doctors were forbidden from seeing the female patients. The hospitals were overcrowded and unsanitary, and many patients died due to lack of medical care. This compounded our fear—what if we stumbled and broke an arm? What if we developed appendicitis? We did not speak of these fears but just went about our business and prayed to stay healthy.

We were all looking forward to *Nowroze,* the Afghan New Year's Day, which takes place at the end of March. This had always been one of my favorite days of the year when I was growing up. When people could, they journeyed to Mazar-e-Sharif to picnic on the ground where Ali—the cousin and son-in-law of Mohammed—is buried. A special flag, called a *janda,* was raised. If the flag ascended the pole and started to fly without difficulty, people congratulated one another and said that it would be a good year. The year that the Mujihaddin took over, I heard that the flag did not go up properly. In fact, it had taken two attempts to get it up the flagpole. People considered this to be a bad omen.

I say I heard about this because I had never personally been to Mazar-e-Sharif. Our celebrations took place at the home of the oldest, most esteemed family member. It was traditional to wear new clothing, to symbolize the start of a new year. All kinds of traditional foods were served. Each food symbolized good luck, sweetness, or new beginnings. For example, it was traditional to eat white rice, white meat from a lamb or a chicken, and green spinach. The white represented purity and a clean slate, while green was the color of good fortune and new beginnings. We used to drink *haft mewa.* This was made out of water in which seven different kinds of dried fruits and nuts had been soaking for twenty-four hours. The sweetness was supposed to symbolize a sweet new year.

Children were encouraged not to cry on that day. I still remember Madarjan, stroking me on the head because I was crying. I must have been about four or so. I don't even remember why I was crying. She said, "If you cry today, you will spend your whole year crying. But if you are happy, you will be happy all year."

Nowroze was also a time for games. Men participated in playing *buz kashi*—a traditional game played on horseback. Young girls were encouraged to walk barefoot on green grass. There was music and laughter. There was a sense of family and a wonderful feeling that the world could be renewed again and again.

The Taliban outlawed all new year's practices, from raising the flag to games. "These frivolous activities are relics of a pagan time, before the coming of the Prophet. They are not fit for Muslims, only for infidels. Anyone celebrating *Nowroze* will be whipped."

Although our celebrations had been toned down during the time of the Mujihaddin—we did not want to venture out to walk on the grass, for example—we always had some kind of celebration. Even when special foods were no longer available, and when we could no longer afford new clothes, we preserved as many of the traditions as we could. But celebrating *Nowroze* had never been forbidden before. We continued to observe as many traditions as we could in the privacy of our homes, but we were afraid. Who knew what they might do next? Maybe they would suddenly decide that even private observances of *Nowroze* were improper and punish us. For the first time, the New Year felt hollow and empty. The year that lay ahead looked equally hollow and empty.

And the fighting was relentless. Even if we had been allowed to go out, we would have been in danger of being shot or stepping on a land mine.

So here we were in Khairkhana—Madarjan, Naim, Surya, and myself. The Taliban presence in Khairkhana was not as strong as in central Kabul, at least at that point in 1997. We occasionally left the house by ourselves without a male escort—always wearing the burqa, of course. But rarely did we venture out. If we needed groceries or other supplies, Naim brought them to us. If he was not free, then Zahir, the husband of Nadima, our neighbor and friend, helped us out.

The phone was ringing. It was Asim, who had moved to the East after his marriage. His wife had been weak and ailing for several months. A routine cold had become the flu but had not disappeared. The lingering cough and listlessness worried all of us.

"Friba is terribly sick. She has back pain and chest pain. She cannot stop coughing. I have listened to her chest. It is not pneumonia or bronchitis. I believe she has cancer of the lungs."

It did not take my medical school training to understand the implications of that.

Asim continued. "It may not be too late. If we could find a surgeon to remove the tumor, and if we could get the medicines for chemotherapy, maybe there would be a chance. But—"

He did not need to finish his sentence. There were no surgeons who could treat a woman. There were no medications. Even if he could get his hands on the medication, without a biopsy, Asim could not know which medication to prescribe.

"I will come immediately," said Madarjan. "Friba will need to be nursed. The baby will need to be taken care of. I will leave tomorrow."

"I'll go with you," Naim offered.

It was decided that my cousin Haseena and her new husband Tawaab would move in with us. It would have been not only improper but actually dangerous for us to live in a household consisting of only two women. Haseena and Tawaab were recently married and had no children, so they were the most mobile. After several weeks, however, Tawaab managed to make arrangements to leave the country. His goal was to reach a European country, such as Switzerland or Holland. Then he planned to send for his wife. Although three women were not allowed to live by themselves, only our neighbors were aware that Tawaab had left. We knew we could trust them and hoped that none of the other neighbors would find out.

Horror stories continued to pour in. Some I saw with my own eyes, others I just heard about. I was walking to the market with Tawaab, who was prepared to say he was my brother if we were questioned by the Religious Police. (A cousin was not considered to be a close enough relative to serve as an escort.) A woman was walking a few paces ahead of us. Her pants were a little too short, and her ankle was showing.

Immediately, a turbaned, bearded man wearing the dreaded white uniform of the Religious Police appeared beside her. He seized her arm and pushed her against a wall.

"*Hey, Kafir!* Infidel! You are exposing your flesh!"

He lashed at her with his whip. Again and again it descended. Muffled cries came from beneath her burqa. Otherwise there was no sound except the whizzing and stinging of the whip. Male passers-by averted their eyes, women hurried past. When he was done he spat a curse at her and she stumbled away.

That night, I could not sleep. I had heard about the beatings—who hadn't? But I had never seen one before. I closed my eyes and heard the snapping of the whip. The crying of the woman. The beating of my own heart. The silence of my lips. I had watched but had not spoken up—of course, what could I say? If I had stepped in, I would have gotten beaten too, possibly killed for insolence or rebellion. My own sense of helplessness felt as stifling and suffocating as the burqa itself. I had dreamed of becoming a doctor to help other people. Helping had always been important to me. Now, I was being barred from this as from so many other things. Someone was suffering before my eyes and I was completely unable to help her.

Some weeks later, my friend Adela came to see me, accompanied by her brother. Neema had committed suicide

I was shocked. "Neema? But why?"

"Her parents betrothed her to a man named Jamal. She hated Jamal. He was her second cousin, and had been part of the Mujihaddin before he joined the Religious Police. He is a cruel man—you don't want to know what he did—and she didn't want to marry him. But she had no choice. Where could she go? Who could she turn to?"

Though I was afraid to ask, I still said, "How did she do it?"

"She hung herself from a beam in her room. She used—"

I didn't want to hear any more. This was the second woman that week I'd heard about who had committed suicide, and it was the third death of a woman—although Neema was the first I knew personally. And again, there was that helplessness. Neema had been a friend. She had been going through a hell beyond my imagining. Even if I had known about it, I would have been powerless to help her.

Those months were shrouded by that sense of helplessness and mounting despair. An increasing number of tales of brutality were reaching us every day. It was like watching some crazed VCR speed up a horror movie. Each scene of blood and terror flashed before our eyes before we could so much as blink or catch our breath. The Religious Police issued new edicts every few weeks. More women were killing themselves. What was there to live for? We could not go out. We could not pursue careers, hobbies, or interests. We could not choose our marriage partners. We could not even celebrate our traditional holidays. The years ahead stretched before us in a monotonous procession of identical days, punctuated only by reports of brutality. More and more, death seemed to be the only way out of our prison.

I prayed. I fasted. I tried to hold on to the sense of peace that came to me with my dream. Because Islam was being used to punish us, it was harder for me to find religion a source of comfort. I continually had to remind myself that the Taliban were not representatives of Mohammed. What they taught was only masquerading as Islam. It was a lie. I closed my eyes and remembered the love, the tender expression on the face of the Prophet as he had appeared to me. There had to be a reason for all this.

But with each new horror story, I felt myself slipping deeper into a new kind of despair. Even the recollection of my dream could not always pull me out of this quicksand. The daily grinding boredom caused by being indoors with nothing to do served as a petri dish for the growth of this dangerous germ of despair. I had to do something to keep my mind alive. By keeping my mind alive, I stood a better chance of keeping myself alive too.

22

My school did not start out as a way of defying the Taliban. It did not even start out as a school. To keep myself alert and stimulated, I went back to my old hobby and pastime—tutoring children. Nadima, my next-door-neighbor and her husband, Zahir, had two daughters named Zakia and Shula, aged ten and seven. Our houses were close by. Surya and I risked moving between the houses without a male escort.

It started as a conversation with Nadima.

"Zakia is so smart. She was such a good student. Zaki, show Hala your last test."

Zakia ran and brought a math test with an excellent grade. She smiled proudly, then her face clouded over.

"She has been so sad since she has not been allowed to go to school. She is afraid she will forget all she knows. She tries to study the books on her own, but they're too hard for her."

"Would you like me to tutor her?"

Zakia's little face lit up. She looked eagerly from me to her mother and back to me again.

"Do you mind?" Nadima asked. Her voice was apologetic. "I never was good in math. In fact, I never got much schooling at all. I left school when I got married."

"Mind? It would be a pleasure."

"Will you work with Shula too?"

"Of course. Just send them over every morning with their schoolbooks. I'll help them review, then I'll pick up where they left off."

Everyone was home-schooling children at that point, so it did not occur to me that I was violating the Taliban's rules. All I felt was excitement. Why hadn't I thought of this before? It was such a pleasure working with ideas, teaching concepts to young children and watching their minds grow.

Zakia and Shula proved to be very cooperative students. Each day they came over and we worked on math, biology, language, and history. They were bright, motivated, and charming. They always asked me for more lessons.

Two weeks later, there was a knock at my door. I opened it to see a woman clad in a burqa. She was together with her husband. When she came indoors and I could see her face, I recognized her, though I did not know her name. We had seen each other around town, and I had a sort of nodding acquaintanceship with her.

Over tea and cookies, she told me why they had come.

"My daughter Efat says you've been tutoring Zakia and Shula."

I nodded.

"Zakia loves going to study with you. She's told Efat all about it. Now Efat wants to come too. Can you work with her?"

Of course I said yes. And yes again to the next mother who asked, and the next. And the next.

"I'm going to need some help with this," I told Surya at the end of the second week. "I already have fifteen children, and more seem to be coming every day. The children are different ages. While I'm working with one student, the others sit and don't do anything. When you have that many kids, it stops being tutoring and you have to run it like a school."

Surya frowned. "Tutoring is one thing. A school is something else. We could get into terrible trouble for running a school. We could be beaten. We could be killed."

"I don't think they'll find out," I said. "None of the parents will tell. It wouldn't make any sense. They would be in as much trouble for sending the children here as we would be for teaching them. And the kids won't tell. So what are we afraid of?"

Surya looked uneasy. "I'll help out," she said finally. "But we'll have to figure out a way to keep this even more secret. I mean, what if someone sees all these kids coming to our house? What are we going to say—that we gave birth to all of them? Without husbands? We could get killed for that too, you know." She laughed, but it was a sad, mirthless sound.

We consulted Haseena, and she came up with an idea. "Let's tell them to come separately. No more than two or three at a time. And we'll have two separate shifts. One group will come in the morning at nine. The second group will come at lunchtime, after the others have gone home. We can start class at twelve-thirty."

I liked the way she said "we."

"So are you going to help too?" I asked.

"You can count me in."

We decided to get organized. We created a curriculum: biology, Pashtu, Dari (which is another Afghan language, similar to Farsi), basic health and hygiene, math, and English. My English was very limited. I had learned Russian in school, not English. But Haseena had studied English, and she taught the children.

We arranged that I would teach Pashtu and Dari to all the classes, and English to second grade. Since my English was so poor, I used picture textbooks. I knew the alphabet and could help quiz students with simple object words, such as *umbrella*, *apple*, *bed*, *book*. I also knew a few sentences. Surya would teach math and biology to all the classes. Haseena would teach everyone health and hygiene, and English to all grades except second. Since there were no textbooks available, we decided to use the children's own schoolbooks and improvise our lessons from them.

Our school grew very quickly. By the end of four months, we had sixty students—thirty in the morning session, thirty in the afternoon. Most of them were girls, but we actually had three boys as well. Many boys' schools had been destroyed in the fighting, including several in our area. I saw no reason why I shouldn't further the education of the boys too.

One boy in particular caught my fancy. His name was Ali, and he was a real charmer. His eyes danced with a special light, and there was always laughter on his lips. He caught on to new material faster than anyone else in the class. I loved his spirit and his sense of humor, and I admired his mind. He was a pleasure to teach.

I started calling him my *jan-jeegar*. This is an Afghan word of endearment that literally means "darling of my liver." Looking back on it now, I realize that this wasn't right. A teacher shouldn't favor one student over the others. But I was young and inexperienced. Besides, I didn't see myself as a "real teacher." I was just someone teaching children because there were no real teachers.

My favoritism caught up with me one day when Ali was absent from school. "Where's my little *jan-jeegar?*" I asked Haseena.

"He hasn't arrived yet," she answered.

A few minutes later, Ali showed up. Layli, a fat, very dark-skinned girl who was also quite smart but not especially attractive, came up to me. "You were asking about your *jan-jeegar.* He just arrived."

I suddenly felt bad. I didn't know that anyone had overheard my question to Haseena. I rumpled Layli's hair—or, to be more precise, I stroked the veil over her hair. "You're all my little *jan-jeegars,*" I said.

Some Americans have asked me if I ever had discipline problems with the children. I can honestly say that I didn't. They were well behaved and polite. They knew that they were taking a great risk by coming to our school, but they came anyway, and they were quite eager to learn. If anything, they were insatiable. They were always clamoring for more than we could deliver. "More studies! More lessons!"

We never talked about the danger. If the children had any fears or worries, they either did not express them, or they spoke to their parents. We did not deal with these issues with them. We felt that they were in school to learn, not to discuss problems that we couldn't solve anyway. We also didn't want to scare them. Dwelling on the danger we were in would have undermined their studies and frightened them. So we just went about our business of teaching math, biology, and the other subjects.

Of course, we talked among ourselves.

"I don't like it," Surya said one day. "Thirty children at one time. No matter how careful they are, someone is bound to notice them one of these days. There are Religious Police everywhere."

"They don't usually come into our neighborhood," I pointed out. "Not unless someone tips them off."

"But there are so many kids coming and going—" Surya began.

I interrupted. "I'm scared too, but what can we do?"

"We can close the school down." Haseena's voice carried no conviction.

I looked at both of them. "Is that what you want to do?"

Slowly Surya shook her head. "No. I can't bear to do it to the children. They love to come here."

"And what we're doing is important," I said. "I can't see giving up now."

We were having these discussions more and more frequently, as the Taliban reached new heights of brutality. I heard of a woman who was beaten because the Religious Police thought she was walking alone. "She is with me," said a man next to her. "I am her husband." They were both beaten—the husband for allowing his wife to walk in front of him, and the wife for walking in front of her husband.

I heard that the Taliban had turned a football stadium that was built with monies donated by the international community into an execution stadium. There were almost daily reports of the horrible executions that took place there. With each report, I wondered if I could be next. Was our school worth the risk? But then I would close my eyes and see Ali's eager eyes or Zakia's dimpled smile. All thoughts of closing the school would vanish. I could not abandon these children.

So I prayed. I continued to believe that the Prophet would help me. I was doing the right thing. God did not want women to be locked up in a prison of ignorance. He wanted women to be free to study, and to learn about His world. I was afraid, but surely God would protect me.

Despite the fear, those months of running the school were among the happiest I ever had. I felt productive. I felt useful. I felt I was doing something important, something that went beyond myself. I woke up in the morning grateful for the children. I realized that not only was I giving them something, but they were giving me something equally important. Maybe more important. They were giving me something to do with my time and my mind. Each time a child smiled, it lit up my world. The children reminded me that there could be innocence and wonder, even at the darkest times. They gave back to me something basic that I had lost, and I will always be grateful to them for that.

I don't want it to seem as though I lived every minute in fear. I didn't. Hours could go by when I hardly thought of the Taliban. The awareness of risk was always there like white noise in the background, but I was able to filter it out and give myself over to the children. At those times, I could almost forget why I was running a school in my house to begin with. I could pretend that things were normal.

But I was living in an artificial bubble that was soon to burst.

23

It happened almost five months after we opened the school. An ordinary morning, or so it seemed—that is, if anything after the arrival of the Taliban could be considered "normal." The first shift of students were in the classroom. I was teaching biology. I had gone into the yard to get a leaf to show the children how the veins bring water to a plant.

I didn't hear the knock on the door at first. When it got louder, I thought it was at my neighbor's house. Only when I heard someone banging hard and shouting did I put on my burqa and answer the door. When I saw who was standing there, I nearly fainted. My knees turned to water. My stomach leaped into my throat and I wanted to throw up. There was no mistaking the white uniform, beard, turban, gun, and unyielding facial expression. I was staring at three members of the Religious Police.

The tallest man scowled at me. "Are you the teacher?"

"Teacher? I don't know what you are talking about."

In my mind, I spoke to the children. I pleaded with them. Please, please stay quiet. Don't move. Don't laugh. And then to God, but without words. A silent prayer for my life. Please.

"I heard there was a school here." The same man was talking.

"You heard the wrong information," I said. "There has been some mistake."

"Are you sure?" The man tried to peer into the house behind me, but I deliberately stood in the door, blocking his view.

"Really." Could he tell from my voice that I was lying? Well, here was one advantage of the burqa. They could not see my face. I had never thought the burqa could protect me.

He stared at me long and hard. I waited for him to say something. I waited for a child to make some noise that would give us all away. Those moments of waiting seemed to last forever.

"I hope you are telling the truth," he finally said. "Because if you're not, we will punish you severely."

The second man spoke up. "We will come back and kill you."

The first man motioned to the others and they left.

My knees were shaking so badly, I could scarcely walk down the hall. My stomach was still heaving and turning over. My palms were sweating.

Surya saw my face. Right away she knew what had happened.

"Don't say anything to the children," I whispered to her. "I don't want to scare them."

She threw me a frightened look. Then she nodded and returned to class. "So we were up to fractions," I heard her say to the children.

I took a deep breath. I must be brave and strong. Must not let the children see how shaken I am. Must not scare them. Brave and strong. Courage.

When I had calmed down, I entered the class. "Here is the leaf I was going to show you."

"Do you want to continue doing this?"

It was night. All the children had gone home. Surya, Haseena, and I were sitting at the table.

"I think so." Surya's voice was so soft, it was almost a whisper. "Every time I think of closing this down, I see the children's faces. I can't bring myself to do it to them."

"That's how I feel," I said.

"I do too, but what if they come back? What if they make good on their threats? They threatened to kill you for this."

"I don't think they will. I think they believed me that there is no school here."

Haseena looked doubtful. "I don't know—"

"They looked like they believed me. They must have done, because they went away without searching the house."

"Maybe we should have a plan, just in case they come again," Surya suggested.

"What kind of plan?'

"Where the children can hide if the house is searched."

We talked late into the night, but by morning, we still had not come up with a plan. I yawned. "Let's pick this up again after school."

"What if they come back today?" Haseena asked.

I stood up and walked over to the sink to wash my face. "I don't think they will."

I was sitting in the front room of the second floor. We called that room the "office" because that was where we handed out assignments to the children. I looked out the window onto the courtyard, and there they were. Four of them this time. All with guns.

Today they didn't knock. They pushed against the door and stormed through the house. Two of them grabbed my hair and pulled me down the stairs and into the courtyard.

"You lied to us!" It was yesterday's man speaking.

"What are you talking about?" I barely recognized my own voice.

He pulled my hair harder and the other man slapped me. "We know who you are. You come from a family of infidels. Your sister was a Communist. Now she's a Christian. You're a Christian too. Lying and heresy run in your blood." The other man slapped me again, shouting about Christianity and teaching English, a language of the corrupt West.

I do not remember all the rest. I remember the pain. I remember the blows. I remember the feeling of fists against my cheek. Of hair being wrenched from my scalp. The sound of a woman crying. The sound of children shrieking. The sound of the men shouting. "Children, go home. If we ever catch any one of you in this house again, we will burn down the house with you in it."

The next thing I knew, I was being pulled to my feet by my hair. "You deserve to die," one of the men said.

"And we will come back for you," the other added. "We will make an example of you. Everyone who finds out what you have done and how you have been punished will learn not to sin against God."

He pushed me and I fell. "We'll be back for you tomorrow!" he called, waving his gun at me.

Surya and Haseena came rushing out. They were crying. They hugged me and helped me to my feet. "Are you all right?" Surya kept asking.

I allowed them to support me as I stumbled into the house.

"Are you okay?" I asked them after they had washed my face and bandaged my head. "Did they hurt you?"

Surya shook her head. "They were really after you. Somehow they knew that you've been the main person running this school, that Haseena and I have only been helping out."

"Are the children okay?"

Surya nodded. "They all went home. They were upset and scared, but they weren't hurt."

My head was throbbing and my face was swollen. Clumps of hair were missing, and my scalp was bleeding. Surya brought me an ice pack.

"How do you think they found out about us?" Haseena asked.

"A neighbor—" Surya began.

"No." I remembered what they had said about the family and related it quickly to Surya and Haseena. "They knew specifics about our family."

Surya's eyes widened. "Do you think—"

I nodded. "There's only one way they could have known all this."

We did not have to say it aloud. Our own relatives had probably betrayed us. Madarjan was living close to the half-cousins and second cousins who had once been Mujihaddin and were now members of the Taliban's Religious Police. Or perhaps it was members of Ibrahim's family, who bore all of us only ill will. Many of them also belonged to the Religious Police. The Taliban who came to close down my school knew too much about our family. They even knew that Sulima had visited churches during her time in Europe—that's why they assumed that she had converted to Christianity and that I was Christian too. They could not have heard all that information from a stranger. And Taliban did not routinely patrol small residential areas such as ours. They usually came only if someone had reported a violation to them.

"We have to leave here," I said.

Surya nodded. "But where will we go?"

"I will go back to my mother's house," Haseena said. "You can both come too."

"No, that wouldn't work." My headache was getting worse. The ice didn't seem to be helping. "They would think of looking there. We can't stay with family."

"So where will you go?"

I racked my brain to think of someone, anyone, who could hide us. "What about Naim's friend, Jabar?"

Surya brought me more ice. "Good idea."

Naim and Jabar had been friends since high school. Jabar was married now and living in another suburb of Kabul. Although he was Naim's friend, he had become a good family friend. Surya and I liked and trusted him. He owned a store a few blocks away from our house. Filled with trepidation—what if the Religious Police saw us walking without a male escort?—we made our way to Jabar's store.

"You must come and stay with my family, until we come up with another plan," Jabar said. He escorted us back home, and we threw some overnight supplies into a suitcase. It did not occur to me to pack identity documents. All I could think of were basics, such as a toothbrush and extra shirts and getting out of the house as fast as possible. I shut the suitcase, then hurried outside. We stood on the doorstep, clinging to one another and crying.

I stepped back and looked at the house that had helped me teach so many wonderful children. Their faces swam before my eyes. Ali, Layli, Zakia, Shula, Efat. I had come to love them, and now I felt as though I was abandoning them. I did not even have the chance to say good-bye.

I didn't have the luxury to reflect for very long. We were in danger every minute we remained. They could come back at any time and make good on their promise to punish me further. We had to leave.

More hugs, kisses, and tears. Then Jabar escorted Haseena to her mother's house. Surya and I followed Jabar to his house.

"You can't stay here very long," Jabar said. "They will probably search the neighborhood houses, looking for you. I live too close by. But I've called my sister. She lives in Now Abad. She said you can stay with her until we can figure out a way to get you out of the country."

Out of the country! What about Madarjan? My brothers and sisters? My friends? How could I leave Haseena, Adela, and all my other friends behind? I started to cry.

Jabar's wife came into the room with a handkerchief and a cup of tea. I dried my tears. "You're right," I said to Jabar. "I won't be safe anywhere in the country. I have to leave."

My head was aching where they had pulled my hair and hit me. Dry blood had crusted on my scalp. My back and legs were swollen and painful where they had dragged me and where I fell when they pushed me. Suddenly, I had no more tears. No more feelings. I was numb. Like a robot, I went through the motions. Drinking tea. Lying down and resting. Smiling at Jabar's children. But a part of me had gone elsewhere. My real self was in hiding.

Surya's presence was comforting, even though she couldn't take the pain away. Jabar's wife was also very nice. So was his sister, whom he took us to after nightfall. "Stay here until I have made arrangements for you," said Jabar. "I know you don't want to leave the country. If I can find a way to get you to the East, where your mother is, I will. Otherwise, I'll have to arrange for you to go to Pakistan."

I tried to thank him, but the words wouldn't come out. He sensed this and waved his hand, as if to brush away my attempts. "Please don't worry. I am glad I can help. I only wish I could help more."

I could not sleep that night. Images of the Taliban police assaulted me like fists. When I wasn't seeing the four men with the guns, I was seeing the sorrowful faces of the children.

Sleep came the next day. I slept much of the time but felt no better when I woke up. The strange, numb feeling continued for three days, until Jabar came back with some information. "I have arranged for you to stay with my friend Khaled in Jalalabad."

"But Jalalabad is full of Taliban police!" I cried.

"I am sorry," Jabar said. "I couldn't work out going to the East. The roads are completely blocked. You'll have to stay in hiding in Jalalabad. I don't think they'll come looking for you there. They would look in your own neighborhood."

"And what happens to me then?"

"Khaled has promised he will help you get out of the country."

I felt a tightening in my chest and a lump forming in my throat. "Thank you," I said.

The numb feeling slowly began to go away during my time with Khaled and his wife, Swita. She was especially loving and nurturing. In her house, I began to heal a little bit. Swita brought us movies, which we watched on the VCR. She played cards with us to distract us and to while away the time. Although I was confined to the inside, Swita was so nice that it took the edge off being unable to go out.

"I've been able to arrange for one of you to go to the United States," Khaled said at the end of two and a half months.

Surya and I exchanged glances. "Only one of us?"

Khaled nodded. "That's all I could organize. Which of you is going?"

"You should go," I said to Surya. "I love you and I wouldn't want you to stay here where it's dangerous."

Surya was shaking her head. "No, you should go. You're younger than I am and I'm responsible for you."

"What does age have to do with it? You're older than I am, so I'm supposed to give you respect."

Surya's voice rose. "You're in more danger than I am. The Taliban didn't threaten to kill me."

"Yes, but you were there too, and so you're in danger," I argued. "I'd never have an easy minute if I knew I was safe and you were still in danger."

"Hala, listen to me." Surya looked deep into my eyes. "I was not threatened. You were. My danger is slight. Yours is great. If I go and something happens to you here, your blood will be on my conscience. Please go. I'll be okay."

I knew that she was right. They had told me they were going to make an example of me. They had not threatened her. In essence, I realized, I had been sentenced to death. And these were people who would carry out their threat.

"I will go," I said. And then I started crying so hard I could say nothing else.

"You are going to be my sister," Khaled told me as we rode the bus to the border. I nodded.

"What if they ask for documents? I left mine behind because—"

"It is better that you have no documents because we do not want them to know who you are," Khaled interrupted. "Documents could only get you in trouble. If I handle this correctly, they will believe that I am your brother and we are visiting relatives in Pakistan."

And if they would not believe him? I was too scared to think what might happen then. My heart was thudding. For the first time in my life, I had no family members to talk to or count on. As dangerous as things had been to this point, I always had someone around—my brothers and sisters, Madarjan, my cousins and aunts—to share the dangers. We supported one another. They gave me advice and comfort. Khaled was certainly courteous and gentlemanly, but he was not family. I felt bereft and frightened.

I watched my home country disappear into the distance. Would I ever see it again? Would I ever see Madarjan, Surya, Haseena, Adela, all my family and beloved friends again? They did not even know I was leaving, and it was too dangerous to try to get a message to them. What if I got caught on the border now? They might kill me, or capture and rape me. And what if I got caught on the airplane without a real passport? What did they do to people who traveled with no documents? And what would America be like? Would I be happy in a new, strange country?

At the same time, I felt a sense of excitement and hope. I would be free! No more burqa. No more hiding or lying or secrecy. I could walk anywhere or do anything. If I made it to the United States, my problems would be over.

We had reached the border. I was covered by the burqa. My head was lowered modestly. I heard Khaled murmuring with the guards. "She is my sister," he said. They nodded and let us go, and soon we were in Pakistan.

One step removed from the Taliban's power—at least, their official power. But even in Pakistan, there were Taliban sympathizers everywhere. Many of the Taliban soldiers had been trained in Pakistan. They had studied at the madressas and still had friends and teachers there. I was not safe even here. I had to hide.

"We are going to Rajab and his wife in Peshawar," Khaled told me as we rode on. "They're my friends. You can stay in their basement for a few days while I finalize arrangements for your ticket."

I tried to thank him then. Now that we were out of Afghanistan, I broke into tears. "*Tashaker*. Thank you." But he shook his head.

"Please. Don't think anything of it. It's the right thing to do."

Rajab and his wife were welcoming and friendly. Perhaps I could have integrated myself into their household. But I felt more comfortable staying in their basement. Nothing should get in my way now. Nothing should stop my safe departure. His wife brought me dinners on a tray. I stayed downstairs, reading books and trying to sleep. I would need to rest. Who knew what lay ahead?

On the third day, Khaled was back. "We're going to the airport," he said, opening the door to his car. "A man is waiting for us there. You don't need to know his name. He has false documents that have been prepared. You are not to show your face, even at the airport. You are to remain covered and look down. He will take care of all the rest."

"What if they ask me about our relationship? Am I supposed to be his wife, his sister—"

He cut me off. "Leave it to him. He has done this before. He will handle the airport officials."

We pulled up to the airport and Khaled got out of the car. He nodded at a man who was standing near the curb. The man came over to us.

"Here she is," Khaled said. He handed the man an envelope. Then he turned to me. "*Khuda hafiz*! Good-bye, Hala. And good luck!"

As I watched him walk away, I blinked back tears. He was taking part of me with him. I had felt alone when I left Afghanistan with him because he was not family. But by now, Khaled had become a friend. It felt as though he had become family. He was also my last connection to home.

For the first time in my life, I was completely on my own.

As Khaled had predicted, the man had no difficulty getting me onto a plane. We walked like any other good Muslim couple, with me a few paces behind him, through the hallways of the airport. I didn't know what airline I was flying. I didn't know what name I was supposed to be using. Nothing. I just followed the man blindly. Like an obedient Muslim woman.

He handed the documents to the official. I don't know what they said to each other. It was common enough for men to handle all transactions for their wives so that the wife wouldn't have communication with a male other than her husband, so this didn't strike the official as unusual. Besides, it was clear that the man had done this before. The official knew him. Few words were exchanged, and the official pointed to a door. I walked through an enclosed corridor onto the plane.

As I watched my country get smaller and smaller, I silently prayed for Madarjan, Surya, and all my family.

And for the country itself.

24

Ladies and gentlemen, we are starting our final descent into JFK Airport, where the local time is nine A.M. In preparation for landing, the captain has asked you to fasten your seat belts. Make sure your seats are in the full upright position and that your tray tables are stowed away for the duration of our flight. . . ."

The announcement, first in English and then in Arabic, woke me from a restless doze. Where was I? I rubbed my eyes and looked around. Wasn't I still in the basement? Why was the basement swaying? Who were all these strange people? Next to me was a man, someone I had never met. How could I be sitting so close to a strange man? I could be flogged, I could be killed—

It took a few minutes for me to get reoriented. I had to remind myself of everything. I was not in Afghanistan. I was not in Pakistan. I had escaped. I was on an Air Egypt plane to the United States. I could sit next to anyone I wanted. I could talk to anyone I wanted, whether the person was a man or a woman. I would never have to hide again. I would never be treated badly by a government again. America was a free country, and I would be free. Soon I would walk around the streets for the first time in three years, and no one would ever lock me indoors again.

When the plane landed, I stood up. My insides were swaying, as though I were still in the air. Pain was pulling at my abdomen and I wanted to throw up. I urgently needed to get to the bathroom.

"Are you all right?" one of the airline attendants asked me. "You look a little pale."

I was embarrassed to tell her about my time of the month, and how sick I always became. "I'm fine."

"Probably just a little airsickness. You'll feel better in no time."

Sulima would take care of me. She would take me to her house. I would lie down in a comfortable bed and rest. By tomorrow, the worst pain would be over. At least I was finally here, in the United States, where my sister would help me and the government would protect me. I gripped the handle of my suitcase and forced my feet to walk down the aisle and into the airport. I followed the other passengers to a series of desks. People in uniforms were asking passengers to display their travel documents.

It was my turn.

A big man with a bristly moustache held out his hand. "Passport? Visa?" His voice sounded bored.

"No passport, no visa." My English was broken and I hoped he would understand. "Asylum."

His face changed. His eyes got smaller and his mouth got tighter. He motioned with his hand. "Come with me."

His voice was different now. It was hard and sharp. What was he angry about?

I followed him down several long hallways to a large room. I saw a series of desks with computer terminals at each desk. At a distance from the desks, I saw rows of metal benches with funny metal rings attached to them in a waiting area. The man pointed first to the waiting area, then to the desks. "Sit here. You're going to talk to one of these people."

I wanted to ask him where the ladies' room was, but he had already walked away. I looked around. Two black men with tired faces were sitting in the row in front of me. A young Chinese woman was twisting a tissue in her hand, obviously trying not to cry. She was so petite, she looked almost like a child. Several people of various racial and ethnic backgrounds were standing in front of the desks, talking to the officers behind them.

I hoped Sulima would turn up soon. My English was not adequate to explain the situation to these people behind the desk. I needed her to help me, and then to take me home and care for me. For a moment, I felt uneasy. Would Sulima know where to find me? But then I put the question out of my mind. Sulima had been living in the United States for many years. She knew the system. She knew her way around the airport. I was sure she would be here any minute to help me out.

I was right . . . and I was wrong. Sulima did come to help me out, but not because she knew the system or her way around the airport. She almost did not find me. Later she told me how she managed to locate me.

A day earlier, Sulima had received a one-minute call that I was arriving at JFK some time the next morning. No further information. Not the airline, not my flight number, not my time of arrival. The smuggler would not know until the last minute which airline official he might succeed in bribing, so he could not inform anyone in advance which airline I would be taking.

Sulima arrived at the airport at five-thirty that morning, after a frantic last-minute scramble to find someone to cover the plant store for her. Bob was lecturing at a conference in Sweden, so she had to make the long drive to New York alone.

When she arrived, she went to the Air Pakistan terminal, assuming that I would probably be on an Air Pakistan flight. An hour passed, then two. She began walking through the airport, searching for me. She wandered from terminal to terminal for three hours. By ten she was exhausted, distraught, and crying.

A uniformed man came over to her. He had a black moustache and an Italian accent. "I work for Customs. I couldn't help noticing you walking around. You look lost. Can I help you?"

Sulima started to cry again. "I'm looking for my sister."

"What flight is she on?"

"That's the problem. I don't know. I got a phone call that she was arriving today, but they didn't tell me her flight number."

"What country is she arriving from?" he asked.

She told him I was arriving from Pakistan, that I was running away from persecution, and that I had taken the first plane that could be arranged for me. When she said this, his face changed. He became serious. "Let me think about this for a minute," he said.

After a few moments of silence, he motioned for her to follow him. While they walked together, he started talking into a radio. His voice was low and Sulima could not understand what he was saying. "I'm not supposed to do this," he said when he had put his radio away. "Immigration doesn't allow relatives to see new arrivals until they've cleared security and been officially admitted to the country. But you're so upset, I'd like to help you out."

They turned a corner and saw another uniformed official who looked like a police officer walking along the hallway toward them. "Here she is," the Customs official told the policeman. He disappeared before Sulima could even thank him. We don't know the name of this compassionate man. We don't know how to thank him. I hope he is reading this book, because then he will know how much his help meant to Sulima and me.

The policeman took Sulima to the room where I was waiting to see the Immigration officials. He opened the door a crack. "Do you see your sister?"

"I haven't seen her for almost twenty years. I hope I recognize her," Sulima said. She looked around the room and had no trouble spotting me. The policeman opened the door and Sulima rushed over to me. We both started to cry. We hugged and hugged and did not want to let go. Eventually, we pulled apart and looked at each other. I had been only nine years old when she left Afghanistan, and I did not remember her very well.

"You still have the same face," she told me in Pashtu. "Just a little more grown up, that's all."

I squeezed her hand tightly as I began to tell her what had happened to me. I had just reached the part about escaping over the Pakistani border when a woman at one of the desks called to me. Sulima and I went over and stood in front of her.

"Where are you from?" The woman's voice was harsh.

"My sister is originally from Afghanistan," Sulima said. "But she just arrived from Pakistan."

"What did she want to know?" I asked Sulima in Pashtu. I understood enough English to figure out what she said, but I wanted to be sure.

Sulima translated, then said to the woman, "My sister does not speak much English. I will translate for her."

The woman frowned. "That's not good enough. We have professional translators. One of them must translate for her. A relative is not allowed. What language does she speak?"

"Pashtu," Sulima answered.

"What's that? I've never heard of it."

"That's the language we speak in Afghanistan."

She consulted a folder. "I don't have any translator who speaks that language.

"She also speaks Dari," Sulima said.

"Never heard of it. We don't have any translators who speak that language either. I'll have to get someone else." She picked up a phone receiver and said something into it, then turned her back to us.

"Where are your travel documents?"

Sulima said, "She has no travel documents. She is seeking asylum."

"What are you running away from?" She sounded as though she didn't believe us.

"My sister is fleeing the Taliban. They want to kill her."

"What does *Tali ban* mean?"

Had I heard right? I thought everyone knew about the Taliban and the terrible things they were doing to women.

"She was teaching girls," Sulima said.

The woman snorted. "And what's wrong with teaching girls?"

I couldn't believe it. Here was someone who worked at the airport with people from other countries but did not know anything about those countries. I heard Sulima talking rapidly in English, and I knew she was explaining the situation in Afghanistan to this ignorant official.

My stomach was hurting more and I needed to go to the bathroom. "Please tell her I need the bathroom," I said to Sulima.

"My sister needs to use the bathroom," Sulima said.

"In a little while. We have some more questions for her."

The pain got even worse and I thought my bladder would burst. "Tell her it's urgent," I whispered.

"My sister—" Sulima began.

"You're not in a position to argue," the woman interrupted. She looked at me. "The sooner you cooperate, the sooner we can decide what to do with you."

What to do with me?

She continued. "We have to decide if we believe your story. If we're not convinced, we will put you on the next plane to wherever you came from."

I started to cry. After everything I had gone through, how could they even think to send me back? This couldn't be happening. This was America. This was where they had the Statue of Liberty. Sulima had told me about it in a letter once. The sign on the statue said everyone was welcome if they had been persecuted in their own country. So maybe this wasn't America after all. Maybe I was still in Pakistan or on the plane, having a bad dream.

But my stomach hurt from both hunger and menstrual cramps. My bladder was screaming. I had been standing in front of the desk for close to an hour. My body was telling me that this was not a dream. I was at the airport in the United States with a cold, unpleasant official. How could I make her understand?

"My sister needs to use the ladies' room," Sulima said firmly in English.

"All right." The woman's voice was impatient. It was a tone I might have taken with a child who was trying to avoid her lessons by pretending to need the bathroom. "But I'll have to get someone to go with her. And she has to be searched first."

She picked up the phone receiver again.

"What's happening to me? Why won't they let me go home with you?"

"I don't know, but I'm going to find out."

I started to cry again. "I'm scared. What if they beat me?"

"This is the United States, not Afghanistan. The American police aren't like the Taliban."

Another female officer arrived. I picked up my suitcase and prepared to follow her.

"You can't take the suitcase with you," she snapped.

"Please," I said. "My suitcase?"

"You can't take your suitcase," she repeated.

"But—" I whispered something to Sulima.

"My sister needs her suitcase," Sulima said firmly.

"Our rules are—"

"She has her period and needs a pad."

I did not know enough English at that time to recognize the word *pad*, but I guessed what she was saying. My face got very red, and I felt like I wanted to die. There were men walking around the room. What if they heard Sulima talk about my female functions?

Sulima and I both started to follow her, but the officer shook her head. "No. The relative cannot come with you."

I was led alone into a small room with tile walls, concrete floor, a metal desk, and a few metal folding chairs. It was cold and dreary.

"Take off your clothes."

My eyes grew wide. This woman, this stranger, wanted me to strip. But why?

She saw me hesitate. Her voice grew louder and more strident. "I said, take off your clothes!"

My fingers fumbled with the buttonholes. I was shivering with cold and with embarrassment as I pulled off my blouse and skirt. Did she want me to remove my underwear too? I thought of the time of month, and my cheeks grew hot. I squeezed my eyes shut so she wouldn't see the tears.

She looked at my feet. "Your socks and shoes too." she said.

I stood there shaking while she ran her hands over my body. My torso, my stomach, and the insides of my thighs. Then she made me turn around and put my hands on the wall, while she repeated her search. Finally she pointed to my clothes. "Get dressed and I'll take you to the bathroom."

She stood outside the door. When I was done, she led me back to the room where Sulima was waiting. A man was standing next to her. He started talking to me in Arabic.

"Who's that?" I asked Sulima.

She made a face. "He's a translator. They think you speak Arabic."

"I do, but not very well. Only enough to pray."

Sulima turned to the woman behind the desk. "I told you my sister doesn't speak Arabic."

"Then we will try someone who speaks Urdu. That's the language they speak in Pakistan."

"She doesn't know Urdu either," Sulima said. I could hear impatience and weariness in her voice. "Please let me translate for her."

After much further arguing, the woman behind the desk gave in and started a barrage of questions. Why had I left Afghanistan? Who were the Taliban? Why did they want to kill me for teaching girls? Why did I not have valid travel documents? Why didn't I want to go back to Pakistan? What was I afraid of? If I didn't have travel documents, how had I gotten onto the plane? And how did I manage to get an education if women were not allowed to go to school? On and on, again and again. She questioned me for over two hours.

I tried to answer as best I could. The process was awkward, because I had to tell everything to Sulima and then wait for her to translate. I was still in pain. My feet ached from standing so long. Why didn't they have chairs in front of these desks? I kept asking them for pain medication, but they refused to give it to me. I hadn't eaten anything since I left Pakistan. I had felt too sad and sick to eat. Now I felt dizzy and nauseated and scared.

After two hours of interrogation, the woman behind the desk reached for the telephone receiver. When she hung up she said to Sulima, "We're finished with this stage of the process. She's not going back on the plane."

Sulima's relief and elation showed in her face. We hugged each other. I asked her to thank the woman, then turned around to leave.

"Where are you going?" The woman's voice was sharp and angry. "You can't just walk out of here!"

Sulima motioned for me to wait. "I don't understand," she said.

"She's come into this country without travel documents. We don't know who she is. We don't know if her story is true. We can't make the decision to let her just walk out of here. Only a judge can make that decision."

"Can't she come home with me while a date is set to see the judge?"

The woman shook her head. "No, she has to go to detention."

Sulima frowned. "Detention? What's that?"

Before the woman could answer, a police officer appeared. "Ma'am, you have to leave," he said to Sulima.

I clung to her. "Please don't go! Don't leave me alone here!"

"You must leave right now," the police officer repeated. His face was as hard as the concrete floor. "I don't know who gave you permission to be back here but you'd better get out in a hurry."

"I don't want to get the nice man who helped me into trouble," Sulima said. "I'd better go." She hugged me hard. "I'll help you. I'll get to the bottom of what's going on. I promise. Meanwhile, you have to be brave."

"I've been brave." I was sobbing loudly now. "I've been strong and I've been brave and I thought I'd be safe and now they're not letting me go and maybe they'll hurt me like the Taliban did."

"Just go on being brave." Sulima's arms were around me. "You believe in God. Pray that he will help you while I try to sort this out."

When I saw her disappear through the door, I started to cry again.

"We're going to take you someplace," the man said. He took a chain out of his pocket and attached it to my feet.

They were chaining me like an animal! They were going to lock me up! The room began to swirl, everything turned gray, my skin felt cold and clammy, and my legs began to buckle. Everything was turning around, spinning faster and faster. I heard someone's far-away voice saying, "She's going down!" Then I felt a thud on the back of my head as I fell onto the lap of a man sitting on one of the metal benches.

When I came to, I was on a stretcher. My vision was blurred and I blinked a few times until my surroundings came into focus. I was in some kind of medical facility. It looked very different from the hospitals in Afghanistan, but I could tell that it was a hospital. Someone was standing next to me. A woman dressed in a white shirt and white pants. A nurse, I guessed. She was talking to the officers who had brought me in.

"You can take her back to the airport. She's going to be all right."

Back to the airport? I tried to sit up. "No!"

I begged for pain medication. At first they refused, then the nurse gave me two pills. When she heard how long it had been since my last meal, she brought me some tea and a sandwich. I realized how hungry I was and ate the food gratefully. When I finished eating, I asked them to call Sulima.

"Who's Sulima?" the nurse asked.

"My sister." I struggled to sit up again and took her phone number from my pocket. "Please say where I am. Please give me phone and I talk."

They tried to call Sulima, but of course, she was not home because she was on her way from New York. I had no idea how far Pittsburgh was from the airport, so I thought she would be home by now.

Sulima's daughter answered the phone and said that her mother was not home.

"Please try store?" I pleaded.

The nurse became irritated. "You're wasting my time," she said.

At that moment, Sulima came running up to me. "How did you find out I was here?" I cried joyfully.

Sulima explained that she had just called home, to tell them that she was on the way. Her daughter had given her the message that I had just called and where I was. "This very kind officer let me come and see you, although she's not really allowed to do that. She told me I could stay, but only for a little while."

Sulima held my hand and we talked. I thought my heart would break when she was finally asked to leave and the officer came back to take me to the airport.

Still in chains, I was led through the corridors of the hospital, out to a police van of some sort, and back to the airport. I found myself in the same waiting area, with the desks and the computers. This time, the officer brought me to a bench at the back of the room. She shackled me to the bench by my ankle. Now I knew what those strange metal circles on the bench were for.

"Please—"

There was no answer. Only the sound of the officer's shoes and the clinking of her keys as she turned to walk away.

I sank onto the bench and leaned my back against it. How long would I be here? When were they coming back for me? What if I fainted again or got sick? Would they help me? And what was going to happen to me next?

I had hardly stopped crying all the way back to the airport, and by now, I was all cried out. Totally spent. My head slumped down onto my shoulder and I closed my eyes.

It was a terrible sleep. The chain was painful. It cut off my circulation, and my foot was numb and icy. The position in which I was chained prevented me from lying down or moving my foot. I had not brought any warm clothes with me, and the metal bench was cold and hard. They had taken my suitcase away, so I could not even take out the lightweight clothes I had. I was shivering and my cramps hurt more than ever. When I finally managed to doze, I saw men standing over me, waving whips. They had beards and turbans but were dressed in the uniforms of American policemen. I awoke with a start. Everything was numb, from the waist down. I tried to move my legs and wiggle my toes to get the blood flow started.

I must have been dozing again when I heard, "Wake up and get moving!"

It was a different police officer. A redheaded man with a long nose.

"What time?" I asked.

"It's three in the morning," he said. "Time to go."

"Go where?"

"To a place where you can rest up. A place where people like you wait to see the judge."

He removed my ankle shackle. I stumbled to my feet and tried to follow him as best as I could. The pins-and-needles feeling in my feet made it hard to walk. He brought me over to another woman, unchained her, and handcuffed us to each other. The handcuff was so large, that it fell off my hand. He tightened some screws and now it fit—too well.

"How long to see judge?"

He shrugged. "Not long. A couple of days, maybe."

A rest home sounded nice. Comforting. Someplace where new-comers like me would be taken care of by people who understood them. I thought of a warm bed, hot soup, and a kindly nurse. Then I would see the judge and he would let me go and live with Sulima. What had happened in the airport had been a terrible mistake. A giant misunderstanding. While I was sleeping, they must have realized their mistake. Now they were correcting it. They were taking me to a place where I belonged.

They put me into a large van, together with two men from Liberia and the woman from Jamaica, my partner in handcuffs. The two men were handcuffed to each other. I strained to see out the window, but it was still dark, and I did not know where we were going. There was a chill in the air. I huddled against the seat to keep warm. Lights winked on and off in the distance as we sped by.

Soon I saw more lights. The car had turned into a parking lot, which was surrounded by a tall chain fence crowned by barbed wire. There was another uniformed officer standing by a gate. The officer driving the car opened his window and said something to the officer at the gate, who waved the car on.

I looked at the building in front of us. It had thick doors and bars on the windows. My stomach heaved violently and I thought I would throw up. This was no rest home. This was a jail!

I had gone from one prison to another.

25

J stumbled out of the van. The handcuffs clinked as the Jamaican woman and I awkwardly tried to move in unison. We were led to a large room. A woman in the corner sat at a small desk.

The officer handed her four slips of paper. "Hala Obaidi and Martha Marston!" she barked.

We stepped forward, and she opened our handcuffs. Then she pointed to a door. "Go into that room."

We followed the direction of her finger. The door to the room had bars on it. When we were through the door, we heard it slam after us. A key turned in the lock.

We were in some kind of holding cell. It was a tiny room, about the same size as the cubicle at the airport where they had searched me. A cement bench was built into one wall. I sat down and looked around.

The room was divided in the middle by a cinderblock partition that came halfway up to the ceiling. I peered over the partition. On the other side stood a toilet and sink. I shuddered. How would I ever get used to this? The top half of whoever sat on that toilet was completely visible to anyone sitting in the other room. Someone standing could probably peek over the wall and see everything.

I shivered and tried to draw my sweater around me, but it was no protection against the unheated room with its stone floor and cement bench. Martha and I exchanged glances. I felt so helpless and so alone. She looked like a nice, caring person, but we did not speak the same language, and there was nothing she could do to help me. I pressed my knuckles to my eyes. I wanted Madarjan.

It was getting colder. I banged on the window. After a few minutes, the lady came to the door. I heard the key turn in the lock, and then she was standing in front of me, scowling.

"What do you want?"

My teeth were chattering. "I'm cold."

"Sorry, there's nothing I can do about that."

She was about to close the door again. "Please, my suitcase?"

"I'm not allowed to let you get anything from your suitcase." She slammed the door again.

An hour went by. I sat huddled on the bench, shivering. I felt the cramps building again in my stomach. I would need to use the toilet after all. And I would have to find some way to get to the feminine pads in my suitcase.

I tapped on the window again. This time it took longer for her to come, and when she did, I could tell she was angrier. "What is it now?"

I pointed to my stomach area. "Period," I said. "Need pad."

She looked extremely annoyed, as if I had gotten my period just to bother her. "I'll see what I can do." Again the door slammed.

She was back a few minutes later. "Follow me." She motioned with her hand.

I followed her into another room, where my suitcase stood among several other pieces of luggage. "Go and take what you need. And hurry."

I took out my pad, as well as a blouse. Though the blouse was thin it would at least provide an extra layer.

When I returned to the cell, I knew I would have to use the bathroom, and put modesty aside.

It was another two hours before we were released from the holding cell. We were taken to a shower area by a different female officer. She ordered us to strip and take a shower. The curtains were flimsy and too small for the shower stall, but the lady insisted on watching us. What did she think we would do? Escape through the drain?

When we were finished, we were given a prison uniform—an ugly orange jumpsuit. Then they took our photograph and attached it to some kind of ID card with a number. I now had a new name and identity. I was prisoner number 427. She handed me a sheet of paper and a booklet. "On the paper, you'll find a list of lawyers. You can call them after your credible fear interview. In the booklet, you'll find the rules of Wackenhut. That is the facility you're in. Make sure you keep them carefully, or you'll be miserable."

As if I wasn't already miserable. I glanced at the book. It was written in English! How was I supposed to know the rules if I didn't understand the language in which they were written? And what was a credible fear interview?

She handed us a pillowcase filled with our prison supplies. I looked inside and saw a blanket, sheet, pillowcase, and two towels. We were also given a toothbrush, toothpaste, comb, soap, three bras, three pairs of underwear, and strange cotton shoes with plastic soles.

We were led to a room with telephones and told we could make one free call. I called Sulima.

When I heard her voice, I burst out crying again. "I'm in jail! It's called Wackenhut. I'm number four-two-seven. They're locking me up! I'm scared. I'm cold. There's no privacy. Please, get me out of here!" The words tumbled out and I couldn't stop them.

Sulima's voice was firm but loving. "You have to calm down, Hala. I will do everything I can to get you released as soon as possible. Just stay strong and don't give up hope. Now let me talk to someone in charge."

I handed the receiver to the officer and heard him explain how she could contact me. I would be allowed to call her collect, but she would not be allowed to call me. If she wanted to reach me, she had to leave a message at the prison office center and I would call her back.

I was sobbing when I hung up the phone. "Come on, we don't have all day," the officer snapped. I followed until we reached a room that looked like a medical clinic. A white-coated doctor stuck her head out. "Next!"

I was ushered into a chilly examination room. The doctor handed me a cup and opened the door to the bathroom. I gathered that they wanted a urine specimen. Fortunately, the door to the bathroom closed this time. Then I was asked to sit on the table while she drew blood, took my blood pressure, and examined my vital signs. When she was done, she wrote something on a paper and handed it to me. "Take this to your sleeping quarters," she said, walking me to the door and sticking her head out. "Next!"

I followed the officer to a dormitory. She unlocked the door. "This is your room." Then she called a guard over. "Here are two new ones," she said, pointing to my Jamaican companion and me.

The guard looked weary and irritated. "Follow me."

Then she led us to our room and pointed to two beds. "Use your linens and make your beds."

I obeyed, then looked around. The sleeping area had six bunk beds, three on either side of the room. The other detainees were still sleeping. Next to the sleeping area was a dayroom, separated from the beds by a cinder block partition reaching halfway to the ceiling. I saw some plastic tables and chairs, and a television that was attached to the wall. In one corner of the dayroom stood a small desk. An officer was leaning over some papers. In the other corner was the bathroom area, consisting of one shower and three toilet stalls. It was separated from the dayroom and sleeping area by another one of those partitions. My heart sank. It was the same kind of setup we had in the holding cell. Anyone could watch us using the bathroom.

It was even worse than I thought, as I discovered the first time I needed the bathroom. The security camera was pointed right at the shower stalls. Here too the curtain did not close properly. Would I have to wash with someone staring through a camera at me?

I sank into bed and covered my face. Had I escaped the Taliban only to come to this cold, friendless place? At least in Afghanistan I had my family and friends. We sustained one another with laughter and love. I could walk freely from one room of my house to another. I could make my bed—or leave it messy. Was this really America?

I felt a light tap on my shoulder. Looking up, I saw a girl not much older than myself. She smiled. "Where from?" she asked in broken English.

"Afghanistan," I replied.

She threw her arms around me and began speaking rapidly in Dari. "It's so wonderful to have someone I can talk to! My name is Nasima."

It was like finding a sister. I introduced myself and asked her about her life. She cried as she told me her story. The Mujihaddin had killed her entire family. They had come and burned the family's house during the night. Nasima had been spared because she was at a friend's house. She had no one left in Afghanistan. Additionally, she felt that if her family had been targeted, she could be next. I never found out the details of how she got out of Afghanistan, but apparently she chose to come to the United States because she had an aunt living in this country.

She was granted asylum on my third day. Although I had known her less than seventy-two hours, I cried. I had lost another piece of home.

It was harder to get to know the other women. For starters, there was a language barrier. Most of us spoke some broken English, but between my limited vocabulary and theirs, it was difficult to communicate. Some were reluctant to share their stories or reasons for being there. Others used sign language and the few English words they knew. Two women from Ghana and one from Uganda were fleeing some type of hideous war. They seemed unfriendly and suspicious at first. I gathered that they had been cruelly treated by white people and that they did not trust me because I was white. Later, when they saw that I meant them no harm, they became friendlier. I didn't understand all they were saying. It seemed that they saw their closest family members being killed or horribly tortured. Two were granted asylum, but one was deported. We all cried when her asylum claim was denied. The terror in her eyes stays with me to this day. And of course, we were crying not only for her but also for ourselves. Each one of us knew that we could be the next one deported.

I became especially friendly with two Pakistani girls. Since I had stayed in Pakistan, I felt a kinship with them. I tried to learn their language. They had both gone through some terrible experience, but neither was willing to talk much about it. So we studied language to pass the time. I also tried to learn English and asked any detainees who knew English to help me.

So I got along with the other detainees, but I was still lonely. There was no one with whom I could share my soul—no human being, that is. I could share only with God.

Prayer became even more important to me now. I started to organize my day around prayer times. I woke up at six, when they brought us breakfast. We did not go back to sleep after breakfast because at seven, when they changed shifts, we had to line up to be counted. We were required to wear our plastic shoes, shirt, and uniform. After roll call, I usually went back to bed until around noon, when we were woken for lunch—unless it was my turn to do cleaning. Then I did my chores first. We were not allowed to sleep through lunch and had to present ourselves in the dayroom whether or not we were hungry. After lunch, I said my short prayer, the second prayer of the day. Then I slept, watched television, talked to the others, and prayed some more.

Dinner was served at five. After dinner I usually prayed, instead of hanging out with the others in the dayroom. Often I spent as much as two to four hours at a time in prayer. During the night, I got up at midnight, went back to sleep, then rose again and then at 2 A.M. If I went to sleep at eleven, I woke up at one. This is called *Ta'ajud*. It is considered especially virtuous to wake up and pray two hours after you have fallen asleep. It is believed that if you do this for several days, God will grant your wishes.

Since there were a few other Muslim women with me, we took turns waking one another up during the night. Two Christian detainees also prayed during the night, so they participated in our group wake-up calls. Sometimes, we would ask the officer on duty to wake us. At first, the officer was cooperative. Then she found out that she was not allowed to wake a prisoner at any time other than for breakfast, or to inform a prisoner that she was being deported. So she refused to help us. But by this time, my body had become accustomed to waking up during the night. I no longer needed anyone to wake me.

I had never before prayed with someone of a different religion. I discovered that although we were all using different words, we were actually doing the same thing. We were appealing to a Higher Power to help us. We were turning our lives over to Him. We were all sisters in suffering and all created by the same God.

My prayer caused some problems. We were required to wear uniforms and were not allowed to wear head coverings. In the Islamic faith, it is traditional for women to cover their hair during prayer. And even when it was not prayer time, I had been covering my hair since I had my dream. But they would not let me wear my veil in prison. "Why should you look different from the other prisoners?" the guard had snapped when I asked. I felt uncomfortable walking around with my hair exposed all the time, but especially during prayer.

I also missed the presence of a prayer rug. Much of prayer is spent kneeling on the floor and bowing down. It is considered disrespectful to kneel on the bare floor, and Muslims always use some kind of floor covering. In our language, it is called *juoy namaz*. If you don't have a specially designed prayer rug available, you spread out whatever clean piece of cloth you can find.

At first, I used my sheet.

"Obaidi! Number four-two-seven! You know you're not allowed to leave your area like a pigsty. Make your bed!"

"But floor cover for prayer."

"Then you won't cover the floor."

I started to cry.

"All right, all right," she said. "I'm not really supposed to do this, but I'll let you have an extra sheet you can use for prayer."

Should I go for more? I tried. "Can—maybe I have two? Another cover hair?"

She scowled but handed me two sheets.

The next guard on duty saw me praying. "Where did you get those extra sheets?" she demanded.

I did not want to get the first guard in trouble, so I simply said, "For prayer."

"Well, you can't have them. No one here gets extra linens. Give them to me right now!"

I asked the imam—the Islamic prison chaplain—to see if he could arrange to have the prison rules changed, just for prayer times. The next time I saw him, I knew right away that they had said no.

"I not understand," I said to the imam. "America land of freedom. But they not let me do my religion."

"I will try again to help you," he promised.

It was the beginning of Ramadan, so it was especially distressing for me to pray without my rug and hair covering. Maybe the awareness of how important Ramadan is to Muslims influenced the authorities, because a few days later, the imam came back. He was holding a small prayer rug and a shawl. "You can use these only when you pray. You can't take them into the dayroom or even use them in your sleeping area unless you are praying."

My schedule changed during Ramadan because Muslims fast during the day and eat only at night. So I skipped breakfast. I wanted spiritual food to nourish my soul, not physical food to nourish my body. (Not that any of the prison food was nourishing. The vegetables, when they came, were always overcooked and limp. The gray "mystery meat" was fatty. The oatmeal was loose and watery. The food was tasteless. It was a diet to make people feel physically sick and mentally punished.) Instead, I prayed during breakfast. Although I had to appear at lunch, I did not eat. I saved the food and ate it either late at night, when eating is permissible, or I gave it to someone else.

The officers generally were nasty. One in particular, a large African American woman named Doris, had it in for me and for some of the other white girls. She gave us double the cleaning while she allowed the black girls to sleep.

One day I had forgotten to take off my shawl. You would think I had murdered someone. "Take that thing off your head!" Doris yelled. Another time I was still praying when they served lunch. "Get off your knees, get your tray, put your food on the table, and then do your prayers. Don't pray on our time."

I wanted to argue. To point out the injustice of it. To ask her why she was treating me so badly. But I did not want to antagonize her further. I saw what happened when people talked back to the guards.

Kim was a Chinese girl who had fled a forced abortion. She had violated China's one-child-per-family rule and become pregnant a second time. She was caught when she was in her fifth month and her belly started to show. They dragged her to the police station, then to the clinic. She was held down while they removed the baby, a boy. I knew all these details because Kim was outspoken and willing to tell her story to anyone. Her English was quite good, and there was no problem understanding her. She often talked about the little boy who died. "He was a baby, not a fetus," she kept saying. "They killed a person." She also talked about her daughter, now living with her mother in China.

Kim was not only outspoken, but also angry. Curse words came easily to her lips. She refused to be pushed around by anyone, including the guards. "I've been treated badly enough in my own country. No one is going to do this to me here."

One day, I was praying. I was so absorbed that I didn't hear the commotion that broke out. I found out later that Kim had started cursing Doris. The next thing I knew, two security guards rushed into our dorm. They grabbed Kim by the arms and dragged her to the segregation cell. I never saw the cell personally—thank God—but other prisoners told me about it. From what I gathered, it looked like the holding cell I was in when I had first arrived. The prisoner was chained to the wall by her wrists and ankles. There was no bed, not even a mattress or a blanket. The room was cold. There was a toilet in the cell, but in order to use it, the prisoner had to call a guard. Of course, the guard could see her using the bathroom over the partition.

Kim was there for an entire week. Then they transferred her to another dorm. I don't know what happened to her.

After seeing what happened to Kim, I was determined to be a good girl and not cause any trouble.

Only one person could make me laugh. Her name was Marguerite. We called her Maggie. She was fleeing some type of domestic violence situation in France, but originally she was from Nigeria. She didn't talk much about her own problems. Instead, she was the prison clown.

She would grab my hand. "Come on and dance with me, honey!" Then she would twirl me around. "You gonna let them get to you? Wheee!"

She would take words of popular songs and adapt them to prison life. I don't remember any specific songs because my language skills were poor and I wasn't familiar with the songs she was imitating. But I know they were funny at the time. Sometimes she would lead us in calisthenics. "Now, move your butts, ladies. One, two, three, four, one, two, three, four. No, don't just stand there. Let's run. Ready? Up and down the room. Here we go!"

She was the only black inmate that Doris did not like. "You're crazy," Doris said to her flatly.

Maggie's face got serious. "Sure I'm crazy. And you know what? You're an officer. That's why you're not crazy. Believe me, if you was in here, you'd be crazy too."

Maggie was streetwise. She had been in Wackenhut for a long time and she knew all the ropes and procedures. She was invaluable in helping me understand some of what was going on.

"You know, you're one of the lucky ones," she said. "They could have sent you right back at the airport."

"No trial? On TV, program about America. There is judge. At big desk. He bang with hammer—"

She started to laugh. "Only Americans can be sure of seeing a judge. Not us. We're foreigners. So we're nobody. We don't got the same rights as Americans. The officers at the airport are your judges when you get off that plane. They don't like you and wham!" She banged her hand on the table. "You're back on the plane to wherever you came from."

I later found out that this process is called "expedited removal." The Immigration officials at the airport can decide the fate of people like me who do not have valid travel documents. If the person specifically requests asylum, they are supposed to pass the case along to other authorities, as they did with me. But if the person does not use the word *asylum* or explain the situation properly—and of course, many foreigners do not speak enough English to know the word *asylum* or express themselves adequately—then these airport officials can send the person home. And many of these immigration officials at the airport send people back anyway, often due to whim, prejudice, or just plain ignorance. I shudder to think what would have happened to me if Sulima had not been there to translate and explain my situation.

Nor did we have any way to appeal our treatment in jail. Abusive guards, nasty officers—we had to put up with whatever they dished out.

Once when Sulima was visiting, she saw how the guards spoke to me. "I must talk to them about this. It's outrageous!" But I begged her not to. I was afraid I might get into more trouble. "If you challenge them, they will make life terrible for me here." Sulima is a brave and outspoken person. She always sticks up for someone who is being mistreated. It must have been maddening for her to see me treated like this and not explode.

She told me later that she did confront one of the guards after I had been taken back to my room.

"Why do you treat these people like criminals?"

"Listen, lady. They're in jail. As far as I'm concerned, they're all criminals."

Women of all colors and religions came and went. It was like a carousel of suffering. We felt like throwing a party every time someone was granted asylum. But when someone's request was denied, we all felt the blow as if it were happening to us.

The question of whether we would be granted asylum hung over us at all times. Each of us was at a different point in our legal proceedings. For all of us, healing from the wounds inflicted by our own governments was almost impossible. We felt no safety. We were in a harsh and alien world. And we had been caught completely off guard. We had come to the United States with high expectations. Of course, we had expected that we would get into some kind of trouble for traveling without proper documents. We thought we would probably have to deal with some kind of legal authority. But it never occurred to any of us that we might end up in jail. All of us came to the United States with preconceptions about what America represented. I know that when I was in Afghanistan, I thought people in America were treated equally. But when I came here, I found out that this wasn't true. Bad things happen to people who come from other countries. You can be put into jail for no reason other than leaving your country to save your life.

So once again, I lived by looking only at the present moment. Hope was too dangerous. I could be denied asylum. I could be sent back. It was better to focus on getting through each day. Better not to think about tomorrow. So I spent time with the other detainees. I worked on my English. I prayed. I did my chores. And I wrote poetry. Only on paper could I dare to express how lost and hopeless I really felt.

"Stranger"

I am the dry leaf on a garden branch
Where no dream passes, only the wind
Fluttering, it clings to its flimsy stem
But its struggle for life does not succeed

I am the endless desert spread beneath the sun
No passers-by, except the caravan of sorrow
The sun of hopelessness burns fissures so deep
That even the tears of clouds cannot heal

I am the bereft bird that from fear of sorrow
Buries its head silently under its wing
From the depth of hopelessness or the peak of grief
Soundlessly cries for itself

I am the unsung poem hidden in a heart
That, from fear of silence cannot begin
It knows no one will heed its words
And it chooses to remain voiceless

26

During all this time, my asylum claim was making its way through the complicated bureaucratic immigration system. It started with an interview with an immigration officer two days after my arrival at Wackenhut. I later found out that this is called a "credible fear" interview. It is designed to let the Immigration and Naturalization Service—the INS—know whether the person has good reason to be afraid of returning to his or her own country.

I had been told that I would be allowed to have someone of my choosing present for this interview, and of course, I chose Sulima. But when I was led into the room, I was surprised to see another woman standing with her.

"Who's that?" I asked.

Sulima explained that this was a lawyer. She did not get far in explaining why the lawyer was here, and how the authorities had allowed her to bring someone else with her—after all, I was allowed to request only one person—because the asylum officer came into the room and said it was time to get started.

Later, she told me the story. After returning from the airport, Sulima began calling friends to find out about how to get a relative out of detention. One friend referred her to the Lawyers Committee for Human Rights. She was so anxious to meet with a lawyer as soon as possible that she hung up the phone and immediately drove back to New York, where the organization's office is located. She slept in her car outside the office, so as to be there at 9 A.M. when they opened. It must have been very cold and uncomfortable for her. To this day I am awed by how much she did for me.

The Lawyers Committee for Human Rights agreed to help out. They found out when my credible fear interview would be held. Then they sent a lawyer—the woman standing next to Sulima now—to accompany her. Somehow, Sulima had managed to convince the authorities to allow an extra person to be present at the interview.

But I didn't know any of this at the time. The official was talking, and I had to pay attention.

He explained that I had to tell my story and answer some questions. They were giving me a Farsi translator, who provided his services via a speakerphone on the desk. They were providing me with a Farsi translator because Farsi is similar to Dari and they did not have a Dari or Pashtu translator available.

I found out later from Maggie that I was one of the fortunate ones. I knew what a phone was. There were people from underdeveloped areas of the world who had never seen a phone in their lives. The small cell and strange object terrified them. They were convinced that this was some new instrument of torture.

We started. I was asked my name, my address in Afghanistan, and some other basic information. Then the questions became more complicated. I started to explain the situation in Afghanistan with the Taliban. "When the Taliban came to power, women had to stay inside." But before I could even finish my sentence, the translator jumped in with a question of his own. "I thought women were allowed to go out with a male relative."

"Well, yes. Women were allowed to go out with a male relative," I said. "But not just any male relative. Only a close one, like a husband or son—"

He finished my sentence. "—or brother or father or cousin."

"No, not cousins," I corrected him.

The interview was excruciatingly slow. It would have been difficult in the best of circumstances, because working through a translator always slows down a conversation. But the translator kept interrupting. I kept having to explain what I really meant.

"Please," the officer said to the translator. "Let her finish her statement without interrupting. Your job is to translate, not to ask questions or make comments."

We continued.

I started to explain the law that women who went out had to wear a burqa. *Burqa* is actually an Arabic word that has fallen into common use. But in our colloquial Dari language, it is called a *chadari*. In Afghanistan, the word *chadari* refers to the full burqa. But in Iran, where this translator came from, *chadari* means *chador*—the veil that covers the head and shoulders, but not the face.

When the translator explained the word *chadari* to the officer, I realized that he was not explaining it correctly. This was clear, even though my English was limited. Sulima noticed too, of course. She immediately spoke up.

"That's not what a *chadari* is in Afghanistan," she broke in. She described the *burqa*.

The translator began to argue, but Sulima held her ground. This happened several times. The Farsi dialect spoken in Iran is slightly different from the Dari dialect spoken in Afghanistan. Either the translator was not familiar with our idioms, or he was too impatient to hear my full sentence. Finally the officer got fed up.

"Thank you for your services," he told the man on the phone, "but they are no longer needed." He turned to Sulima. "Please translate for your sister."

What a lovely man he was! Kindly and pleasant. And clearly filled with sadness about what I was telling him. Many times during my story, he frowned and said "that's terrible" or "I'm sorry this happened to you."

"You believe me?" I asked him when I was done. "I can go?"

"I do believe you. And if it were up to me, I would open the door and let you out right now." He sighed and shook his head. "But my job is to ask you questions, not to make decisions. I have written down everything you told me. I will pass it along to other people. They will make this decision."

Sulima asked, "Does it have to show in the document you are writing that I was the one who translated, since a relative is not allowed to do that?"

He smiled at Sulima. "We did use the telephone interpreter, didn't we? Besides, your translation was more accurate than his." Then he smiled at me. "You're very fortunate to have a sister who is so proactive and willing to help you out."

"And we are fortunate," Sulima said, "to have an officer as nice as you."

I wholeheartedly agreed. I thanked him as well. "Many people here not nice," I said. "You nice and helpful. Thank you."

Two days after the credible fear interview, I received a formal document. An immigration officer came and handed it to me personally.

The letter was dated the day after my interview. It informed me that I was in something called Removal Proceedings. I sounded out the words at the top of the page. "Notice to Appear." Maggie read me the rest. She explained the difficult words.

You are an arriving alien. The Service alleges that:

1. You are not a citizen or national of the United States.

2. You are a native of Afghanistan and a citizen of Afghanistan.

3. You did not then possess or present a valid immigration visa, reentry permit, border crossing identification card, or other valid entry documents.

4. On the basis of the foregoing, it is charged that you are subject to removal from the United States pursuant to the following provision(s) of law:

I asked Maggie to stop reading the intricate laws that followed. The language was difficult, and anyway, I was far too distressed to listen. Attached to the back of the document was a written transcript of my interview at the airport and my credible fear interview.

"Don't worry," Maggie said, giving me a hug. "This is good news. It means you passed your credible fear interview! Now you can see a judge and ask for asylum." She hugged me again. "Just make sure you get a good lawyer. Ask your sister to go through the list they gave you when you first came here."

But Sulima had already retained a lawyer from the Lawyers Committee for Human Rights.

"How about the money?" I asked her. "I don't want you to spend a lot of money. Some of the lawyers on my list are free."

"These people are free too," Sulima told me. "The lady who arranged for me to be at your credible fear interview is from the same organization. So is the lawyer who came with me. But she won't be your lawyer. Some other volunteer lawyer who works with the organization will come and see you."

A week later, two lawyers showed up. Sulima was with them, serving as the translator. Kalpana Vajramati came from an Indian family but her mother was American. She was familiar with Eastern culture, which helped me in telling my story. Lenore Smith was a beautiful, blonde American woman, dressed neatly in a business suit. She looked professional, but under her business suit beat a warm heart and a wealth of caring and compassion. We sat together in the special cubicle they have for prisoners to consult with their lawyers. We shook hands a little awkwardly. Then Kalpana pulled out a chair for me to sit on. Lenore opened her briefcase and took out a yellow legal pad and a pen.

"Thank you for coming," I said. My English sounded stilted. I wondered if I was really conveying to them how grateful I felt that they were taking my case for free. I asked Sulima to tell them.

I was nervous at first, and it showed. Would I be able to make them understand what happened to me, even with a translator? "I was—I mean, in my country." I took a breath and started again. It was not going very well.

Lenore put her hand on my arm. "Just take your time and don't worry."

Slowly, painfully, I told my story. They took notes. They asked questions. They talked to each other, then asked more questions. Did I have any documentation from home to show that the Taliban were after me? I explained as best as I could that it didn't work that way. Did I have a birth certificate, or any other official papers to prove who I was? I explained that I had fled without being able to gather any documents together. Sometimes they seemed puzzled while I explained how things were in my home country. But Sulima helped them to understand and she filled in missing information.

By the end of the interview, I was feeling much better. These people were on my side. When they hugged me, I knew I had made two new friends.

Kalpana stood up to leave. "We'll come back to clarify any further questions."

They were back later that week with a list of questions. Many were about my family members. Apparently it was important for them to understand who everyone was. They also wanted to know what role, if any, my family had played in my life and in the running of my school. Considering the size of my family, this was no easy task.

"Now tell me again, which of your brothers is a doctor? And which one is an engineer? You say your sister is a veterinarian? Is that a common profession in your country? I see, and where are they living now?"

On their next visit, they had some news. "Your first court appearance has been scheduled for next week," Kalpana said.

I immediately felt my stomach tighten. "What do I to do in court?"

"This is a preliminary appearance. It's called a Master Calendar Hearing. That means no decisions will be made at this first court date. The purpose is for us to introduce ourselves to the judge and for the judge to see you in person and to take care of some preliminary matters. Then the judge will set a date for your next appearance."

"Sulima too?" I asked

Kalpana shook her head. "They are much stricter in a court than they were at your credible fear interview. They won't let her be there."

It was easy for them to say don't worry. I was very nervous in court. It was scary to see a judge and to know that my entire future lay in the hands of this one person. But I was not as nervous as I thought I would be. Maybe that's because I had no real role to play, except to appear.

I listened to Lenore explain that she and Kalpana were pro bono attorneys. I later found out that this meant they were taking my case for free. She explained that they had just met me and were still studying my case. Then she told him that I was requesting asylum.

The judge nodded and opened a calendar. They set a date for the second Master Calendar Hearing, two weeks later. The judge told them to bring some preliminary documents to substantiate my case.

"What next court for?" I asked after we had left the courtroom. "Does judge decide asylum?"

Lenore shook her head. "An asylum claim has to be filed in person, in court. It can't be mailed. At the next hearing, we will formally file your claim for asylum. Then a date will be set for your trial."

"What is affi—affy Davids and letters?"

Kalpana laughed. "The word is *affidavit*. This is a legal document where someone makes a statement. You are going to tell us your complete story, starting with your childhood. We will write it down. We're going to get Sulima to tell the story of your family. We're going to contact Husna and Gula and have them tell their stories as well. If their stories support your statements, as I'm sure they will, this will help the judge to believe that you are telling the truth."

"What letters did judge talk about?"

"If there are any letters from your family that describe the situation, or refer to you—let's say, a letter from your mom to your sister saying how proud she is that you were accepted to medical school. Something like that."

I had tried to be brave, but now I started to cry. "Do I stay in prison?"

"We will try to arrange for parole," Lenore said.

"What is parole?"

"They let you go free, but you haven't been given asylum yet. You still have to come back to court."

I dried my eyes. "I don't have to stay in jail?"

She held up her hand. "Whoa there. Don't get your hopes up. Most people in your situation don't get paroled. The INS can be very difficult that way."

"Even when person have relative? And can live with relative? Like I have Sulima? That not make good sense."

Lenore's face darkened. "The whole system makes no sense. There is no good reason for people like you to be locked up, for my tax dollars to pay for you to be in jail if you could be living with your sister, who is a U.S. citizen. That's why I'm doing this work. To help you, and others like you."

I squeezed her hand. But I still had one more question.

"Why they afraid?"

"They're afraid you'll run away and not go to your hearing," Lenore replied.

I started to laugh. "That crazy! I do not know country. My English no good. I have to hide. If I want to hide, I stay in my own country."

Lenore laughed too. "You're a lot more sensible than they are." Then she sighed. "We're not going to change the laws overnight. But we can help you."

"Does today judge decide parole?"

Kalpana shook her head. "It's up to the district on deportation. Believe me, they're not as fair as the judge and they don't have the understanding of your asylum claim. And if they deny your claim, you can't appeal to the judge. But even if you don't get paroled, don't worry. It doesn't mean anything about your chances of winning this case."

My formal application for asylum was submitted at my second Master Calendar Hearing, which was held a few weeks later.

My request for parole was denied. "I'm sorry," she said. "But there's no appeal to a judge about parole. In this situation, the INS acts as judge, prosecutor, and jailer. There's really nothing we can do about it."

But Sulima does not take no for an answer. She is a strong, stubborn person. She allows nothing to stop her in her quest for justice. She worked tirelessly. Aside from collecting the documents for my asylum application, she did everything she could to get me paroled. She went to her local members of Congress. She urged them to put pressure on the INS to give me parole and grant me asylum. She contacted a television station, and a reporter came to Wackenhut to interview me. She contacted the Vera Center for Justice.

I think that Sulima's hard work was responsible for my parole. I bet it also had something to do with the relatively quick and efficient handling of my case. Most of the other detainees were not treated so well. Some had been in prison for several years. They were still awaiting final trial dates and parole.

It started with a dream.

The first was not my own dream. It was Marina's dream. She was one of my Christian partners in prayer. She came over to me during the second week of my third month of detention.

"Last night when I was sleeping, I heard the voice of God. He told me that He has answered your prayers. You will be released."

Oh, how I wanted to believe her. Could I trust her dream? She spoke with such confidence. But maybe it was just her good heart talking. Maybe she was simply having a wish-fulfillment dream because she so badly wanted my release.

But the following week, I had a dream.

I am in Kabul, outside the house where I grew up. It is springtime. The rosebushes are blooming. I feel the sun on my face. I look up, and suddenly, I am flying. The trees beneath me are a rich green color and are surrounded by bright red roses. I am on my way to visit Husna. I feel safe and confident. I am happy. I am free!

The feelings of hope and happiness lingered long after I woke up. I believed—and still believe—that God sent that dream to give me hope. My religion teaches that if we pray with sincere faith in our hearts, we will be given a sign before a miracle happens. My dream was that sign. The green colors represent happiness, faith, regeneration, and good luck. Red symbolizes prosperity and honor. Flying symbolizes freedom and reaching for the heavens.

For the first time since my arrival at Wackenhut, I allowed myself to think of the future and to hope. Something good was about to happen.

I was given parole one week after my dream.

I will never forget the day I was informed that I had been paroled. My lawyers had come to see me to work on the draft of my affidavit for the judge. Sulima came with them as translator. She was always delighted for an excuse to come visit. She willingly spent all those hours in the car in order to see me.

We were sitting around the table. It was January 1999. Ramadan. I was fasting, but Lenore, Kalpana, and Sulima had sandwiches and coffee. Suddenly the door opened. An officer came in.

"Who is the lawyer?"

"I am," Lenore answered.

"So am I," Kalpana added.

"And who is the sister?"

"I am," Sulima said.

He put an official-looking document in front of Sulima. My heart stopped. She had been coming to do translation, and now we were in trouble because she was my sister.

"You have one hour to leave," the officer was saying.

Oh no. Sulima was being thrown out! We were in trouble after all.

Then Sulima screamed, "They're letting her out!" She jumped up and threw her arms around me. The coffee spilled all over the papers. Lenore and Kalpana hugged each other. They ran over to hug Sulima and me. We were hugging and crying and laughing when the officer repeated himself. "I said, you have to be out of here in an hour."

Lenore and Kalpana stayed behind to mop up the coffee while I went to the dorm to say good-bye. I saw in the eyes of the other detainees the same mixture of joy for me and fear for themselves that I had also felt when others had left. I left amid hugs and kisses and tears.

"Your dream was right," I said to Marina.

"I never doubted it," she answered.

"I will pray for your release," I promised her. And indeed, she was given asylum three weeks after I was paroled.

"Don't forget us!" Maggie called. She was wiping her eyes.

As if I could forget any of them, especially Maggie.

When I left the dorm, the officer returned my suitcase to me. "Go and change into your clothes."

For the first time in three months, and fourteen days, I was wearing normal clothes again. No prison uniform. No burqa. Just regular clothes.

Lenore greeted me with a hug. "Look at you! You're so pretty in clothes."

Kalpana nudged Lenore with her elbow. "She was pretty in her uniform too, you know."

"Do you want to go out to dinner?" Lenore asked as we walked to the car.

Out to a restaurant? I had not been out to a restaurant since before the Mujihaddin came to power. This was luxury. "Oh, yes!"

"Shall we call a taxi?" Lenore asked. "Kalpana and I don't have our car here. We came by cab."

"Why bother?" Sulima said. "My car is right here in the parking lot."

We opened the door to Sulima's car. An avalanche of stuff came tumbling out. There were papers, mostly about my case. There were candy wrappers. Books. Gardening tools. Fertilizer. Seeds, bulbs, bags of potting soil, and a bag of potatoes that Sulima had bought to cook for the family tonight.

Lenore burst out laughing. "What do you do, grow potatoes in your car?"

We shoveled the contents of the car into the trunk and pushed it shut. Then we drove to the restaurant.

I looked out of the car window. I could not believe it. The sight of people walking free and unafraid dazzled me. I was overwhelmed and almost awed by the neon lights of the stores. I opened the window, even though it was cold, and breathed in the fresh air. I gawked at women without burqas, just walking around the streets. I stared at men and women who were walking hand in hand. I was filled with wonder and gratitude at the freedom. The beauty. The utter vastness of it all.

We ate at a Middle Eastern restaurant in Manhattan. I had my first cup of tea in three months and fourteen days. After the prison food, it was wonderful to be eating tasty, nutritious food again, especially foods like lamb and rice, which we also ate at home in Afghanistan. I could not believe that I could actually choose my food again. I could eat on pretty dishes instead of the plastic tray with four compartments that we used in prison. All around us, people were chatting and enjoying their dinner. They did not know how fortunate they were to have this freedom. To them, this was just an ordinary night out. To me it was a banquet.

It was starting to snow by the time dinner was over. "I was hoping to take you to see the Empire State Building," Kalpana said regretfully. "But you've got a long drive ahead, and the weather might get worse."

"Plus, she doesn't have warm clothes," Sulima added. She put her arm around my shoulder.

"What I can't get over is the amazing timing of this," Sulima said to me in the car. "I had driven all these hours to meet you and your lawyers, and it just happened to coincide with the day they decided to parole you. Let's say it had been tomorrow or the next day. I would have had to drive all the way back. This way, I was right on the spot."

"It's not coincidence," I said. "When God wants to perform a miracle, He really does it right."

My final court appearance took place fifteen days after I was paroled. I was quiet and withdrawn during the long drive to New York. I had been fasting and praying even though Ramadan was over. I felt weak and my stomach was tied in knots. What if the judge took away this new, glorious freedom I had just found? What if he made me go back to Afghanistan?

I was especially nervous because the attorney for the INS had a reputation for being nasty to asylum seekers. "Watch out for her,"

Maggie had warned me. "When you're in the hole as long as I am, you hear about all these creeps. Just don't let her rattle you. She might yell at you, implying that you were lying, or trying to rob the American people, or something. She'll ask questions to trip you up. You know. Were the people who hurt you driving a blue car or a green car? What do you mean you don't remember?"

"They weren't driving," I said.

She laughed. "That was just an example, silly. She'll pick apart every detail of your story—dumb questions about things that people don't remember when they are trying to run for their lives. Then she'll make you out like you're lying because you can't remember. Don't let her get to you, kid."

After we all filed in and got settled, Lenore rose to make an opening statement. After introducing herself and Kalpana she said, "Asylum can be granted on the basis of a well-founded fear of persecution on account of political opinions, religions beliefs, family membership, or gender. I contend that all four are applicable here."

She looked from me to the judge, then continued. "Ms. Obaidi believed that women's education was not wrong and disagreed with Taliban policy to restrict women from schooling. She was accused of having Christian orientation by the Taliban when they came to shut down her school. The Mujihaddin destroyed the family home in Kabul because her older sister was involved with the women's right movement and had Communist affiliations. Also because all the children in the family had received some form of higher education and were professionals. And finally, the Taliban imposed harsh restrictions on women. Ms. Obaidi was virtually a prisoner in her own home. Driven from medical school and deprived of a career, deprived of freedom and medical care at risk of extreme punishment, she qualifies to be considered someone persecuted on account of gender."

When Lenore had finished her opening statement, she informed the court as to the order of witnesses to be called and documents included in the fat legal submission she had prepared. "Please note the affidavits from Ms. Obaidi's sisters and letters from other Afghan family members." Sulima, Husna, and Gula had all submitted affidavits. So had several experts from human rights organizations, such as Human Rights Watch. There were articles about Taliban policy and Afghan history and a stack of letters from family members that made mention of me—newsy family letters from Gula to Husna, or from Naim to Sulima describing what everyone was up to—including my graduation from high school and my attendance at medical school.

When she had completed her introductory statement, she gestured toward me again. "Thank you. Now we would like to call our first witness, Hala Obaidi, to testify."

My heart was beating so fast, I was sure the judge would hear the thumping noise and would throw me out of the courtroom. But Lenore smiled at me.

"State your name," the judge said to me.

"Hala Obaidi," I answered immediately.

The judge frowned. "I know that you understand some English and that you have even learned to speak some English. But you must wait for the translator to tell you what I said. That's the law."

"Okay. Sorry," I said.

He shook his head. "You did it again. You were supposed to wait for the translator to translate what I just said."

I nodded, and Lenore started going through the questions we had reviewed. Name. Country of origin. Citizenship. Age. Level of education. I was starting to relax. Then I began answering questions about the Mujihaddin and the Taliban. I explained my reasons for fleeing, and my fear of returning.

After a few questions, I began to realize that the translator was taking liberties with my statement. He was embellishing my statements and improvising, based on his own knowledge of Afghanistan. Here we go again, I thought.

I was explaining that I believed some of my own distant relatives had informed the Taliban about my secret school.

"She says, 'my family may have told the Taliban about my secret school, or maybe a neighbor noticed the children because houses in Afghanistan are very close to one another.'"

"That's not what I said!" I told him. We argued back and forth until he gave the judge an exact translation of what I had said.

A few minutes later, I said that the men had hit me with their hands and fists. When he translated, he added that they had also hit me with metal cables.

"That's not how it happened," I corrected him.

"But I know that many women have been hit with cables," he argued.

"Yes, but that's not what happened to me."

When he repeated his statement, I turned to Lenore. I tried to signal to her with my eyes that the translator was messing up. But she shook her head. I understood her to mean that I should simply stay with the process, even if it meant correcting him.

I did the best I could, and eventually I had given a coherent and correct statement.

Now it was time for the INS attorney to question at me. I braced myself for her trick questions. Lenore and Kalpana had prepared me for the type of questions I might be asked. For example, "You say you were in medical school. Describe the digestive process, using appropriate medical terminology." Or "If you are really from Afghanistan as you claim, then why are you using a Farsi translator? Farsi is spoken in Iran, not Afghanistan." I had my answers ready for the trick questions I knew, but what about the trick questions for which Lenore and Kalpana could not prepare me?

It was her reaction that I was most unprepared for. She was crying! This woman, who had struck fear into the hearts of so many other asylum seekers, was crying for me. Then she dried her eyes and asked a series of basic questions. Name, address in Afghanistan, family members, why I was fleeing. She questioned me extensively about differences in names. Why was I referring to my brother as Naim, when the legal documents called him AbdelNaim? I explained the complicated Afghan naming system.

Finally, she asked me to list the names of some of my family members. When she asked me which uncle Sulima lived with in college, I answered, Uncle Nayk. She smiled and said she was done. Lenore flashed me a "thumbs-up" sign. Now Sulima was called into the room.

She was asked the same series of questions—her history, reasons for leaving Afghanistan, and current circumstances. Then specifics about the political situation in Afghanistan. Then questions about me. When Lenore was done, the INS attorney asked Sulima a barrage of questions.

"What was the name of the uncle you lived with when you were in college?"

"His name was Nayk-Mohammed."

I was staring. No one had ever called him Nayk-Mohammed in front of me. Sulima caught my eye and added, "But the children all called him Uncle Nayk, which was his nickname in the family."

"How did you know that this really was Hala?" the INS attorney asked. "After all, you had not seen her for over twenty years."

What a ridiculous question! Sulima started to laugh. Then my lawyers began to laugh. Then the INS lawyer started laughing. I was worried that the judge would get angry, but then I saw his face. Even the judge was smiling.

The INS lawyer got serious again. "I have no further questions."

Lenore rose to give her closing statement. "Ms. Obaidi has met the burden of proof and she is entitled to political asylum." The passion and love in her voice did not seem to match the carefully worded statement with its legal terminology. "Discretionary factors weigh heavily in favor of granting asylum. Ms. Obaidi is an educated young woman who will undoubtedly become a productive member of American society. She never participated in the persecution of another human being in Afghanistan. Rather, she risked her life to support human rights for women by educating girls, in contravention of Taliban dictates." Lenore tossed her hair back as she reached her conclusion. "For the foregoing reasons, we respectfully ask that you grant Hala Obaidi's application for political asylum."

I had been warned by my friends at Wackenhut that most cases take several hours. My court appearance lasted only an hour and twenty minutes. Then the judge retired to his chambers to think about it.

"It was so short. Does that mean anything bad?" I asked Lenore anxiously.

She laughed. "Relax, Hala. I have a good feeling about this."

The INS attorney overheard us. She walked over to the table where we were sitting. Her expression was reassuring. "Don't worry. Everything will be fine."

When the judge came out, my heart was beating quickly. Lenore drew me a little smiley face on her legal pad.

"Petition for asylum has been granted!" the judge announced.

It was real. God had not let me down. I was a bird released from her cage, soaring over the green trees, happy and free.

27

I live with Sulima and her family now. There are no words to express how much I love them and how grateful I am to be here. Sulima's daughters are like my own siblings. We giggle together, as my sisters and I used to do. And her husband, Bob, is a generous and caring person. He has been a real friend and support to me. He also has two wonderful sons from his first marriage, who have become like brothers. After being in prison, being among family again feels wonderful.

But there have also been many adjustments. My first weeks here were filled with joy and wonder, but also with a great deal of confusion, even about simple things. The array of choices was overwhelming. It had been years since I had last shopped for clothes. We did not need new outfits to wear under our burqas, even if we could have afforded to buy them. How did one choose clothing from amid such an enormous selection? What were American fashions? And even once I had finally selected some clothes, the choices continued to bewilder me. Should I wear the blue sweater or the red? How did you put on makeup? What hairstyle should I choose? For so many years I had been restricted in what I could wear, first by the Taliban and then in Wackenhut. I also had not been allowed to use cosmetics. I felt as though I was from another planet.

Just walking through the streets was terrifying, although it was also exhilarating. I kept looking for the bearded men with the familiar white uniform to turn the corner and chase me with their whips. Every time an American woman passed me on the street, my heart skipped a beat. Her hair was showing. Didn't she know she was in terrible danger, walking around like that? Then I had to remind myself. We were not in Afghanistan. There were no Taliban here.

I had many choices to make. The hardest was giving up my dream of becoming a doctor. Where would the money for medical school come from? And even if I had the money, I would not be finished for another ten years. I would be almost forty before I could emerge from behind the textbooks and start enjoying life. I did not want to postpone my life further. Too many years had already been lost. So I enrolled in a community college. I registered for a broad base of general courses. Hopefully, the way would become clear as I got more accustomed to the country and to my freedom.

I started classes. I worked on my English language skills. I experimented with taking various types of courses, such as poetry, history, and sociology. The only class I dropped was a communications class. It involved giving speeches. I was self-conscious about my English and also shy. Coming from a society ruled by the Taliban, the idea of getting up in front of a group of people to make a speech was daunting.

I am still not sure what career I will pursue when I have finished college. I am taking only three courses each semester because I am also working in Sulima's store. It is hard to balance a full-time job and a full schedule of classes. And of course I want to help Sulima out because she has been so good to me. Her small flower store has been expanded into a greenhouse. It is much larger than a one-person-behind-the-counter establishment.

During those first weeks, I allowed myself to mourn my losses—something I did not have the luxury to do in Afghanistan, or in prison. I cried with longing for Madarjan, for Surya, for Husna and Gula, for Haseena and Adela, and for the country I loved and lost. Nights were particularly difficult. Taliban men and American guards rode roughshod through my dreams. It was months before I got a full night's sleep. I saw the faces of the children—Ali, Efat, Layli, Zakia, Shula and the others. Sometimes they looked happy and free. I would see them bending over their schoolbooks or raising their hand to ask a question. But sometimes they looked reproachful. I was sure they were upset with me for abandoning them. Even though I knew it was not my fault, I still woke up sad and missed them. Sometimes I felt that Madarjan was angry with me for doing something wrong. I wondered if I had let Surya down by leaving her behind. I woke up and begged Sulima to contact them and tell them how much I loved them. Unfortunately, she was unable to get in touch with them. They did not have phones in the East. Even people in Kabul no longer had phones. Eventually, we made contact with my uncle Daoud, and he got a message through to Madarjan. After that I slept better. And I found out that no one was upset with me.

Adjusting to American society was far more challenging than I had thought it would be. For one thing, I was extremely disillusioned. I felt bitter about how America had treated me. I thought about my friends in detention. I was angry that America was continuing to lock them up. I was angry at the country and its leadership. I even found myself getting angry with people on the streets. They took their freedoms for granted. And they didn't care about foreigners. Why weren't they pounding on the doors of their congresspeople to get detained asylum-seekers released from prison?

It has helped to realize that many American citizens actually do not know about the detention system and that they need to be educated, rather than judged. Teaching has always been important to me, and I have come to understand that education takes many forms. In Afghanistan, I taught math, science, and other academic subjects to girls, who had been banned from school. Now that I am in the United States, I want to teach Americans about what happens to people like me when they come to the United States without the right documents. I want to open the eyes of Americans to conditions in detention centers.

It is gratifying for me to know that I am playing some role in this education process. In May 2001, I testified before a congressional subcommittee about my experiences in detention. Other witnesses included a Tibetan monk, and a teenage boy from the Ivory Coast. His story was especially upsetting because he had been incarcerated in seven different detention centers and had shared a cell with adult American criminals, one of whom had been a murderer! I was amazed by the shocked expression on the faces of the senators. Even lawmakers were unaware of what was going on!

After the hearing was over, a woman approached me. "I am Senator Brownback's assistant. The senator would like to speak to you."

She brought me over to him. "I am so sorry for how you were treated," he said. "We will do whatever is possible to help."

I was touched by the senator's offer. It made me feel that Americans were simply ignorant of what was going on and that if they were educated, they would care a great deal and want to help.

Around the same time, I was approached by the Lutheran Immigration and Refugee Service, an organization that provides a variety of services to people seeking asylum—including extensive programs to educate the public. They were publishing a booklet about asylum seekers in American detention centers and wanted their writer to interview me. I was glad to have another opportunity to inform people about asylum and detention issues. Expanding the short write-up into this full-length book is a continuation of that educational process.

I found myself judging Americans for other reasons. I had no patience hearing Americans complain. "I only got a B on the exam. I could shoot myself." I thought of the women who had committed suicide under the Taliban. A picture of Neema rose before my eyes. How could someone use such terminology about the grade on a test? Or I would hear, "My boyfriend just dumped me—my life is over." I would think, I'll tell you stories that would make you feel your life is *really* over. Americans used words like *nightmare* or *ordeal* to describe inconveniences like waiting on line at the bank in the summer heat, or having a flood in the basement. They used words like *tragic loss* to describe having one's team lose a baseball game. At times, there seemed to be an unbridgeable gap between my life and that of my classmates.

Since then, I have learned not to judge others. God knows what He is doing. He gives each one of us the experiences that we need. Some of us seem to have an easier life, some of us have a harder life. But we are all entitled not only to our freedom and religious beliefs, but also to our pain. We all have a right to mourn our losses, whatever they may be.

My religious views have also evolved and changed over the years. I have stopped covering my hair. Religion has become something deeply personal. It is so embedded in my soul that I no longer feel a need to show everyone that I'm a Muslim by wearing a particular kind of clothing. Islam is what lives in my heart, not what I wear on my head.

Living with Sulima has been wonderful. It has also been challenging. We are very different personalities. Sulima is an activist and a zealot. Even now, her life revolves around her work for the liberation of Afghan women. Although I am also committed to seeing changes in Afghanistan, I want to enjoy my life here. I want to have fun. I want to experience everything I was restricted from doing for so long—movies, music, dancing, reading poetry, and dating. It's hard to work and go to school. I don't have time for everything I want to do. Sometimes, I'd just like to skip work and have fun. But I know Sulima needs me to work behind the counter at the store. Sulima also fusses over whether I wear a sweater when it's cold, or whether someone I'm dating is appropriate. I respect her judgment. I know she loves me. But sometimes I want to do things my own way.

Still, I am filled not only with gratitude but also with respect and awe for Sulima. In certain ways, she has suffered much more than I did in her life, and she is a truly selfless human being. I knew about what she went through in Afghanistan. That was remarkable enough. But I had no idea about how much pain and dislocation she went through after her escape until she told me her story.

One of us—maybe it was Gula—once asked Madarjan why she talks so much about Sulima. "I love all of you," she said, "but in some ways, I love Sulima the most. She has had a harder life than any of you. She has suffered a great deal in our family, but she continues to love all of us and make sacrifices for us."

I understand what Madarjan is saying, and I think it is true. Of all of us, Sulima was the most anguished. If I had a good childhood, it is largely because Sulima paved the way. I was the beneficiary of her vision and her self-sacrifice, not only in the family but even in my culture. It was people like Sulima, who fought for equality, who set the stage for the environment in which I grew up.

I will always thank her for that. And for saving my life when I was in detention.

My greatest and most abiding thanks go to God for giving me the strength to endure everything I went through. The light of the Prophet Mohammed guided me through the dark night of oppression. It will continue to guide me, even in freedom.

EPILOGUE

by Sulima and Hala

As of this writing, Karim is living in Pakistan with his family, where he works as an engineer. We are in touch again. We have never thoroughly discussed the past or smoothed over misunderstandings, but on the other hand we are all older now and more settled in our lives and have, hopefully, gotten beyond all that pain.

The war has changed Karim. He has become a gentler person. Sadly, the atrocities he has witnessed have been too much for him, and he continues to turn to alcohol for comfort and escape. We hope that he will find some type of solace and healing in his life.

Husna is married and living in England with her husband and four children. She teaches elementary school and is content with her life.

Asim's wife died of lung cancer right after Hala left Afghanistan. Shortly after that, Asim fled to Pakistan because the Taliban discovered that he was treating women, which was against Taliban edicts prohibiting male doctors from having female patients in their practice. He was tortured and condemned to death, but—like Hala— he managed to escape into Pakistan with his children. Rajab and his wife allowed him to stay with them for a few weeks, as they had so graciously opened their home to Hala after her escape. But Asim felt that he would not be safe in Peshawar because of the strong presence of Taliban sympathizers and Islamic fundamentalists. As with Hala, the people who betrayed him turned out to be fundamentalist members of our own extended family. A cousin warned Asim that several distant relatives were looking for him. These particular relatives had been members of the Religious Police and had close ties with fundamentalists in Peshawar. Asim took his children to a small town, where they live in hiding with a trusted friend.

He sends us E-mails from his friend's computer. In his last communication, he wrote, "I do not know what I will do, and how long we can go on living here. It is not fair to my hosts to take care of my children and me indefinitely, and I am frightened that the people who want to kill me will figure out where I am. I cannot practice medicine properly, although sometimes neighbors who know where I am staying come to see me with their health problems. I have applied to the UNHCR [United Nations High Commission for Refugees], but I have not even gotten an interview yet. There is no end in sight."

We asked him if he regrets treating women. He wrote back, "Of course not, because how could I refuse? I have a duty to relieve suffering, as a doctor. I only hope that one day I can practice medicine again."

Zamin is still in Afghanistan. We have very little contact because of difficulties of staying in touch due to the war. All we know is that he is an assistant professor of chemistry and has two children.

Gula lives in England, not far from Husna. She married a British man last year and is pregnant. She hopes to continue working as a veterinarian after the baby is born.

Surya felt it was not safe to remain in Afghanistan, and Khaled helped her to cross the border. Like Hala and Asim, Surya stayed with Rajab and his wife but felt that she was not safe there either. Rajab arranged for her to live with his sister and her family in Kamalpour, which is a small suburb of Peshawar.

Surya was unable to complete her dental studies because of the Taliban's prohibition against women's education, so she has no formal training for a profession. At present, she works as a hairdresser. Because she is still keeping a low profile, she has only a small, hand-picked group of customers who come to see her where she is staying. She would like to leave Pakistan and resume her dental studies, but like Asim she has been unable to receive refugee status because she has not yet been interviewed by the UNHCR.

We did not know where Naim was for a very long time. We thought he might have been killed by the Taliban and were frantic with worry until we heard that he escaped into Pakistan. We do not know where he is.

Several weeks before the writing of this book, we received a very special blessing. We were able to arrange for Madarjan to come to the United States and live with us. She is seventy years old, but her beautiful face looks older. It has been ravaged by the pain and sorrow she has experienced during these years of brutality, but she does not complain. Her quiet dignity, patient acceptance, and unfailing gentleness inspire both of us. She greets our guests with Afghan hospitality, offering them her chair and personally serving them food. Although she speaks no English, the dignity and graciousness of her demeanor speak louder than words and never fail to move our American friends. It is a gift to have Madarjan in our midst and a source of comfort for both of us.

Afghanistan continues to live on in both of our hearts. As we have watched the drama of the American involvement unfold following September 11, we have been filled with trepidation. Will the new government be any better than the old? Will America abandon Afghanistan again once their military objectives are met? Will women ever be free, as they are in the United States?

We don't know. We are waiting. Meanwhile, we tremble. We hope. And we pray.

HOW YOU CAN HELP

FOR AFGHAN WOMEN AND CHILDREN

RAWA
Rawa@rawa.org
PO Box 374
Quetta, Pakistan
Phone: 0092-300-855-1638

Humanitarian Aid for Women and Children of Afghanistan (HAWCA)
Hawca@hawca.org
PO Box 646
GPO Peshawar
Pakistan
OFFICE:
House #94
Street #7, Phase 1
Hayatabad, Peshawar
Pakistan
Phone: 092-91-811663

Women for Afghan Women
www.womenforafghanwomen.org
info@womenforafghanwomen.org
PO Box 152
Midtown Station

New York, NY 10018
Phone: 212-868-9360

Afghan Women's Mission
260 South Lake Avenue
PMB 165
Pasadena, CA 91101

Equality Now
www.equalitynow.org
info@equalitynow.org
PO Box 20646
Columbus Circle Station
New York, NY 10023

Equality Now has been working to support women in Afghanistan. In December 2001, Equality Now convened a coalition of international women's organizations to host the Afghan Women's Summit for Democracy, a global gathering of Afghan women leaders in Brussels, resulting in the adoption of the Brussels Proclamation—their vision for the future of Afghanistan and the role of women in reconstruction. More recently, Equality Now has been supporting the newly formed Afghan Women Lawyers and Professionals Association, based in Kabul, and mobilizing its membership to urge the United Nations, the international community, and the United States government in particular to ensure security during this transition to democracy through expansion of the scope and mandate of the International Security Assistance Force (ISAF).

FOR ASYLUM-SEEKERS IN THE UNITED STATES

1. **Advocate**
   a. Write letters to your senators or Congressional representative in Washington, D.C., and express your concern about the unnecessary detention of asylum-seekers. For sample text, visit the Lutheran Immigration and Refugee Service (LIRS) Web site at www.lirs.org and click on Advocate. To find out how to reach your senators or representatives, please visit the following sites: http://www.senate.gov/senators/index.cfm

and http://www.house.gov/writerep/. The Lawyers Committee for Human Rights can E-mail your senators or representative directly. You can do this by going to their Web site at www.lchr.org.

b. Find out about important legislation pending in the House and Senate that would restore important rights to men, women, and children "forgotten" in the U.S. asylum system by visiting the LIRS' Web site at www.lirs.org and clicking on Advocate.

c. Join programs that work to advocate for asylum-seekers, like the Forgotten Refugees Campaign, a national advocacy and education outreach effort. Participate in the Forgotten Refugees Campaign Urgent Action Network and receive notifications of donation drives for asylum-seekers and "Postcards of Hope" drives for lonely and vulnerable asylum-seekers in INS detention. Visit LIRS' Web site at www.lirs.org and click on Advocate.

d. Order the "Advocates Handbook: A Guide to Assisting Asylum Seekers in INS Detention." This comprehensive manual details how to write to legislators, organize detention facility tours, set up a visitation project, write an op-ed article, conduct an information session for others in your community, and much more. To get a copy, send your request to lirs@lirs.org, with the subject "Advocates Handbook Order—Asylum and Detention Concerns."

2. Reach Out

Contact the Detention Watch Network, a national network of over a hundred organizations and 1,500 individuals that work to both provide services to detained asylum-seekers and to help you find organizations or churches in your area that are visiting, writing to, and supporting those in detention. Contact LIRS for more information at www.lirs.org.

3. Learn More

a. Lawyers Committee for Human Rights—www.lchr.org
Online report titled: "Refugees Behind Bars: The Imprisonment of Asylum Seekers in the Wake of the 1996 Immigration Act," August 1999 www.lchr.org/refugee/behindbars.htm

b. Amnesty International—www.amnestyusa.org

Online report titled: "Lost in the Labyrinth: Detention of Asylum-seekers," September 1999—www.amnestyusa.org/rightsforall/asylum/ins/index.html

c. Women's Commission on Refugee Women and Children—www.intrescom.org/wcrwc

Online report titled: "Liberty Denied: Women Seeking Asylum Imprisoned in the United States," April 1997—www.intrescom.org/wcrwc/reports/reports.html

3. Educate Others

a. Coordinate educational events in your church, community center, school, university, library, or other public space. Program guides and educational materials are available through the Forgotten Refugees Campaign, including posters, fact sheets, sign-up sheets, videos, "Remember Me" cards, wristbands, and more. All materials and program guides are available free of charge. Contact LIRS at lirs@lirs.org with the subject "FRC Event—Asylum and Detention Concerns."

4. Donate Your Expertise

a. *If you are a doctor, or a mental health professional,* you can play a crucial role in the legal proceedings of a torture survivor by providing expert testimony corroborating physical consequences of torture, such as scars. Doctors of the World at www.doctorsoftheworld.org and Physicians for Human Rights at www.phrusa.org can make these arrangements.

b. *If you are a lawyer,* you can donate your services on a pro bono basis, as Lenore and Kalpana did for Hala. The Lawyers Committee for Human Rights at www.lchr.org can arrange this, or can refer you to a similar organization in your own area.

c. *If you are facile with words,* you can write an op-ed or some other piece for local publications on detention issues in general, or about a particular detainee. The INS is very sensitive to public opinion, and many detainees have been granted asylum following an outcry of public outrage generated by a newspaper article. If you yourself cannot do the writing, you can still call your local paper and ask if they would like to assign a staff reporter to cover the story.

6. Give Money

Make a monetary donation to the following organizations, which are involved with helping refugees and detainees:

LIRS (www.lirs.org)

Lawyers Committee for Human Rights (www.lchr.org)

Physicians for Human Rights (www.phrusa.org)

Doctors of the World (www.doctorsoftheworld.org)

Women's Committee for Refugee Women and Children (www.intrescom.org/wcrwc)

Hebrew Immigration and Aid Society (www.hias.org)

Equality Now (www.equalitynow.org)